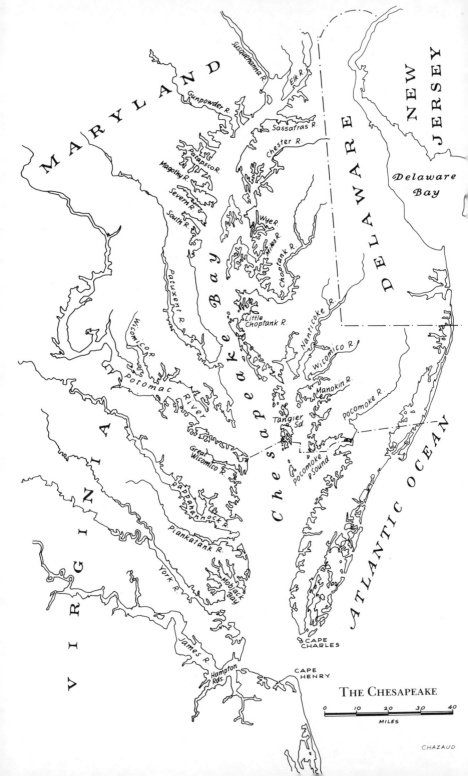

THE CHESAPEAKE

0   10   20   30   40
MILES

CHAZAUD

A Place in Time

Middlesex County, Virginia

1650-1750

DARRETT B. AND ANITA H. RUTMAN

———

W · W · NORTON & COMPANY

NEW YORK · LONDON

The frontispiece map is based upon one published in Arthur P. Middleton, *Tobacco Coast: A Maritime History of Chesapeake Bay in the Colonial Era* (Newport News, Va., 1953) and is used courtesy of the Mariners' Museum, Newport News, Virginia.

Portions of chapter 1 were originally published in *Historical Methods* 13:1 (1980), 29–41 and *Virginia Magazine of History and Biography* 88:1 (1980), 37–74 and are reprinted with the permission of the editors of those journals.

Portions of chapter 4 are reprinted with permission from *The Chesapeake in the Seventeenth Century: Essays on Anglo-American Society*, edited by Thad W. Tate and David L. Ammerman. Copyright 1979 The University of North Carolina Press. Published for the Institute of Early American History and Culture, Williamsburg.

The lines that introduce chapter 4 are from *John Brown's Body* by Stephen Vincent Benét. From: *The Selected Works of Stephen Vincent Benét*. Holt, Rinehart and Winston, Inc. Copyright renewed 1955, 1956 by Rosemary Carr Benét. Reprinted by permission of Brandt & Brandt Literary Agents, Inc.

Printed in the United States of America.

FIRST EDITION

The text of this book is composed in VIP Baskerville. The display type is Typositor Modern No. 20 and Baskerville. Composition and manufacturing are by The Maple-Vail Book Manufacturing Group. Book design by Marjorie J. Flock.

Library of Congress Cataloging in Publication Data
Rutman, Darrett Bruce.
   A place in time.
   Includes index.
   1. Middlesex County (Va.)—History.   2. Middlesex
County (Va.)—Social conditions.   I. Rutman, Anita H.
II. Title.
F232.M6R87   1984   975.5'33   83-13378

ISBN 0-393-01801-6

W. W. Norton & Company, Inc., 500 Fifth Avenue, New York, N.Y. 10110
W. W. Norton & Company Ltd., 37 Great Russell Street, London WC1B 3NU

1 2 3 4 5 6 7 8 9 0

For our sisters, Harriet and Sally,
who bring home a meaning of family

Contents

NOTE

THE CORPUS OF *A Place in Time* appears in the present volume. A supplementary second part dealing with underlying statistical evidence is published as *A Place in Time: Explicatus* and is available directly from W. W. Norton & Company. All references to *Explicatus* in the notes in this volume refer to that volume.

Maps/Illustrations

Preface

DURING THE YEARS in which this book was being researched and written, we often visited the Virginia county that is its subject. Usually we entered from the northwest, driving down from Fredericksburg to cross the invisible line that separates Essex County from our Middlesex, then continuing through the center of the county to Saluda, the modern county seat, and beyond. On one such occasion, it suddenly dawned on us that this road from the northwest was essentially *our* road—that is to say, the road we knew so well in the seventeenth and eighteenth centuries. With the realization came familiarity. Here was Mickleburrough's bridge where Tobias had his store. Just beyond Saluda was George Wortham's and the ordinary where Benjamin Davis died. We had no need to consult a map when we came to a branch a half-mile farther on. We knew that the left led toward Ralph Wormeley's Rosegill Plantation and the Mother Church, that the right would loop toward the Piankatank River, and that the two roads would join together farther down. We took the right and, after a mile or so, I said, "The turnoff to Turk's farm and the ferry should be coming up." Within a hundred yards, we passed the overgrown entrance of a lane and a sign: "Turk's Ferry Farm." Momentarily, it seemed, we had been transported across time. Yet we remained in an automobile, a product of the twentieth century; the road was macadam, not dirt. The feeling passed, but not the eeriness of this name from another time being so exactly where it ought to be.

In truth, this eerie familiarity across time—better put, this destruction of time or evocation of timelessness that allows us to intermix past and present—is a common enough feeling among those deeply involved in history. It flows from the simple fact that the past is always parent to the present, that barring the cataclysmic the vestiges of other days perpetually surround us and, if we allow them to, will succor our knowledge of a finite temporality with evidence of immortality. It is what makes history attractive to so many and what, as an artist or poet, the historian strives to evoke.

Evoking this familiarity cannot be the central purpose of writing history, however—at least not to us. Ours is one of the several disciplines devoted to the systematic study of human behavior, set apart from the others by the materials the historian uses—the remnants of past times—and the historian's preoccupation with the passage of time itself. To frame an imperfect analogy: Sociologists, psychologists, political scientists, and even most anthropologists tend to present aspects of human behavior in still life; the historian strives to convey via print a moving picture, in our case of the evolving web of associations among the English settled in a small corner of the Chesapeake region, from those people's entry at mid-seventeenth century into the second quarter of the eighteenth. But the point of the moving picture speaks generally to the human condition. The web of associations we write of—that web that makes for a community—*must* exist even in an environment considered by most observers then and now to be hostile to any indigenous sense of community.

To be both artist and social scientist is by no means an easy task. The characters of our story are a disparate lot, yet our intent must be to depict what are called the central tendencies of their society, which requires statistical analysis. We need to convey a sense of the past in terms of those who lived it— what did they feel?—all the while retaining the advantage of the outsider, free to comment from our own vantage point on what it all means. And to be fair to the reader we must make it clear that, as the historians, we are also part of the story being told, even the principal characters around whom all the others circulate and through whom the reader understands the others.

Our way of attempting to resolve the difficulties in what follows has been to bring the historian out of the closet, so to speak. Where normally in works of history the historian is an invisible but omniscient narrator, we have identified ourselves quite openly as visitors to the early Chesapeake. As such, we frankly declare for the reader our paramount concerns and the assumptions we have carried into the work, and we let the reader know the nature of our materials and the limits those materials impose—all in chapter 1. In the subsequent narrative, we consciously summon scenes for the reader's consideration and offer our interpretation of them directly, even indicate where we have had recourse to our "historical imagination"—a phrase the historian applies to impressions drawn from years of study rather than derived from particular pieces of evidence. Our way here is both chronological and cumulative in the sense that we introduce essential elements of the society as they appear and presume them in place as we proceed. These eight chapters form a consistent whole, the corpus of our report of our visit, and for the convenience of the reader are published as a single volume. To them, however, we have added a second and supplementary part, published separately. Here we abandon the narrative style customary in history to present in a series of *explicatus* some of the statistical evidence that has silently colored the entire work. We are explicit as a matter of principle—the materials and methods of our analyses must be available if they are to be judged. We are also to an extent pedagogical, in recognition of the fact that our methods will not be completely familiar to everyone. In both parts of the work, but particularly in the second, our intent is to involve the reader so thoroughly in our literal visit to the materials of the past that he or she will accept the reality of our figurative visit.

Some technical matters: Much of the book is based upon computer files containing some 12,200-odd biographies of Middlesex people, the creation of which is described in chapter 1. Note 24 of that chapter is, in effect, a sample of the annotation that could be supplied throughout. Obviously such extensive annotation would be both expensive and irrelevant. Hence we have adopted a policy of citing the sources only of direct quotations and key events. Where the source of data relative to individuals, families, or aggregations is not specifically given, it is implicitly the Middlesex biographical files. For much the same reason, we have eschewed a formal bibliography. Thad W. Tate's excellent review, "The Seventeenth-Century Chesapeake and Its Modern Historians," in Tate and David L. Ammerman, eds., *The Chesapeake in the Seventeenth Century: Essays on Anglo-American Society* (1979) makes any general discussion of the literature largely redundant, while in the *explicatus* and in our notes throughout we relate our work to the continuing scholarship of the time and place.

In the text and notes, we have consistently modernized quotations to the extent of expanding standard seventeenth- and eighteenth-century abbreviations and contractions, changing the characters thorn "y" to "th" and, where they have been used interchangeably, "v" to "u" and "i" to "j." Superscript letters have been reduced to line and numbers recorded in roman style have been changed to our more customary form. Where applicable, dates have been rendered Old Style, except the years, which have been modernized to make January 1 a consistent New Year's Day. The variant spellings of proper names have been standardized to the form most commonly found in the records. (The occasional instances where modernization exceeds these limits are indicated in an appropriate note.) In stipulating category boundaries—as, for example, 1650–99—we have, with one exception, opted for the historian's rather than statistician's way in that the boundaries are inclusive at both ends. The one exception is our retention for literary purposes of the mid-century mark, 1750. Where this occurs as a boundary, the reader should understand "to 1750" rather than "through 1750." And we have used the abbreviations *li*, *s*, and *d* for pounds, shillings, and pence. Where a money value is known to be sterling as against current money of Virginia or where we have converted or adjusted it in some fashion, the fact is explicitly stated in the text or accompanying note; where there is no explicit statement, the value is as given in the pertinent source.

To simplify footnote references to the manuscript materials of Middlesex and its parent county, Lancaster, in the Virginia State Library, Richmond, the volumes have been cited by county, followed by a keyword and inclusive dates taken from the library's own finder list, for example, "Middlesex Wills, 1698–1713." It should be noted that, particularly for the earliest volumes, the keyword and contents do not always agree. Thus, Lancaster Deeds, 1652–57 consists largely of court orders, while Middlesex Orders, 1673–80 contains wills from the period.

Research of the kind we have engaged in as we prepared to write this book has been extraordinarily expensive. For the most part these expenses have been met by grants-in-aid-of-research from a number of agencies: the Central University Research Fund of the University of New Hampshire and the university's Research Office (which provided internal funding for computer services during more years than we like to remember), the American Council of Learned Societies through its Committee for Computer-Oriented Research in the Humanities, and the National Endowment for the Humanities.

Ours has also been collaborative research in a number of other ways. Over the years many individuals have personally facilitated the work: in their entirety, the staffs of Dimond Library and Computer Services of the University of New Hampshire, Virginia State Library, and Alderman Library at the University of Virginia; Cary Carson and the research staff, Colonial Williamsburg Foundation; the late William M. E. Rachal and the staff at the Virginia Historical Society; Ransom True of the Association for the Preservation of Virginia Antiquities.

Some of our conceptualizations and various technical matters have been set before our historian colleagues in the form of papers and articles.* We have drawn freely from these, even incorporating parts into the book itself with the permission of the appropriate publisher. Thus in chapter 1 whole sections are from our "Community Study," published in *Historical Methods* (1980), and from " 'More True and Perfect Lists': The Reconstruction of Censuses for Middlesex County, Virginia, 1668–1704," published in *Virginia Magazine of History and Biography* (1980); chapter 4 includes parts of our " 'Now-Wives and Sons-in-Law': Parental Death in a Seventeenth-Century Virginia County," which appeared in Tate and Ammerman, eds., *The Chesapeake in the Seventeenth Century*. Needless to say, we have drawn heavily upon the criticism of our "trial balloons" offered by many scholars, including Daniel Scott Smith (who was kind enough to read all of the demographic discussions of the *explicatus* in typescript); Gloria L. Main; and members of what is frequently referred to as "the Chesapeake family": Lois Green Carr, Russell R. Menard, Allan Kulikoff, P. M. G. Harris, Lorena S. Walsh, and Daniel Blake Smith. Through their own work, too, these scholars have contributed to ours. We are particularly grateful to two who allowed us to read in advance of publication their major studies: Main's *Tobacco Colony: Life in Early Maryland, 1650–1720*, and Kulikoff's *Tobacco and Slaves: The Development of Southern Cultures in the Chesapeake Colonies, 1680–1780*. Our conclusions differ from theirs in many instances, but that in no way lessens our appreciation.

Over the years, too, Middlesex has been a continuing project for the faculty and graduate students in history at the University of New Hampshire. On occasion we have presented formal drafts of articles, papers, chapters, and parts of chapters to our faculty seminar, while every graduate seminar for the past decade has to an extent served as an audience for (and critic of) our impressions and conclusions. Some students have chosen allied topics and their research has directly supported ours—Peter V. Bergstrom on the Chesapeake economy, James M. Vaughan on agricultural practices, Karen D. Heydon on architecture, John W. Durel on marriage patterns, and Karen E. Andresen on wealth. Five graduate students worked directly on the project as assistants: Andresen, Dennis E. Barbour, Bergstrom, Fleurange Jacques, and Charles Wetherell. The appearance of the last as a joint author with us of published articles and computer routines testifies to his invaluable contribution. But the work of all has been of enormous help, while the gay enthusiasm of all has regularly rekindled our own sometimes flagging verve. One visiting historian might well remember entering our front door and interrupting the uncontrollable laughter of a group crowded around a map of Middlesex covering our dining room table— a spontaneous outburst prompted by the sudden realization of the absurd futility of an hour spent trying to puzzle out the boundaries of a particular property from a conveyance that described one of its lines as proceeding "northerly up the hill from a little stream then westerly from the mulbery bush."

Knowing they will read this preface, we take the opportunity to tell the group that a stray document found later allowed the completion of the plat and of the map itself.

Finally, we note our particular gratitude to our children, Morgan and Elizabeth, whose patience with their parents has been consummate, to Elizabeth again and Mrs. Cheryl Grimes of Dover, New Hampshire, for suggesting the word *"explicatus,"* and to those people with roots deep in the county who, on becoming aware of our work, wrote without solicitation to supply us with information on their Middlesex ancestors. As in the case of the map, certain puzzles encountered on our visit to this Chesapeake society required some stray fact for solution; not infrequently it was supplied to us in this fashion.

D.B.R.; A.H.R.

Durham, New Hampshire
August 1982

1. The Visitors

And as imagination bodies forth
The forms of things unknown, the poet's pen
Turns them to shapes, and gives to airy nothing
A local habitation and a name.

— Shakespeare, *A Midsummer Night's Dream*

HISTORICAL community studies are in a very real sense visits to places distant, sometimes in terms of space, always in terms of time. This particular visit to a place in time—to Middlesex County, Virginia, of the late seventeenth and early eighteenth century—began more than a decade ago. It was not begun out of any filiopietistic love of Virginia, or of Middlesex. Neither of the authors can be accounted a Virginian, although we spent four delightful years in Charlottesville and have visited the Old Dominion and Middlesex many times. And while we were amused to find a "Darrett" briefly resident in the county in the early eighteenth century, none of our ancestors, to the best of our knowledge, danced in any of Virginia's great houses or tilled her red soil. Neither was this visit begun out of curiosity about what our children, when young, called "ye olden times," nor out of a belief that somehow the simpler values of those times constitute a lesson for this time. We did not even set out to track in some fashion and to some degree the origins of contemporary American society; we did not intend to make Middlesex into some sort of case in point of what scholars see as a transition from a traditional to modern life-style. Others might find our work illustrative along such lines, but for our part we began—and ended—our visit simply as ethnologists might leave home for a visit to a Brazilian jungle tribe or as ethologists might set out to visit (observe) a troop of hamadryas baboons in eastern Ethiopia. The people of Middlesex, although we came to like some of them and to dislike, even distrust others, were not and still are not important to us in any other way than the tribesmen are important to the ethnologists and the baboons to the ethologists.

Twice before we have made such visits to past places, in both instances to places in the New England of the seventeenth century.[1] On those occasions, and on the occasion of the present visit to Middlesex, our purpose has always been the same: to see how people organize their lives and relationships under the conditions prevailing at the particular time and place. For essentially we are interested in the variations and similarities to be found in communal life.

The central question that we have asked during this visit to Middlesex can be brought into focus by alluding to an incident in the county's history. The date: August 20, 1736. Somewhere in the northwestern or "Upper Part" of the county, a group of "Freeholders and Inhabitants" met to draw up a petition to Virginia's colonial legislature. The petitioners noted that the county was "but one Parish" with three churches, but "that Divine Service is not alternately performed at each of those Churches, to the great Grievance of the Upper Inhabitants." To rectify the situation, the petitioners prayed "that the said Parish may be divided, and made Two distinct Parishes."[2]

Had the petitioners been New England townsmen and the legislature to which they applied been that of Massachusetts or Connecticut, their activities would not be construed as anything unusual. A rhetoric of order, of natural or organic hierarchy, and of the primacy of the group—of the community—over the desires of its individual members permeates that section, from John Winthrop speaking to his settlers aboard ship for America in 1630, through church covenants, to Jonathan Edwards in the eighteenth century:

Wee must be knitt together in this worke as one man. . . . Wee must uphold a familiar Commerce together in all meekenes, gentlnes, patience and liberallity, wee must delight in eache other, make others Condicions our owne, rejoyce together, mourne together, labour, and suffer together, allwayes haveing before our eyes our Commis-

sion and Community in the worke, our Community as members of
the same body.[3]

We whose names are here unto subscribed do, in the fear and rever-
ence of our Almighty God, mutually and severally promise amongst
ourselves and each other to profess and practice one truth according
to that most perfect rule, the foundation whereof is everlasting love.[4]

There is a beauty of order in society, as when the different members
. . . have all their appointed offices, places and station, according to
their several capacities and talents, and everyone keeps his place,
and continues in his proper business.[5]

New England settlement patterns, family life, town government, and even the separation of one group of townsmen
from the rest under the guise of forming a new church are all
viewed by historians in the context of the intense (albeit
declining) communalism defined by such rhetoric.[6] And all
are in sharp contrast to our present understanding of the early
Chesapeake, a region devoid of rhetoric, randomly settled, its
geography, economic base, and labor system so different from
New England. Looking at this southern landscape, even contemporaries complained of the absence of community life:

The saddest Consequent of their dispersed manner of Planting
themselves . . . is the great want of Christian Neighbourhood, or
brotherly admonition, of holy Examples of religious Persons, of the
Comfort of theirs, and their Ministers Administrations in Sicknesse
and Distresses, of the Benefit of Christian and Civil Conference and
Commerce.[7]

By reason of the unfortunate Method of the Settlement . . . they
depend altogether upon the Liberality of Nature, without endeavouring to improve its Gifts, by Art or Industry. They spunge upon
the Blessings of a warm Sun, and a fruitful Soil, and almost grutch
the Pains of gathering in the Bounties of the Earth. I should be
asham'd to publish this slothful Indolence of my Countrymen, but
that I hope it will rouse them out of their Lethargy, and excite them
to make the most of all those happy Advantages which Nature has
given them.[8]

In this situation, we are not at all sure what to make of
Middlesex's 1736 petitioners. Conceivably we could accept their
words at face value. These freeholders and inhabitants simply
felt the need of a preacher and a church of their own. But

then, Virginians of this period are not perceived by historians as being particularly religious either. We certainly cannot read into their words any broad set of communal values. Virginians, and the Chesapeake as a whole, did not have communities. Or did they? Perhaps historians have endowed one form of community with so much emotional content that they do not see the varieties of community life.

At this point, it should be noted that historians are not alone in studying places and the concept of community. Anthropologists and sociologists have long been doing such work. Indeed, historians are latecomers to the field, although entering late they seem to have entered with a vengeance. Among historians of early America, the onslaught on local records over the past decade or two has been so indefatigable, the list of locally oriented books and articles has become so lengthy, that one critic has been led to comment, only partly tongue in cheek, on an academic revivalism akin to the "Great Awakening" of the eighteenth century: historians rushing into community studies now with the same enthusiasm and ardor displayed then in a rush to God.[9] For the most part, their studies have dealt with seventeenth- and early eighteenth-century New England and are extensions of Puritan studies. The very meaning of community is taken by these historians from the particular time and place, and the communal life of New England is seen as epitomizing "the world we have lost." Conversely, the disappearance or nonappearance of that life anywhere is seen in terms of a transition into the modern world we have gained. Community is construed as something that existed in pristine form in the New England past and that either does not exist today or exists in a very much diluted form; hence its disappearance or decline is a historical event to be explored.

Kenneth A. Lockridge's *A New England Town* is a prime example of this sort of approach, the story of "A Utopian Commune" collapsing into "A Provincial Town" and one well worth the telling, according to its author, because from it "emerges the certainty that the village community had physically disintegrated, [and] the probability that a society more accustomed to social diversity and political dissent had begun to evolve." But the locus for such studies has not always been the single community. Michael Zuckerman spanned fifteen Massachusetts towns to depict "a broadly diffused desire for consensual communalism as the operative premise of group life." John Waters used the towns of one Massachusetts county to depict "an old model" of community with "peaceful, consensual, and participatory peasant villages." Richard Bushman took all of Connecticut as his laboratory in demonstrating the end between 1690 and 1765 of "the close-knit, tightly controlled, homogeneous community" of a past time and the appearance of a new, open, pluralistic, and voluntaristic social order.[10] What holds such studies together is the exploration of community as a particular reality of the past involving specific values and behavior patterns and, if you will, a nostalgic view of that past.

Indeed, nostalgia has been the bête noire of community studies from the very birth of community as an analytic concept, when Ferdinand Toennies first made a distinction between *Gemeinschaft* (community) and *Gesellschaft* (society or association). For Toennies, community involved an old, warm, personal, and friendly way of village life that he viewed with sadness as disappearing from his late nineteenth-century Germany; society involved the cold, impersonal, fragmented, atomistic life emerging. "In community with one's family, one lives from birth on, bound to it in weal and woe," Toennies wrote. But "one goes into society as one goes into a strange country. A young man is warned against bad society, but the expression bad community violates the meaning of the word." "Community is old; society is new as a name as well as phenomenon."[11] The same duality was transmuted into a folk-urban continuum by anthropologist Robert Redfield. Redfield's folk-village had "a Rousseauean quality," wrote his most vigorous critic, a "homogeneous, isolated, smoothly functioning and well-integrated society made up of a contented and well adjusted people," more the product of the scholar's values than a reflection of reality.[12] Transmuted into still newer dichotomies (peasant villager and commercial farmer, the world of tradition and the modernized world), the duality persists. Somehow that which is passing is better. So it is, for example, in Lockridge's Dedham. The descriptive words and phrases ring with values. "Simplicity," "stability," and "tranquility" describe the passing "Closed Corporate Peasant" and Puritan communities of New England, and that passing involves "disintegration" before "powerful divisive forces" as men "heeded the voice of mere convenience" and "abandoned" their village communities for isolated farmsteads and profit.[13]

Perhaps because they have been at the business of studying communities longer, anthropologists and sociologists have sensed earlier than historians the damage that such nostalgia inflicts upon our understanding.[14] And to rescue the genre, they have begun to make a necessary distinction between community as ideal and community as simply a field of social interaction, thereby allowing themselves to see varieties of community where, too many times, they also have seen only idealizations.

A modern glossary of terms makes clear their distinction, defining community in two entirely separate ways: (1) "a group of people living together in some identifiable territory and sharing a set of interests embracing their lifeways"; and (2) "that mythical state of social wholeness in which each member has his place and in which life is regulated by cooperation rather than by competition. It . . . always seems to be in decline at any given historical present. Thus community is that which each generation feels it must rediscover and re-create."[15]

We can restate the distinction in terms of historical situations. When, for example, Winthrop spoke of the necessity of his Massachusetts settlers being "knitt together . . . as one man . . . allwayes having before our eyes our Commission and Community," he was reflecting an ideal; when, later, he entered Robert Keayne's Boston store to buy a plow for his farm or sought a wife among the widows of the town after the death of his beloved Margaret, he was interacting socially within a communal setting whether the community met the terms of his ideal or not. Again, when Virginia's Roger Green, a minister, complained of the "dispersed manner of Planting" in that colony, of the Virginians living helter-skelter about the landscape rather than clustering their houses around churches to form village communities, he was reflecting his ideal of community, one very much akin to Winthrop's. But when he mounted the pulpit to speak to the planters on a Sunday, he was taking part in a communal rite of some kind, even though the community was so far removed from his ideal that he could deny its very existence. Similarly, when the student of community idealizes the concept in terms of particular values or behavior patterns—peaceful, consensual, tight-knit—the subjects within his locale will be interacting socially on a local (or communal) scale, whether reflecting the scholar's idealization or not.

In sum, sociologists and anthropologists are consciously attempting to divorce the concept of community from any and every particular set of values and behavior. Community is being considered simply an inevitable concomitant of the fact that people live and associate territorially; hence the nature of associations within territories and, because no group is ever completely isolated, between those within and those without, can be studied on the level of territory. Community is real— the concurrence of group and place—but it is so diverse a social phenomenon as to defy every attempt to define it in terms of specific behavior or values. It is, to use Talcott Parsons's definition, merely "that aspect of the structure of social systems . . . observable and analysable with reference to location as a focus of attention." [16]

In any event, it is just such an understanding of community that has guided our visit. We have journeyed to Middlesex in order to study the people of the county, the patterns of their associations among themselves and with others beyond the locale, and, the changes in those patterns over time. We have carried with us no assumption that community involves particular values or behavior. The values and behavior of this time and place—the very things that at one and the same time lie behind the petition of 1736 and allow us to give it meaning—are yet to be discovered.

If we began our visit without assuming an identity between community and a particular set of values and behavior, we have nevertheless carried certain assumptions with us on our journey, five in number, and these have tended to delineate the sorts of specific questions we have asked in the county.

The first assumption is fundamental, the essential postulate from which all our concerns flow, a truism needing expression only because of a contemporary exaltation of individualism. Simply put, it is the assumption that people inevitably associate in groups, that with regard to humankind nature abhors the solitary individual. As sociologist Gerhard Lenski put it "The starting point . . . is the deceptively simple assertion that *man is a social being obliged by nature to live with others as a member of society.*" John Donne was more lyrical: "No man is an *Iland,* intire of it selfe." [17]

Second, we have assumed that associations among people are never chaotic, but are necessarily ordered in the sense that people tend to relate to each other through certain well-defined nodal points. For personal and group purposes—and the two cannot really be separated—they come together at particular locations where they act together in formal and informal ways. In our own New Hampshire town, the nodal points around which our lives, apart from Middlesex, have revolved over the past decade are clear: our home, our university, the town meeting and its ancillary offices of town government, a shopping center, and a youth athletic association—over these same years our children (male and female) have progressed from "little league" baseball through high school teams, and we have progressed right along with them. But what were the nodal points around which the lives of our Middlesex people revolved?

Third, we have assumed that associations between individuals are to some extent related to land form, distance, and technology. The assumption is taken from geography and can be summed up in truisms. People living on opposite sides of a mile-wide river will associate less than people living on the same side. People constrained by the level of their technology to walking or riding horseback will have a more limited geographic circle of active relationships than those who drive cars or ride Boeing jumbo jets. The river is a "barrier" to relationships between those on opposite sides or, from the vantage point of one group, a "boundary" separating it from that on the other side. Distance relative to technology is "friction." [18]

Fourth, just as associations are related to the physical topography of the locale, they are related to the social topography. We can, in other words, presume the existence of social friction as summed up, again, in a truism: The scullery maid has little occasion to meet and marry the king. And just as spatial friction is dependent upon technology, social friction is dependent upon the extent to which a hierarchical ordering, or other differentiation, is accepted within the locale.

Finally, we assume that relationships among people form observable networks. To put the matter simply, any single individual lives in some relationship with other individuals, and these others with still others, some of whom live in relationship with the first, some not. In the abstract, one could start tracing these relationships with a single individual and proceed infinitely in time and space; in this sense, the "human community" is boundless. In the abstract, too, the nature of the relationship being considered can be defined in such a way as to make viable such terms as "community of scholars" and "the Christian community." But in the reality of community study, a venture that begins with the notion of *locale*—in our case a single Chesapeake county—the visitor at one and the same time isolates a geographic segment of the human community and attempts to deal with the totality of the isolate—scholars, Christians, and all.[19]

The assumption as to interpersonal relationships forming networks among people opens for us a formal mode of analysis developed first in geography and recently applied in anthropology and sociology.[20] The accompanying illustration exemplifies the analysis. Each point symbolizes an individual within a spatial or social context, while each line between points depicts the existence of an active (but for purposes of illustration unspecified) relationship between individuals. And the whole complex is considered a single network. The analysis is in part subjective and qualitative, an underscoring of the paramountcy of questions relative to the intensity of relationships and the way participants look upon them—the last alluding to the different viewpoints of, for example, employer and employee, client and patron, master and slave. But the analysis can also involve mathematics. Among any given number of network members, there is a maximum number of possible linkages; the percent of all such possibilities actually existing defines the "density" of the network, a statistic representing the probability of a member chosen at random being linked to another also chosen at random. The clustering that we intuitively sense in the figure—the fact that the members

form two groups—can be tested by comparing the density of
the whole network with that for each cluster. In this case, all
possible relationships within the clusters considered independently are active; hence each has a density of 100 percent; the
density of the network as a whole is 46 percent. The clustering might well reflect the presence of a boundary or barrier
between groups, perhaps a physical obstacle, or the fact of
spatial or social friction between them, or the centripetal effect
of nodes within each that create a proclivity toward relationships within (in contrast to barriers that act as constraints to
relationships without).

A HYPOTHETICAL NETWORK
WITH TWO CLUSTERS

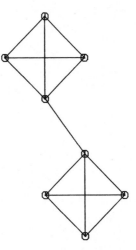

Obviously the logic of the analysis is reversible. If demonstrable clustering (as in the figure) suggests the possibility of
barriers, friction, and nodes, then the demonstration that
barriers, friction, and nodes do indeed exist at a particular
time and place ought to suggest the possibility that social relationships are clustered. The historian, although unable to
undertake in every instance the formal mathematical analysis,
can still be guided by the theoretical framework underlying

the mathematics. Such has frequently been the case during our visit to Middlesex.

The logic of a network approach, moreover, opens the way for us to catch the linkages that bind Middlesex to the broader society. We visit an isolate—a place—but in the firm knowledge that the place is not, in reality, isolated. In an earlier grappling with the notion of community, we put the point in terms of the people of any early American locale, for the most part looking "inward toward the community itself, their activities and their contemplations confined, localized," but with a few here and there "whose activities and thoughts" went beyond the locale: "The storekeeper who takes in the surplus agricultural commodities raised by his neighbors, passes the surplus into channels of commerce, receiving back articles which the community cannot produce for itself. . . . The minister, on the one hand shepherd of his local flock, on the other drawn irresistibly into associations with his compeers throughout the area. . . . Those who, by virtue of their offices, are part of an elaborate political web stretching from the lowly poundkeeper obliged to enforce the colony laws relative to stray animals, through the leadership in the colonial capital, to officers of the Crown in London."[21]

We can, in essence, think of our visit to Middlesex as involving the exploration of relational networks sketched on two planes, one horizontal and (to use Parsons's words again) "analysable with reference to location," the other vertical, bisecting our locale and extending upward and downward, bisecting countless other locations in turn. Thus the figure might depict horizontal networks within two geographically bounded locales linked by an element of a vertical network— that relationship drawn between the apex of the lower diamond and nadir of the upper. Again, the logic is reversible. We will not be able to trace in all of its complexities the vertical network that binds the Chesapeake as a region and the region to an Atlantic complex, but we can presume the existence of the vertical if we can spot the points at which it bisects the horizontal plane of the county.

Five assumptions: People come in groups; their relationships are effected through nodal points; relationships are subject to friction imposed by the interplay of geography and technology; they are delimited in part by social distance; and, finally, relationships form discernible networks. Carried with us on our visit, the five have framed the specific questions we have asked. How are the individuals and families of the county distributed spatially and socially? What features of the land, of technology, of social thought, and of economics divide them or force them together? Where and for what purposes do they congregate? With whom do particular individuals associate, and what configurations do their personal networks assume? What vertical networks link them to the wider world? In a phrase: What was the form of this community on Chesapeake Bay?

All analogies ultimately reach their limit, and we must at this point admit the obvious. Ours has been only a vicarious visit to early Middlesex, performed not in the flesh but through the medium of the materials of that time and place that have managed to survive into ours. The respondents to our questions have not, therefore, been people but documents (for the most part) and artifacts—a gravestone, a miscolored patch of dirt that an archaeologist assures us is the remnant of a house foundation. The surrogate nature of our respondents clearly sets limits to the answers we report. They are neither as full nor as definitive as we would like.

Still, the surviving records of the county are extensive. Indeed, Middlesex was chosen as the object of our visit solely on the basis of the quality and quantity of its remnant materials. Once we had decided on a journey to a Chesapeake community, our first step was to review the extant records of all those Chesapeake counties that dated back to the mid-seventeenth century. The records of Middlesex, when combined with those of its parent county, Lancaster (from which Middlesex was formed in the late 1660s), seemed on balance the most complete—a record series embracing vital events (birth, marriage, death), land patents and conveyances, probate, and the affairs of church, judiciary, and government, extending with only occasional breaks from first settlement well beyond the halfway mark of the eighteenth century.[22]

Our approach to these records has taken two forms. First—but not necessarily first in importance—we have used what modern social historians refer to as "record stripping," a process of disassembling all of the records pertaining to a place and reassembling them on a name basis. Thus the birth and perhaps the baptism of an individual are extracted from the vital records and linked to the probate of a father's will that names the individual an heir, to a marriage entry, to a land conveyance, to a debt instrument, and potentially to scores of other record entries and documents, ultimately perhaps to a cemetery inscription that establishes the individual's death.[23] In effect, the records reassembled on a name basis form biographies, in the case of Middlesex 12,215 in all, biographies of men and women, gentlemen and slaves, artisans and criminals, all resident in the county at some time or other between 1650 and 1750.

As this stripping was in process, moreover, we extracted material on a subject basis—prices and values of commodities, for example, which allow the approximation of price series; the metes and bounds of plots of land, which, once put together in the fashion of a crossword puzzle, allow us to link people with particular farms and plantations in the county. The biographies themselves have been stored in the electronic gizzard of a computer and can be accessed individually—that is, all that we know of a particular individual can be extracted at one time. They can be accessed collectively to track, among other things, kinship, the computer itself sifting through thousands of births and marriages to locate all of an individual's known aunts and uncles, cousins and nephews, by blood and by marriage. And they can be accessed to create aggregations, searching out, for example, all those alive and heading households in the county at a given time for the purpose of examining the aggregation for particular characteristics, perhaps the age of the household heads or the percentage holding public office.

How deep do the biographies take us into the lives of our people? How much information have we been able to obtain? Benjamin Davis of Middlesex was illiterate by the only test historians have available: In witnessing a document for a neighbor, he used a mark rather than his signature. He had no schooling. As a child, he was a bound orphan. As a man, he had little of those things that denominate status and posi-

tion to the historian. Yet his imprint in the records from which
we have drawn is deep and firm.

From a variety of sources, we can establish Davis's parentage and descendants, sketching four generations of his family from an immigrant servant arriving in the county before
1662, through Benjamin in the second generation and the
third generation marriages of Davis cousins to Sanders brothers, to their fourth generation offspring.[24] Benjamin's own
baptism in September 1680 is recorded in the vital records,
verifying an adjudgment of age by the county court when the
death of his father left him orphaned in 1688. The county
court records allow us to track him through thirteen years of
service to three masters. We follow him into marriage to a
young widow in 1706 and glimpse in patent, conveyance, and
probate records the real and personal property that he came
to control by this marriage: one hundred acres of land and
110*li* worth of personal property, including a black slave couple and their son. We see his own family as it grew—his stepson, born to his wife during her first marriage and one year
old at the time Benjamin married, and his daughters, born in
1707 and 1709. We follow his public service, first as a grand,
then petit juror, and, in 1708, his appointment as surveyor of
highways, caring for the county roads from Turk's Ferry to
the courthouse and from the courthouse to Christ Church,
six miles in all as drawn upon a modern topographic map.

All of the records delimit the geographic area in which
Davis spent his life. Neither as a child nor as a man does he
seem to have left the roughly ten square miles of the Gloucester side of Middlesex's middle precinct where he was born
and the adjacent northern edge of Gloucester County where
his Uncle Pritchard lived. Suits at law and the probate of his
estate (when debts he owed and debts owed him were
accounted) allow us to place him within a credit network, one
roughly coterminous with the geographic bounds within which
he lived. Finally, the records establish the time and place of
his death—Thursday evening, September 13, 1711, outside
the ordinary at the courthouse, after muster and horse races.
His death came at the hands of George Wortham, captain of
his militia company, a man who seems not only to have borne
Davis no malice but to have talked to him a little earlier in the

day about the possibility of hiring him as an overseer. For the first and only time, in the testimony of witnesses to his death, the historical record offers us Davis's own words, ironically only the angry, drunken words of the obscure quarrel preceding a confused duel. All witnesses to the fracas agreed that Benjamin ran himself on Wortham's outstretched sword.

Among our biographies, Davis's entry, aside from the detailed information as to the manner of his death, is roughly average. Of some of Middlesex's people we know a great deal more, of others less. There is, for example, the single entry that tells us of a man working in the county as a laborer at a particular time. We do not know where he came from, how long he stayed, or where he went. There is the woman of unknown birth and parentage who simply appears as a resident by virtue of an isolated entry that tells us she is a wife giving birth to a child. Clearly there are biases in the data, extensive as it is, biases that the very fullness of the Davis biography suggests. His entire life was spent in Middlesex; hence he had greater chance of entry into the county records, and consequently our files, than had a transient or short-term sojourner. He was male and as such could leave a mark on the record as a juryman or surveyor of highways that a woman automatically could not, a mark that not only gives detail as to his public service, but tells us he was still alive and in Middlesex at the time. Davis was white and for a third of his life a free adult; hence he was far more apt to enter the records than was a child who died before maturity, or a servant who left the county immediately upon gaining his freedom, or any black slave. The unevenness of our entries—reflecting the biases of the recording processes of the seventeenth and early eighteenth centuries, upon which we must rely—underscores a point already made: In reporting upon our vicarious visit to Middlesex, we cannot be taken to be definitive, only suggestive.[25]

Record stripping has been for us but one of two approaches to the records of Middlesex. Through it we have a view of behavior and of relationships between people—a marriage, a man mortgaging his property to another, an orphan being bound to a tanner. Using the biographies, we can establish particular linkages between individuals—determine that this person was cousin to that person or that a group of individuals had regular, face-to-face contact in church or court. But behavior only occasionally implies the thoughts and feelings that lie behind it. To put the point bluntly: Behavior in beds might ultimately result in cousins, but did the biological fact of cousinship mean anything socially to the cousins themselves? Before assuming that it did, we must sense something more than the original bedroom behavior.

Yet what we need most desperately in order to couple thought and feeling with behavior, that is, direct evidence of the minds and hearts of the people of the Chesapeake and of Middlesex, is the one thing that they almost obstinately deny us. They were not a people inclined to put much more than their business affairs on paper. They did not produce a literature. They were not, in the main, given to diaries. And the few letters they wrote—or the few that have survived—communicate more of markets than of mind.

To compensate for this lack, we have combed the records of Middlesex for vignettes, social dramas, if you will, on one level insignificant to all but the players, on another seemingly encapsulating some part of the mentality of the time and place.[26] Benjamin Davis's duel with George Wortham—the setting, the events leading up to it, even the confused words during the duel itself, all conveyed to us in sterile depositions—is one such drama. In it we sense the character of Davis, his aspirations and frustrations, feelings that, by extrapolation to others of Davis's sort, we assume to be general.[27] A lengthy argument between the county's justices and Ralph Wormeley, the county's preeminent gentleman, an argument that ultimately came down to the matter of an ear of corn and dovecotes, is another such vignette, implying again aspirations—in this case Wormeley's—but also implying something in general about the evolving character of the county's gentlemen.

We have, too, searched elsewhere in the evidence from the early Chesapeake for such small dramas, extrapolating into the county from outside where it seemed warranted and the county's materials themselves were lacking. A wedding in nearby Gloucester described by a passing traveler could just as easily have taken place in Middlesex, as could a neighborhood celebration precipitated by the visit home of a young man who had earlier emigrated from his New Kent County birthplace. On occasion we have introduced such scenes directly into our narrative of Middlesex, but frequently they have simply informed our understanding of county matters generally. John Clayton's argument with the overseer of a Gloucester plantation in the 1680s, for example: The good parson argued for what was then the most modern agricultural technique; the overseer answered that Clayton "understood better how to make a Sermon than manageing Tobacco," then walked away in a huff. The scene speaks to us of the innate conservatism of the Chesapeake (and Middlesex) farmer and of the definition of social roles at the time.[28]

Clearly there are limits to this use of the insignificant. It is akin to using the single churchyard scene—Hamlet, Horatio, and the skull—to try to understand the totality of Shakespeare's *Prince of Denmark*. But to admit as much is simply to admit the limits of all history.

Shakespeare in another play described the poet as one who shapes things unknown and "gives to airy nothing / A local habitation and a name." Historians are something more and something less than poets, for they build form and essence out of real fragments from the past. Yet historians are not pure empiricists, and they should not be taken as such. Their reality, the fragments that they read or view and inevitably puzzle over, only hints at the reality of the past that they try to capture. For the rest, they must fall back upon imagination, conceptualization, analogies, and models—Shakespeare's "airy nothing" once again. As visitors to the past, to this county on Chesapeake Bay, we confess ourselves neither poets nor empiricists but something in between: travelers in twilight who only hope to see things as they really were.

2. Entry

From harmony, from heavenly harmony
  This universal frame began:
When Nature underneath a heap
    Of jarring atoms lay,
  And could not heave her head,
The tuneful voice was heard from high: . . .
Then cold, and hot, and moist, and dry,
In order to their stations leap,
    And Music's power obey.

— Dryden, *A Song for St. Cecilia's Day*

CHESAPEAKE BAY is a great slash of blue water cutting into the North American continent at roughly thirty seven degrees north latitude and extending northward some 195 miles. A third of the way up the bay, where the Potomac River enters from the west, an imaginary line divides the upper bay and Maryland from the lower bay and Virginia, separate political entities in the seventeenth and eighteenth centuries, as they are today. In speaking of the Chesapeake as a region, however, a second imaginary line is more important, one to be traced on a modern map. Start to the south of the mouth of the bay, where the Virginia–North Carolina border meets the Atlantic, and trace a line northwestward through Suffolk, Virginia, on the Nansemond River, to Petersburg, then north through Richmond and Fredericksburg to Washington, northeast through the western outskirts of Baltimore, and finally a bit more easterly toward Wilmington, Delaware. The area encompassed by this line, on both sides of the bay itself but excluding modern Delaware, is the Chesapeake, a low-lying land of estuaries, necks, rivers, creeks,

coves, and swamps, where even on "the freshes"—the upper
reaches of the rivers—one is never far from the smell of salt.
There is, and was during the years that concern us, some
measure of diversity in the area. But a history common to the
whole area in the early seventeenth century commands our
initial attention as the setting for the entrance of the English
to the land that became our county.

The Chesapeake was "the tobacco coast." [1] It was not such
by design. Those in England who, in the last decade of the
sixteenth and first decade of the seventeenth centuries, propounded, planned, and financed the American adventure that
led to the first permanent settlement in the region—Jamestown, Virginia, in 1607—did so from a variety of high motives.
Organized eventually as the Virginia Company of London,
they wrote grandiloquently of Christianizing the Indians,
relieving England of her burdensome poor, establishing a
bulwark against the power of Catholic Spain, and freeing
England from dependence upon other nations for necessary
products ranging from ship timbers to spices. They then dispatched a motley array of gentlemen, artisans, and a few
laborers to make a reality of their vague dreams. In Virginia
the gentlemen bickered, provoked the native Indians to hos-
tility, and both gentlemen and commoners died. A few fell to
Indian arrows and hatchets, but having built their tiny village
at one of the most unhealthy locations along the James River,
most succumbed to typhoid fever, dysentery, and salt poison-
ing. [2]

One hundred four settlers arrived at Jamestown in mid-
1607. No more than forty were alive when a second "supply"
arrived in January 1608. The leadership of Captain John Smith
offered some respite from death; Smith scattered the settlers
to live off the land. Fear of the wilderness and its Indians
soon clustered them again, and the winter of 1609–10 was
known even then as "the starving time." Almost half of those
alive in the fall of 1609 were dead by spring; and except for
the providential arrival of a new supply, the settlement would
have been abandoned. The company appointed new leaders
and imposed a military regime that ultimately enforced order
and sanitation, dispersed the settlers into places far healthier

than Jamestown, and made peace with the Indians.[3] For all
the effort, however—the hundreds of lives lost and thousands
of pounds sterling invested—the dreams that had inspired the
venture went unfulfilled. Indeed, through 1615 the settlers
had returned to England little more than pyrite (fool's gold),
sassafras twigs, clapboards, and, portending the future, a few
hundred pounds of tobacco.

In 1617 the near-moribund Virginia Company roused itself
for one last effort. The military regime was done away with
and, in a series of instructions to a new governor in 1618—
instructions that the settlers promptly dubbed their "greate
charter"—private property was instituted. Thus far all settlers
had been in effect employees of the company, servants. Now
the old servants were declared free to work land of their own.
And in the future, while company servants would still be dispatched to do company business and work company land, those
paying their own passage to the Chesapeake, or paying for
the passage of others, would receive land to own and work
for their own profit. In this way, the company hoped, land
would serve as a bait to attract people to Virginia; the company itself would profit by monopolizing shipping to and from
the colony.

Tobacco and the "headright" instituted in 1618—the "right"
of an individual to claim fifty acres of land for each "head"
for whom he paid the cost of transportation to the colony—
rescued the failing enterprise. Tobacco was already a minor
rage in England. Moralists might link tobacco houses with
brothels and condemn both; anatomists might point out that
autopsies performed on smokers revealed "inward parts . . .
soiled and infected with an oily kind of soot"; even the king
might rail against smoking as a "custom loathsome to the eye,
hateful to the nose, harmful to the brain, dangerous to the
lungs, and in the black stinking fume thereof, nearest resem-
bling the horrible Stygian smoke of the pit that is bottomless."
But gentlemen and even a few common folk were puffing
pipefuls enough to consume fifty thousand pounds of imported
Spanish leaf a year and were paying twelve shillings a pound
and more for it.[4] Tobacco was, therefore, a product that could
be produced in the Chesapeake, carried into England cheaply,
and there sold dearly. In combination with the headright, it

invited private investment in Virginia, for men of even modest means could recruit servants in England, transport them to the Chesapeake to grow tobacco on land free to the investor by virtue of the transportation, and (at least initially) pocket profits of 200 and 300 percent over cost.

The combination peopled Virginia. In 1616 a few hundred settlers on the James River dispatched just over two thousand pounds of tobacco to England. Inferior to the Spanish leaf, Chesapeake tobacco commanded a lesser price but in so doing augmented demand; those for whom twelve-shilling tobacco was too expensive inhaled at seven or five shillings. By 1620 the population of Virginia had risen to roughly two thousand and tobacco exports to over fifty thousand pounds a year. An Indian uprising in 1622 claimed, directly and indirectly, a thousand lives, bankrupted the company, and brought about royal control of the colony in 1624. Yet the influx of English men and women continued. By the early 1630s, some three thousand Virginians were exporting upward of a quarter-million pounds of tobacco a year. The enormous production forced the high price down as, in classic fashion, supply exceeded demand and goods chased customers. Prices did not drop so low as to make Chesapeake production unprofitable, however, and lower-priced tobacco—now within the reach of almost anyone—further augmented demand in England and on the European continent. Chesapeake production and population continued upward. In 1640 the number of English around the bay, including those in Maryland, where settlement had begun in 1634, reached eleven thousand and tobacco exports surpassed a million pounds. By century's end a population of just under ninety thousand would export more than 36 million pounds, roughly four hundred pounds of tobacco for every man, woman, and child in the region.[5]

Ironically, *Nicotiana tabacum,* the export tobacco of the Chesapeake, was itself an immigrant to the bay, having been imported from the Caribbean and planted along the James in lieu of the native tobacco. The latter was a small plant, with few leaves, "poore and weake, and of a byting tast" to English palates. The basic cultivation, however, was borrowed directly from the Virginia Indians in the first flush of tobacco prosperity, when the weed was selling in England for over five shillings a pound and those in Jamestown were breaking up "the market-place, and streets, and all other spare places" to plant.[6]

In Indian fashion, the settlers pulverized small circles of earth with a hoe, each circle several feet in diameter and three to four feet apart, then worked the soil toward the middle to form hills. The tiny tobacco seeds—a whole crop could be cupped in one hand—were spread broadcast in specially prepared seedbeds and covered lightly with dirt or straw. When the seedlings were sturdy enough, they were transplanted into the fields, one to each hill. For the rest, it was a matter of topping each plant in season to prevent the development of seeds and so force growth into the leaves, of hoeing both to grub out weeds and keep the hills about the tobacco stalk for support, of removing excess leaves and suckers—the secondary growths that emerged from the stalks in response to topping—of plucking attacking worms from the leaves, and of hoeing again, finally cutting, drying (or curing), and packing for shipment in great wooden casks called hogsheads. As new people arrived and settlement expanded, or as old settlers abandoned one piece of ground for another, new lands could be put into cultivation with minimum effort. It was not even necessary to clear the woods completely. At the very least, the trees were simply killed by "girdling," a process of cutting circles of bark from around the trunk, and the tobacco planted under the dead limbs. Most often, however, the trees were cut down; the useful wood set aside for fencing, building, or burning as firewood; the rest burned on the spot; and tobacco hills set among the stumps.[7]

In time the farmers of the Chesapeake learned much about "their *darling tobacco.*"[8] Varieties appeared: sweetscented, which grew best on light, sandy soils and commanded a premium price in England—this would be the tobacco favored in our county; and the more common oronoco. Within varieties, favored strains developed, named for the planters on whose land they first grew—Prior's seed, for example, Townsend's, Onedall's, Anchor's, Fleck's. The ubiquitous hoe evolved into a series of specialized implements, ranging from the heavy "grubbing hoe" used to break up previously untilled ground through the successively finer "sprouting hoe," "hilling hoe," and "weeding hoe." Variant practices evolved, and arguments took place over the most advantageous ratio of number of plants to acreage given particular types of soil, the number of leaves to retain on each plant, the proper timing of the various stages of the crop, and curing and packing techniques. Indeed, Virginia and Maryland would diverge widely, the Marylanders adopting practices designed to produce larger and larger crops at the sacrifice of quality and price, the Virginians opting for practices that resulted in smaller yields but better quality and, consequently, higher prices.[9] But the essentials of the hill agriculture adopted so early were virtually unchanged two centuries later, and a description of 1800 can be appropriately applied to any time and place within the early Chesapeake: The laborer with his hoe (or hers, for women too, worked the fields) "chopping the clods until they are sufficiently fine, and then drawing the earth round . . . the projected leg . . . like a mole hill, and nearly as high as the knee; he then draws out his foot, flattens the top of the hill by a *dab* with the flat part of the hoe, and advances forward to [make] the next hill in the same manner," continuing on "until the whole piece of ground is prepared."[10] The passage conveys the hard, tedious regime that tobacco imposed on those who labored to make a crop, a regime, moreover, that spanned the year from January, when the seedbeds were prepared and planted, through transplanting in May, cutting plants in August, and packing in October, to December, when trees and brush were cleared and new fields laid out.[11]

In one sense, the tobacco cultivation of the Chesapeake was crude, even slovenly, a stark contrast to the cross-plowing, harrowing, and ditching of English agriculture—the elaborate working of the soil of an increasingly intensive farming system. In another sense, however, it was a model of efficiency, of the principle of the least effort applied to gain the greatest profit. There was no need for elaboration when, with no more equipment than a hoe, a single laborer could set and tend two to three acres of semicleared land, between six and ten thousand plants, making a crop of eleven to twelve hundred pounds cured and packed in a good year, seven or eight hundred in a bad one, roughly three to six pounds sterling at Virginia's mid-century price.[12]

THE CHESAPEAKE FARMER'S YEAR

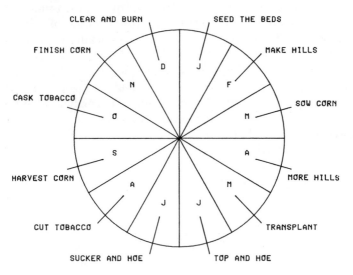

The very efficiency of tobacco cultivation defined and limited the way of farming in the Chesapeake. As tobacco production rose, the price the farmer received dropped, ultimately settling to between one and two pence a pound. But the farmer could not readily respond to lower prices by shifting to other crops. Even at a low price, tobacco retained an assured market of sorts. And, from the 1620s on, it was the circulating medium of the Chesapeake. Accounts might be kept in English pounds, shillings, and pence, but men paid their accounts (even their taxes) with pounds of tobacco. Equally to the point, tobacco cultivation itself dissuaded the farmer from attempting crops that could not be grown as simply, that is, that could not fit his hill and hoe system. Wheat, for example, would have required an investment of money in a plow and oxen and an investment of time in intensive and extensive clearing and soil preparation, money and time that could be spent with greater surety of at least some profit on tobacco. After all, the Chesapeake farmer knew that he need simply semiclear a few more acres and find another laborer and hoe in order to increase the productivity (and profitability) of his farm.

The fact that tobacco demanded intensive labor at particular times of the year further limited the farmer's options. If his seedbed was not prepared and planted on time, or his hills were not ready to receive the seedlings at the moment when the weather demanded, or topping, hoeing, suckering, worming, and cutting were not done in proper season, or the curing was too quickly and carelessly accomplished, a good part of the crop, perhaps all of it, would be ruined. The dependence upon the availability of labor at particular times is well illustrated by a Middlesex planter, Peter Montague, whose one male servant ran away at harvest time, leading Montague to seek relief because of "the whole loss of the . . . Cropp."[13] Any other crop that the Chesapeake farmer might contemplate—oats or wheat or barley—would have to have a crop cycle requiring labor at those times when tobacco did not. Otherwise its adoption would be at the expense of tobacco, the farmer's cash.

Until the end of the seventeenth century, by which time capital accumulation had proceeded to such a point that a few middling and large planters could break into new forms of agriculture, the limitations imposed by the very way in which tobacco was grown held good. Only corn and livestock meshed easily with tobacco. Cattle and hogs could be driven to the outskirts of the farm or onto unclaimed land and there left to graze freely. Corn, like tobacco, could be grown Indian fashion, in hills made with hoes, while its planting in the spring and harvesting in the fall, rather than competing with tobacco, filled interstices in the tobacco year.

Corn and livestock, moreover, filled a real need in the economy. The earliest settlers to Virginia fed themselves with foodstuffs carried from England or bought or stolen from surrounding Indian villages, a parasitism impossible to continue as the number of settlers steadily increased and neighboring Indian societies just as steadily collapsed. During the 1620s and 1630s, therefore, corn and livestock were gradually integrated into the agricultural system of the Chesapeake, and pork, beef, and corn—the last prepared in a multiplicity of ways—became the mainstays of the planters' diet. By mid-century cornfields and grazing livestock were as much hallmarks of the tobacco coast as tobacco itself.

A quarter of the way up Chesapeake Bay, on its western shore, lies Middlesex County. Captain John Smith and a band of explorers from Jamestown were the first Englishmen to see it. Of course, it was not then a county; and the captain and his men did not see all of it, only the southeastern tip, the flat, sandy flare that divides the mouths of two rivers flowing into the bay. Returning from exploring the upper Chesapeake in June 1608, Smith found his barge enmeshed in the currents and shoals that guard the entrance to the larger, northernmost river—the "Toppohannock," he called it—and eventually grounded by the ebbing tide. To while away the time until the next high tide, the men wandered the tidal pools, spearing fish with their swords. In the doing, Smith was stung by his own prey, a fish "of the fashion of a Thornebacke with a longer taile whereon is a most poysoned sting." His hand, arm, and shoulder swelled and, as the chronicler of the expedition wrote, "We al with much sorrow concluded his funerall and prepared his grave in an Ile hard by," calling the island "Stingray" to mark the event. But Smith did not die. Before nightfall his swelling subsided; indeed, the captain revenged himself by eating the culprit fish for dinner. The next day the explorers freed their boat and left, sailing down the bay toward home. Their toponym, Stingray, persisted, however: Stingray Isle until men discovered the flare was linked to the main, then Stingray Point.[14]

Other venturesome Englishmen undoubtedly saw the land over the next few decades. The rivers garnered permanent names, "Rappahannock" being attached to the mile-wide stream to the north, "Piankatank" to the lesser southern river. The tangled swamp from which the Piankatank emerges was named as well: "Dragon Swamp," or, more simply, "the Dragon." But the explorers left no record of themselves, and no Englishmen went to live along the rivers or on the low ridge that bisects the peninsula and holds the waters of the Rappahannock and Piankatank apart. While Jamestown went through its succession of alternating agonies and successes—"Starving

Times" and the propitious arrival of supplies, the military
regime and the "greate charter" of 1618, the Massacre of 1622
and royalization two years later—the land that was to be the
county was home only to some two hundred Indians.[15]

Through the early decades, as tobacco became the mainstay of the economy and Englishmen fanned out from toe-
holds on the James to occupy the Middle Peninsula between
the James and York rivers, the land remained empty of
Englishmen. Yet it was regularly probed by the inquisitive and
acquisitive. Boats scudding the bay on their way to and from
Maryland and the Virginians settling along the south bank of
the Potomac in what would become Northumberland County
passed the mouths of the two rivers and now and again turned
in to explore. Men came to tramp through the forests, blazing
trees to mark claims for the future. John Mattrom was one.
Already settled on the Potomac, he marked and claimed nineteen hundred acres on the Piankatank in 1642. Thomas Trot-
ter of York County was another, laying out five hundred acres
that same year.[16] More names were attached to the land: Mattrom's Mount, Glebeland Creek. The probing hesitated, then
stopped, as new Indian troubles appeared. In the aftermath
of Indian war, the land was acknowledged by treaty to be part
of the Indians' domain, and settlement in what was to become
Middlesex was barred. But in the very year of the treaty (1646),
cattle were being brought into the Piankatank by boat and left
to graze wild on its meadows. And in 1648, because of "the
great and clamorous necessities of divers of the inhabitants"
complaining of "over-wrought grounds and the apparent decay
of their cattle and hoggs for want of sufficient range," all
restrictions to settlement were removed.[17] The English entered
the land to live.

They entered by buying old claims or laying out new claims
of their own, always sprinkling names as they came, new
toponyms. The very act of naming places in the wilderness
made those places familiar and the wilderness less forebod-
ing. The old inhabitants of the peninsula—the Indians—simply disappeared before the newcomers. The latter sought no
title from them. In the minds of Englishmen, the land was the
king's and they need only meet the requirements of laws laid
down in Jamestown. Their records speak of the Indians only

in terms of abandoned towns and empty "Indian cabins."
Rowland Haddaway offers us the flavor of this English entry.
Testifying in a land suit at the end of the 1650s but harking
back to events of 1650 and 1651, Haddaway wrote of sailing
the Rappahannock in search of land with four other men:
"Going into a Creek . . . we gave it the name of Haddaways
Creek and I . . . did take up the land that Hugh Brent now
lives upon, there being three Indian Cabbins upon the said
land." Exploring further, the men came upon a promising
meadow. "Abraham Moone asked Thomas Gaskins whether
he liked the said land or would have any of the same." Gaskins answered, "No, for he thot it would drowne"; to which
Moone replied, "If you wil not, I wil have it myselfe [and he]
took a book out of his pocket and did set down the bounds." [18]
The boundaries so entered would form the basis for Moone's
later application for a patent to the land.

Some entering the land took up broad acres, bringing in
servants and setting them to work building houses, clearing,
and laying out fields. Others had only their own hands to do
the work. Ralph Wormeley and Oliver Seager represent the
extremes. Wormeley, in 1649, patented more than three
thousand acres stretching south and southeast along the banks
of the Rappahannock from the mouth of a small, deepwater
creek that the Indians called "Nimcock" and Captain Ralph
called "Rosegill." The next year he began building his house
on the windy point where the Rosegill enters the Rappahannock, at the same time adding two hundred–odd acres on the
upriver side of the creek. Wormeley died shortly thereafter,
leaving his wife Agatha and two young sons, William and
another Ralph, but Agatha quickly remarried, accepting Sir
Henry Chicheley as her husband. In 1653 Chicheley had seventeen servants at work on his and the Wormeley land—some
thirty-eight hundred acres in all.

Seager's more modest entry was far upriver, in the northwestern tip of what would become the county, where the Rappahannock, eroding the land, had formed a series of low cliffs.
In all likelihood a former servant, Seager arrived in 1652 with
his wife and small son, patenting two hundred acres in partnership with Francis Brown. In 1653 Brown and Seager were
working the land together. The former died soon after, leaving Seager sole owner.

With one strong pair of arms, or with the arms of many servants, the English bit into the wilderness, setting their cattle to graze in the clearings and marshes, putting their axes to the trees to make fields for their corn and tobacco and timber for their homes. In this entry into the county, we find nothing of that self-conscious effort to create a communal life that so marks New England. The Virginians did not move onto the land as a group, but as individuals. They signed no covenant binding themselves as a body politic, as did the settlers of Dedham, Massachusetts, when first entering the lands of their town.[19] Indeed, the county initially had no legal identity of its own, not even a name, being simply an extension of York County until 1651, when all the unorganized lands between the Piankatank and Potomac were joined in one mammoth county of Lancaster. Neither did the settlers on the peninsula attempt to control the parceling out of land in such a way as to hold themselves geographically together. The whole of the county was entered at once, from Seager in the far northwestern corner fronting on the Rappahannock to Thomas Bourne settling at about the same time on the Piankatank, just inside Stingray Point. More than twenty miles separated Seager and Bourne.

To some extent, however, the oncoming English, although entering individually, were already known to each other. This suggests itself when we consider that there must have been a process at work leading particular men and women to this land and not to land elsewhere and that the process was dependent upon familiarity. Clearly, men do not remove themselves from one place to another without at least some knowledge of what lies ahead of them. How then did Haddaway and his companions learn of the Rappahannock? How did Wormeley learn of Nimcock Creek, or Seager of the rich lands along the cliffs? The answer must lie in conversation. This was, after all, a society quite unlike our own, one in which the electronic word (telephone, television, radio) was nonexistent and the written word quite secondary to the word passed face-to-face. It is a point to which we will return frequently, but for now it is enough to sense the paramountcy of conversation in informing men and women of phenomena to which they will react.

Only in our mind's eye, of course, can we see the process

in operation. The extant records are scant and frequently more cryptic than informative; they are fleshed out to project a reality only by the exercise of imagination. When, for example, a visitor to a certain house on the lower bank of the York River in February 1650 wrote of guests gathering for "feasting and carousing," we can—when we realize that the house was that of Ralph Wormeley and that the host and two of the five guests named were even then taking up Middlesex land—imagine the conversation turning to the new area to the north.[20] Similarly, when members of the York County Court met, we can imagine them talking of land in the lacunae between official business, specifically of the land between the Rappahannock and Piankatank, when we realize that four of the court members of the 1640s would later move to that very land: Wormeley, Richard Lee, Rowland Burnham, and William Brocas. And we can imagine conversations begun at court carried into families. Brocas, Wormeley, and Burnham were all brothers-in-law (married to Eleanor, Agatha, and Alice Eltonhead respectively), while Brocas's first wife, Mary, had previously been wife to Ralph Wormeley's brother Christopher. Information passed in conversations at one level of society—that of a Wormeley, Brocas, or Burnham—in all probability passed to other levels as well. Abraham Moone, one of Haddaway's companions, served the York court as undersheriff. Richard Perrott, who would take up land just below Seager on the Rappahannock, worked for Brocas. We are not assuming too much if we assume that when such men turned their minds to finding land of their own they were directed to the land that would become our county by conversations with or between their betters.

If, indeed, familiar, face-to-face conversation was central to the process bringing the first English men and women into the county, then it follows that we ought to think of those who opened the land as relatives, friends, and acquaintances of each other even prior to their entrance onto the peninsula. And this seems born out when, in 1653, we get our first glimpse, however veiled, of the population as a whole. In October of that year, Lancaster County surveyed its tithable persons— essentially males and black females sixteen years of age and over—for the purposes of taxation, charging leading citizens in various parts of the county with the task of collecting the taxes according to the number of tithables in each "family." The list of family "heads" and the number of tithables for which each was responsible has survived, while the geographic organization of the list, together with evidence from extant land records, allows us to isolate those heads living on lands in what would become Middlesex. Of these last (twenty-four in number), over half had previously lived in a cluster along the south bank of the York River. Just under half can be shown to have known each other, a few as relatives, the rest as at least acquaintances.[21]

If we consider all those entering in the 1650s, a tangled skein of relationships approaching Cervantes's "medley of kindred, that . . . would puzzle a convocation of casuists to resolve" appears.[22] We have already noted the Eltonhead sisters: Agatha, her sons by Ralph Wormeley, and current husband Henry Chicheley living on Rosegill Creek; Eleanor and William Brocas; Alice and Rowland Burnham. Just across the Rappahannock was Edwin Connoway, married to still another Eltonhead sister, Martha. Their daughter, Eltonhead Connoway, was the recipient of a black-browed cow called "Thacker," a gift from Aunt Agatha Chicheley "in consideracion of the love and affecion I beare unto my neece."[23] Just downriver from Rosegill was the property of Elizabeth Lunsford, daughter of Chrisopher Wormeley, niece of Ralph, cousin to his sons, stepdaughter to William Brocas, and twice a widow, most recently of Sir Thomas Lunsford and prior to that of Richard Kemp. The latter union related her to Edmund Kemp, whose property lay south and east of her own, on the Piankatank. Kemp's father, Edmund, had been Richard's brother. Upriver and inland from Rosegill lay the land of Cuthbert Potter who, in 1656, received land certificates for the transportation to Virginia of his cousins Richard and Giles Robinson. The latter was managing the Potter land in 1658. Eventually two other members of the Robinson family would arrive from England, Christopher and Frances, brother and sister of Potter's wife.

Marriages among these early settlers made the medley all the more complex. Grey Skipwith (whose mother was a Kemp) entered the county at the end of the first decade, married

Edmund Kemp's widow, and became both neighbor and step-father to Edmund's heir, Matthew, whom Skipwith called "Cozen Matt."[24] Skipwith arrived in Virginia with his sister Diana, who soon afterward married Edward Dale. Dale's home was on the north side of the Rappahannock, but he was linked to Richard Perrott on the south side through kinship with Nicholas Dale, whose widow was Perrott's "now wife." Peter Montague, William Thompson, and John Jadwyn all appear as heads of family on a 1658 list of tithables. Thompson and Jadwyn were Montague's sons-in-law, married to his daughters Ellen and Ann respectively. And Thompson was also Montague's stepson by virtue of Peter's marriage to Thompson's mother, Cicely.

We can, however, go beyond a mere recounting of relationships to suggest a consciousness of the desirability of surrounding oneself with kin on the part of these early settlers. The entry from England of Christopher and Frances Robinson is an example. They could have gone anywhere in the Chesapeake, but they settled in the vicinity of their Robinson and Potter kin. The Lady Lunsford is another. At the death of Sir Thomas she came into control of more than three thousand acres far up the Rappahannock and a separate parcel of but a third that number next to her Wormeley-Chicheley relations. She chose to live on the latter.

Henry Corbin is still a third of those who opted to live among relations. A figure beloved in Virginia legend, Corbin is said to have fought for royalty in the English Civil War, helped Charles II escape capture at the battle of Worcester, and himself escaped Cromwellian vengeance by fleeing abroad.[25] Perhaps. Certainly he was a convivial person, for in Virginia he and two neighbors built a "banqueting hall" where their three properties came together. But we know with even more certainty that he was the second son of a Warwick County, England, family and a London merchant. In 1654, at age twenty-four, he received a four hundred–pound legacy from his father. Shortly thereafter he sailed for the Chesapeake, probably to serve as the American arm of a transatlantic merchant partnership, his brothers Gawin and Thomas staying on in London. In June he was in Maryland, where he probably came to know William Eltonhead, brother of our Eltonhead sisters. By the next year, he was busily establishing himself on the Virginia side of the Potomac. And in 1657, following Rowland Burnham's death, he married Alice Eltonhead. Alice could just as easily have moved north to the Potomac. But instead Corbin moved south to the Rappahannock, assuming control of the widow Burnham's acres. We have no direct entry into motives, of course. But Corbin had no kin on the Potomac; by moving to the Rappahannock, he immediately surrounded himself with relationships.

Such a quest for family meshes well with another aspect of this English entry that we must recognize. The oncoming English carried an English heritage into the county. Virtually all were English-born, and an English sense of family, of kith and kin, and of society as an ordered array of interdependent families committed to the common good was an integral part of their makeup.[26] The very fact of organizing the early tithable lists by "families"—in 1653 subsuming Seager, his wife, child, and partner Francis Brown as one family; Chicheley, Agatha, Agatha's sons, and seventeen servants as another—hints at this cultural background. But Virginians in general reflected such an orientation.

The law itself at this early date subsumed husband, wife, children, and servants into familial units, the master of which was held responsible for an array of public obligations. Thus by law of 1644, "the masters of . . . family . . . shall be responsible for all publique duties, tithes and charges, due from all persons in their family, And shall . . . keep in their . . . custody the cropps and shares of all freemen within their family until satisfaction be made of all such publique duties, tithes and charges." By law of 1646, "all masters of families, upon warning given by the ministers," were to "cause their children and servants to repair to the places appointed to be instructed and catechised." The master of the house was held responsible for the drunkenness and swearing of his "servants and people under age," for maintaining arms for his children and servants over sixteen, for supplying information to the appropriate clerks as to the deaths and births occurring among his charges, and even for sending members of his "family" to clear roads and build and repair bridges. And there was no question as to who in the house was to play the master. When, across the bay in Accomac County, Robert Brace was unable to control the "insolent demeanor" of one servant and fell into rancorous (and public) argument with another, his county court ordered all three punished—Brace because he "hath degenerated so much from a man, as neither to beare Rule over his women Servant, nor govern his house, but made one in that scolding society."[27]

On Thursday, November 17, 1657, a dozen or more heads of families met at the home of Henry Corbin—formerly Burnham's—high on a bluff overlooking the broken shoreline of the Rappahannock, some five miles downriver from Seager's at the cliffs. Perhaps like the Virginia councillors described by a traveler a few years later, they sat about Corbin's great room "booted and with belted sword"; or perhaps they met outside, under the Corbin Oak, where local legend has other such gatherings being held.[28] In any event, those meeting together would hardly look to us like the staid fathers of the vicinage they thought themselves. They ranged in age from twenty to thirty; the foremost amongst them, Corbin himself, was but twenty-seven.

This was their second meeting of the year. In the early spring, they had gathered to write a petition to the Lancaster County Court stipulating that they intended to build a church for themselves and asking for the court's approval of their doings. The court not only placed its imprimatur on their intentions, but authorized them to form a parish embracing the families settled from the cliffs southward along the river for a distance of some ten miles and inland toward the Dragon. Now, in November, they were meeting again. Representing themselves to be "the major part of the Inhabitants" of the vicinity, they proceeded to select vestrymen, churchwardens, and sidemen from among their numbers, officers who would run the affairs of their parish. Equally as important, they met to come to an agreement with a young minister, Samuel Cole. For their part, they agreed to proceed with the building of a church "with all convenient speed," stipulating that it would be built on a point just south of where they sat. They would pay Cole four thousand pounds of "good Tobo in Cask" yearly and make some arrangement for a horse and glebe for him—

the latter a farm dedicated to the support of the church and placed in the occupancy of the incumbent minister. On his side, Cole agreed to preach every other Sabbath and officiate at "all Christenings, burials, marriages, Churchings, and what else is proper to his office."[29]

The meetings of Corbin and his neighbors suggest much about the entry into the county, all the more because they occurred (and were recorded) so early, when evidence of the doings of the county's people is scant and vague. In one sense, they were redundant meetings. The Lancaster County Court had already engaged Cole as a minister for the whole county, presumably to officiate alternately to the settlers north and south of the Rappahannock.[30] Yet to the men gathered, the meetings were not redundant but vital. Parish, church, and minister were elements of their English tradition, important not only for religion but as a "social thing"—sociologist Emile Durkheim's phrase.[31] Through a parish organization, neighbors cared for the indigent among them and for orphaned and bastard children, kept the memory of property boundaries alive by periodic perambulations, set moral boundaries by prosecuting the immoral, and in sundry ways ascribed status to each other. The church building itself was a nexus of neighborhood life, its services a gathering place for gossip, its door a bulletin board, its pulpit a source of news. And christenings, marriages, and burials were the traditional public rites of English families, part religious but also part symbolic displays to the larger group. Corbin and his neighbors, through church and parish, were in effect identifying themselves as living a common life, sorting themselves out by elevating those of worth and substance in the neighborhood to formal positions of leadership, and by their separate dealings with Cole associating his priestly functions directly with their commonality.

Throughout the broad swath of territory organized in 1651 as Lancaster County—twenty-five miles wide and extending without boundary north and west along both sides of the Rappahannock—the same phenomenon was taking place. Entering here and there along the rivers and creeks, the English formed enclaves, scattered but self-conscious neighborhoods, which were increasingly delineated as the larger area dis-

solved into parts. In 1654 the upriver settlers had formed their
own parish and in 1656, at their behest, had been separated
from Lancaster altogether and joined in a new county.[32] What
was left of Lancaster County, almost three hundred square
miles, was itself a collection of neighborhoods. On the north
side of the Rappahannock, the parishes of Christ Church and
St. Mary's White Chapel were already coalescing. Corbin's
neighborhood along the southern bank of the river and now
forming as Lancaster Parish was simply another. And there
was still another on the peninsula that would become Middlesex.

Corbin and his neighbors had entered the land via the
Rappahannock and, although some already were taking up
land inland, away from the water, they were oriented toward
that river. On the lower part of the peninsula, most were
entering via the Piankatank and were oriented toward the
narrower stream. Of the two clusters of families, the Piankatank neighborhood was the smaller in 1657—seventeen families as against twenty-four. Both boasted one or two major
landholders: Corbin and Perrott in Lancaster, the former with
2,250 acres and a dozen servants, the latter 1,250 acres and a
half-dozen laborers; Edmund Kemp on the Piankatank had
1,100 acres and some six servants. Four of the heads of families on the Piankatank—but none in Lancaster—were renting
land. The holdings of the rest in both areas ranged upward
from 100 acres, with most between 300 and 600, worked by
the holder himself and one, at most two, laborers.

Distance and their differing orientation separated the
clusters. But their separation was also a function of the land
structure, for between them lay the most significant properties in the area: the Wormeley-Chicheley land (over 3,000 acres
worked by twenty or more servants); that of the Lady Lunsford (1,700 acres and a dozen servants); that of her "loving
friend" Richard Lee (350 acres and eight servants); and the
more than 1,000 acres formerly belonging to William Brocas
but since his death in the hands of his land-rich but labor-
poor nephew John Jackson.[33] (Brocas's Eltonhead wife,
Eleanor, did not leave the vicinity at his death; marrying John
Carter, she simply moved across the Rappahannock to the
north shore.) Chicheleys, Lunsfords, and Lees were part of

neither of the neighborhoods. Physically scattered, they clustered socially among themselves.

No records of the collective actions of the Piankatank families have survived, but it is obvious that even before the meetings at Corbin's that led to the formation of Lancaster Parish they had reached out toward each other to form a proto-parish of sorts. By 1657 they had a churchwarden, George Keeble; the county court recognized him as such in April, although it had not to this point authorized their parish organization.[34] Certainly by midsummer of that year, the Piankatank families were sufficiently conscious of themselves as a group to enter instant and heated objection to the boundaries the court established for Lancaster Parish, thereby precipitating a decade-long dispute between the two neighborhoods, the crux of which was the allocation of the scattered holdings intervening between them.

The court's first order (May 1657) extended Lancaster Parish southward along the river so far as to include the Lady Lunsford and possibly Richard Lee. This, the Piankatank neighbors complained, had been done "without their knowledge and consent and contrary to the acte of Assembly for layeing out of parishes"—the latter apparently a reference to a recent act of the Virginia legislature providing that "all countys not yet laid out into parishes shall be divided . . . the next county court after publication hereof." Their not having had knowledge that the court was about to proceed, they seem to have argued, was prima facie evidence that the act had not been suitably published. The court responded (September 1657) by rescinding its earlier order and issuing a new one authorizing the formation of two parishes south of the river, Lancaster and Piankatank, and drawing the boundary between them in such a way that the Wormeley-Chicheley land fell to Lancaster and the Lunsford (and presumably Lee) land fell to Piankatank.[35] The partition sat ill with Lancaster, which continued to insist on including Lunsford land even while appealing the division to the government in Jamestown.[36]

In 1659 something of a truce was arrived at, Lancaster agreeing to the court's boundaries but with the proviso that parish taxes "due from the Lady Lunsfords plantacion and other plantacions for the time past" be paid to Lancaster. The wrangling continued, however, and each new holding laid out in the disputed area precipitated discussion as to which parish it belonged. As late as 1665, in instructing the churchwarden John Curtis to collect levies in the lower part of Lancaster Parish, the vestry carefully instructed him that if he "conceives any late Seated Plantacion within our bounds," he was to demand "The Leveys of Them, but forbeare the receiving of it."[37] The forbearance was called for insamuch as the two parishes were then in the process of negotiating their union.

In and of themselves neither Piankatank nor Lancaster was viable as an independent entity. They were mere neighborhoods, each too few in numbers to generate enough revenue to support the parish, church, and minister to which it aspired. The very fact of their smallness made the argument between Lancaster and Piankatank all the more intense, for they were not debating parishioners—the Lady Lunsford and, after 1659, her new husband, Robert Smith, do not seem to have taken part in the affairs of either parish—but revenues. The lady's fourteen tithables in 1658 represented a levy of roughly 280 pounds of tobacco, 7 percent of what Lancaster had promised to pay Minister Cole.[38] Lancaster, moreover, was itself physically divided by deepwater creeks flowing into the Rappahannock, particularly Sunderland Creek just below Corbin's, and Rosegill, which set off the Chicheleys (although it is doubtful that the Chicheleys felt any more attached to Lancaster than the Lady Lunsford felt attached to Piankatank). Thus, while their Piankatank rivals proceeded to build a church, the Lancaster men—despite their promise to Cole—argued about the site of theirs, using private houses for services in the meantime. Not until 1665 would they settle their internecine dispute, and then only by resorting to a choice by lot.[39]

Lancaster divided, each parish too small, the two perforce cooperated even as they argued their bounds. In 1657, when promising Minister Cole a horse and glebe, the Lancaster men counted on the Piankatank families to share the cost. In 1658 and 1659 the two parishes shared Minister Cole's services and jointly paid his salary, having early weaned him away from the notion of officiating on both sides of the Rappahannock. Cole died in 1659, leaving both parishes empty. Soon after, the parishes north of the Rappahannock lost their incumbent as well (Cole's successor). When a search for a replacement proved futile, the county court declared the reason to be "the smallnes of the parishes, not able to give such a competency as may invite Mynisters to officiate amongst us." Its solution was to ask the inhabitants of all the parishes to meet to consider creating a single, countywide parish. But Lancaster and Piankatank preferred to cooperate between themselves, their vestries in 1664 negotiating "Concerning The Settlement and payment of Mr Morris" as a common minister to reside with them. The very next year the Lancaster vestrymen delegated two of their members to "treat" with Piankatank "for the Firme Settleing of the Bounds of our Pish, or the Uniteing of both Parishes into one." The negotiations proved lengthy for it was not until January 1667 that the two vestries met together as "a Generall Vestry for the South Side" to "accord and Agree that the Two parishes . . . be united as one, and called Christ Church parish," dispatching Robert Smith and Henry Corbin to Jamestown to gain approval by the colony government of their work.[40]

All the while the families of the peninsula were increasingly isolated from the neighborhoods north of the Rappahannock to which they were attached as a county. The mile-wide river was a boundary, an obstruction to any sense of commonality between what were more and more being referred to as "Northside" and "Southside." In the earliest years, county court meetings had been held occasionally to the south of the river, but the building of a county courthouse on the Northside ended the practice. All courts in the 1660s were held on the Northside, and, indeed, the members of the court were by and large residents of Northside. County business south of the river had, of necessity, to be done via surrogates, sometimes through the parishes but increasingly in such a way as to recognize the Southside as an entity unto itself. In 1664, for example, separate commissioners were appointed to the Northside and Southside to "clere the highways." In 1666, "For the ease of the inhabitants of the Southside," the county court allowed petitions to be submitted through Cuthbert Potter, who was to transmit them to the clerk of the court.[41] The isolation led the Southsiders to appeal to the colony's

assembly for separate county status, and in 1664 an order to
divide Lancaster was issued from Jamestown. The county court,
however, "thought good to adjourne the same" and wrote the
governor asking that the whole business be deferred.[42] In
September 1667, after the union of their parishes, the Southsiders tried another approach, asking "that Every other Court
might bee kept" on their side of the river. The Northside-
dominated court would have none of it, answering that "they
conceave it very just and reasonable, that the Court bee continued where it hath for many yeres past beene dew kept,"
adding peevishly that "if the Southside . . . shalbe pleased to
devide themselves and make a County . . . they are lefte to
their own librti when they thinke fitt." The two Southside
members present, John Curtis and eighteen-year-old Ralph
Wormeley, abstained from the vote and at its conclusion stalked
from the courtroom.[43] Within a year, the Southsiders, through
Christ Church vestry, were petitioning the assembly in Jamestown asking that its 1664 order be put into effect. Six months
later they had won separation as Middlesex County.[44]

    Two separate but mutually reinforcing movements—one
to unify the parishes, the other to separate politically from the
parent county—had led to the creation of Middlesex and the
coterminous parish of Christ Church. Without doubt geography was a root cause. The parent county was split by the
river, while Middlesex–Christ Church nestled within natural
bounds drawn by river, bay, and swamp. Yet the peninsula
was itself divided, at times bitterly, between two competing
neighborhoods, and, as we will have occasion to see, these early
divisions survived the creation of the county. What seems to
have drawn the county together was not simply nature but the
influence of an amorphous, ill-defined third neighborhood
forming at mid-peninsula. Here initially were a few large and
significant holdings. In the decade after 1657, even as the area
grew in number of families, this remained true; indeed, by
purchase of large blocks of Brocas land, the Wormeley-Chicheley property came to extend halfway across the peninsula
from river to swamp. Here, too, the contested parish boundary meandered between properties, attaching some families,
at least for levy purposes, to Lancaster, some to Piankatank,
and some, apparently, to limbo. But far from the center of

either parish, few mid-peninsula families received much by way of either services or a sense of shared community for levies paid.

We do not, of course, know for sure that the mid-peninsula families—specifically the most prominent among them, Chicheley, his young stepson Ralph Wormeley, Robert Smith—inspired the union of rival Lancaster and Piankatank and the subseqent formation of Middlesex. Historians are privy to very little beyond results. Certainly, however, the results favored what would soon be called the "Middle Precinct." The formal agreement uniting the parishes, held at Chicheley's on Rosegill Creek, provided that "the late reputed" parishes of Piankatank and Lancaster would be levied separately one last time, the former to pay for repairs to their already-built church, the latter to undertake the long-delayed building of theirs. [45] But both churches would be only "chappels at Ease" to "a Mother Church"—Christ Church itself. This would be built on an old Indian field on Wormeley land, "it being Adjudged . . . to be about the Middle of the parish," and the whole parish would pay for its construction.[46]

Contemporaries and subsequent historians have dwelt on the scattered way in which the English of the Chesapeake settled the land. The former—Roger Green, for example, quoted in chapter 1—bewailed "the scatter'd living" and recounted the consequent evils: "The great want of Christian Neighbourhood, or brotherly admonition, of holy Examples of religious Persons, of the Comfort of theirs, and their Ministers Administrations in Sicknesse and Distresses, of the Benefit of Christian and Civil Conference and Commerce."[47] The latter, more often than not, have been content to quote the former and let the matter go.

But the scattered entry into Middlesex was only a matter of geography. The awful consequence—the "want of Christian Neighborhood"—does not apply. Dispersed as they were, those who ran the affairs of Middlesex consciously sought to order their lives around families and the neighborhood institutions with which they were familiar. For them, as for their critics, it seems that disorder was anathema, even sinful. Nature, in John Dryden's poetry, was but "a heap / Of jarring atoms," and order, the response of nature to a commanding but "tuneful voice . . . from high." Middlesex reflected the lyrical, albeit in mundane fashion and from human and cultural imperatives. Nature—Virginia's wilderness, broken now by clearings here and there, by houses, fences, and fields—would have been jarring without order, unlivable; and order to the men of Middlesex was a matter of men of family and substance, through vestry and court, supplying themselves and their neighbors with a church, good minister, and fair judgments, a matter even of making sure that "the Scald head" of the orphan child "of William Baldwins Decd." was properly cured.[48] The wonder is not so much that the families of Middlesex entered in scattered fashion and lived in the midst of their own lands rather than in villages, but that they ordered themselves in their own fashion so very quickly.

3. The Road

As the Dictates of Nature are of Force sufficient for securing the Safety of Particular Beings . . . So the Ties we are under, from the Relation which we bear to Communities, and as we all are link'd together in Society, engage our Care for their Defence, and our Concern for their Welfare. Both the Country where we Live, and the Prince that does Protect us, claim from us a particular Regard for their Interest and Happiness.

— Sir Thomas Grantham, *An Historical Account of Some Memorable Actions . . .*

FROM THE NORTHWEST where the county began, the road stretched south and east twenty-two miles as the crow would fly, over thirty-five miles by the course the road actually took, ending only when the land fell away and the waters of the bay began. The road was little more than a broad path, beaten flat by the feet of men and women and the hooves of animals, its red soil so compacted as to discourage all but the hardiest weed from growing. In general, the road kept to the high ground between the rivers. But here and there it dropped into an abrupt declivity to meander in seemingly aimless fashion until a rude timber bridge carried it across a stream or swamp. It was almost as though the first person traversing the ground had searched about for the easiest crossing and all those coming after had followed his track. Sometimes, however, abrupt turnings were the product of manmade, not natural obstacles; for now and again as the road was in the process of becoming a road, some county man, in order to make better use of his land, would

block one path with fencing or brush, forcing passersby to
beat another.

Dusty in summer, mired by spring rains, laid down with
minimal plan, the road nevertheless was part of a reasonable
scheme of things. It was the central nerve of the county. The
families had originally entered by way of the waterways—the
Rappahannock and Piankatank—and the waterways carried
their tobacco to markets across the sea. But the road linked
them to each other.

As the county formed in late 1668 and early 1669, eighty-
three families, just over nine hundred men, women, and children lived on and about the road, and large sections of the
county were still unpopulated. In the far northwest, the land
to the south and west of the road as far as the Dragon, what
would be called Jamaica Land, was virtually empty; the heart
of old Lancaster Parish—now the upper precinct—lay between
the road and the Rappahannock. Here a spider web of paths
and lanes threaded through the woods to join houses to each
other, to the road itself, and the the newly built Upper Chapel,
high on the ridge between Sunderland and Perrott's creeks.
A side road branched northeasterly some five miles below the
county line, linking the road to the chapel. Near the juncture,
Randolph Seager—Oliver's son—would, late in the 1680s, lay
out the county's most prominent racetrack; in 1700 it would
be referred to as the "publick Race Ground Commonly Called
Seagers."[1] Two miles below, at the Mickleburrough property,
the road reached the south branch of Sunderland Creek, the
first major barrier across its path. Mickleburrough's bridge
carried it across and, two miles further on, the road entered
the middle precinct.

Here, in the center of the county, the road branched several times. On the high ground between Rosegill Creek and
Dragon Swamp, just above where the courthouse would eventually be built, a path cut abruptly south to cross the Dragon
into Gloucester County. At the moment, the route was used
only infrequently, for the crossing was dangerous, but there
had been talk of building a bridge since 1662, and its construction followed shortly on the formation of the county.[2] A
mile beyond this first junction, the road branched again. The

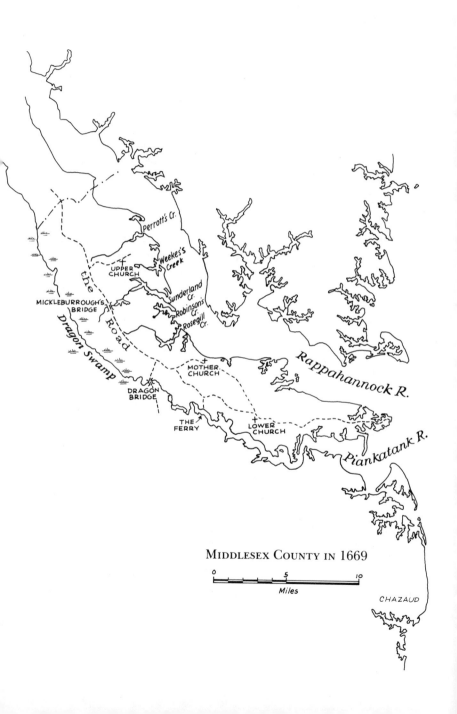

Perrott's Cr.

Weekes's Creek

UPPER CHURCH

Sunderland Cr.

Robinsons Cr.

Rosegill Cr.

the Road

MICKLEBURROUGH'S BRIDGE

Dragon Swamp

DRAGON BRIDGE

MOTHER CHURCH

THE FERRY

LOWER CHURCH

Rappahannock R.

Piankatank R.

MIDDLESEX COUNTY IN 1669

0   5   10

Miles

CHAZAUD

main path edged southeasterly toward the Piankatank and on into the lower precinct, traversing an area of alternating hills and swamps—"My Lady's Swamp," "the Beaver Dams"—before emerging onto level ground at the Lower Chapel. Halfway down this course, still another path cut away to a ferry across the Piankatank, the safest way into Gloucester before the building of the Dragon Bridge. The second path headed north from the road and onto Wormeley land, now generally called "Rosegill Plantation," turned to parallel the Rappahannock along the heights to reach the Mother Church, then continued on through the Lady Lunsford's "Brandon Plantation" before looping southward to rejoin the main road just above the chapel.

The Lower Chapel itself stood roughly in the middle of its precinct and here, as in old Lancaster Parish, there was a cluster of relatively small holdings joined together by a spider web of subsidiary paths. Through this web, increasingly unrecognizable as anything other than simply another strand, the road stretched eastward, past Skipwith's and Kemp's, finally crossing the "neck of land" that attached the main to Stingray. There on the point it ended.

To a modern traveler along the road, any part of the countryside could only appear desolate, the middle precinct a bit more so than the rest. There the rugged terrain between the main road and the northern loop, an area broken by the headwaters of My Lady's Swamp and the Beaver Dams, was all but empty of people and only vaguely surveyed; small gores of land would still be unclaimed well into the eighteenth century. The northern loop, "the Church path" as it was frequently called, ran for half its length through Rosegill, and while this was the most populated holding in the county—forty-eight tithables in 1668, 10 percent of all the tithables in Middlesex—most were laborers clustered on the several "quarters" of the plantation. The largest of these, that immediately surrounding the Wormeley-Chicheley house, lay on the waterside a mile from the church path. A traveler described it in the mid-1680s as "a rather large village" of "at least twenty houses in a lovely plain along the Rappahannock."[3] But the rest of Rosegill's thousands of acres were woods and natural clearings, broken only here and there by an occasional tenant farm.

In the emptiness of the middle precinct, the paths tended to be routes to places—the road to Mickleburrough's bridge, to the Mother Church, to the Piankatank, to the ferry—in contrast to the upper and lower precincts, where the paths linked families. Everywhere, however, in 1668, the road and its subsidiary paths passed through woods more often than through a landscape improved by man. The experience of a visitor of the 1680s would not have been atypical. Wandering away from his host's home "a simpling"—that is, collecting wild herbs—he soon found himself lost and subsequently wrote home of "gazeing round to spie an opening that is a Plantation."[4]

Even man's improvements would appear rough, crude, desolate to a modern eye, certainly in the spring before the tobacco and corn had grown high enough to hide the stumps among which the planters set their hills. Rail fences surrounded the cultivated fields, the farmers laboriously collecting logs to lay lengthwise as a base for the fence—"great timber trees" one traveler called them, heavy enough "so that piggs may not creep" under and into the crop—then pounding stakes into the ground on either side of the logs so that the stakes leaned against the logs to form forks to carry four or more rails.[5] Tobacco houses were ubiquitous—long, narrow wooden structures in which the tobacco was hung in tiers to dry. In the midst of the railed fields stood the farmers' houses, small framed affairs of unpainted, weathering wood, pleasant enough within (according to another traveler) if the planter were well-enough off to coat his walls with a plaster made from oyster shells and "white as snow," but "ugly from the outside, where only the wood can be seen."[6] More than likely one or the other corner of the house would be sagging. For in a land where stone was scarce, skilled bricklayers few in number and expensive to hire, and capital committed to things conducive to income rather than comfort—to land and laborers and cattle—even the prominent planters eschewed foundation walls. Houses were framed with earthfast posts sunk in the ground and extending upward to the plates supporting the rafters. Or, more commonly as the century progressed, the posts were truncated into piers that held the entire structure above ground. In the first instance, the floor of the house was frequently tamped earth, in the second planks. In either event, deterioration was inevitable. Cedar and cypress posts from the Dragon were the best available, but the best was not always used and even it in time fell prey to dampness or termites or both. Houses, even public buildings, constructed also on wooden piers, were in constant need of repairs, eventually replacement.[7] The glebe house that Christ Church Parish finally provided for its minister illustrates the problem.

Situated in mid-county a half-mile off the road, between the road and Rosegill Creek, the house was probably built by Cuthbert Potter in the late 1650s, conveyed to Alexander Smith in 1666, and sometime before 1673 conveyed by Smith to Richard Robinson who, that year, sold it and four hundred acres to the parish for 20,000 pounds of tobacco. But whoever owned it, minister John Shepherd (Robinson's cousin-in-law) was renting it in 1671 when the vestry allowed him 490 pounds of tobacco to undertake minor repairs. Following purchase, the vestry allowed major work, voting 5,030 pounds of tobacco to reimburse Master Shepherd for the cost, a quarter of the purchase price of the house and land, carefully specifying that he was "to leave The Dwelling house . . . in as good repaire at his Departure from the Gleab as now when finished." Twelve years later, with the advent of a new minister, 4,000 pounds of tobacco were required to make the glebe "Tenantable." More repairs were necessary in 1691 and 1693, but it was all a stopgap. In the late 1690s, an entirely new house was built for the minister at a cost of 6,480 pounds of tobacco—an unreasonably high price, the vestry thought—while another 1,000 pounds were apparently sunk in the old house to keep it standing until its replacement was completed. Only ten years later the vestrymen were considering another remodeling, ordering that the house "be forthwith framed and removed out of the place where it now stands and set upon blocks in the Most Commodious place that may be." They decided instead to build anew, planning on spending 18,000 pounds of tobacco. Construction was slow and costs spiraled upward; the builder was ordered paid 18,000 in 1707, 24,000 in 1708, 18,000 for "goeing on with the glebe" in 1709, and 1,600 at completion in 1711. Still, the chimneys needed alteration in 1719 (3,590 pounds of tobacco), and in 1728 the then-minister informed the vestry that "the Mansion house" and outbuildings were "in so ruinous a Condition" that he would have to resign. "The Vestry being very Sensible that in case Mr. Yates Should resign . . . no other Minister would receive the Buildings in the condition they are at present" voted unanimously to undertake to repair the old structure as a make-do until a new one could be built. The record: Over an eighty-year span, one dwelling house was built, twice rebuilt, and replaced completely three times.[8]

In terms of social and economic position within the county, the minister was clearly something more than a Seager yet less than a Wormeley. His income from salary alone (sixteen thousand pounds of tobacco a year) was matched or bettered by only a minority of his parishioners. Hence his glebe house can serve to illustrate the size and style of an above-average planter's home. That which Minister Shepherd took possession of in the early 1670s was described as "a 25 foot Dwelling," implying twenty-five feet long and no more than sixteen to eighteen feet in breadth. In all likelihood, it consisted of a single room on the ground floor and another upstairs under the eaves, the two joined by a ladder or a narrow stairway tucked beside a framed and wattled chimney. A massive fireplace at one end of the ground floor room was Frances Shepherd's kitchen, a corner of the common table the good parson's study, and a curtained bedstead in the corner the couple's bedroom. Children and maidservants slept in the windowless room upstairs, pallets and beds competing for space with the produce and odd "lumber" stored there. Male servants slept in a separate building nearby.

The glebe house built in the 1690s was larger, forty feet long by twenty feet wide, with brick chimneys and ground-floor fireplaces at both ends. The larger size allowed the first-floor room to be divided by a partition separating an "inner room" from the "hall" or "great hall" or "common room," the latter still the setting for cooking, eating, and entertaining, the inner room allowing the minister and his wife a modicum of privacy for sleeping and study. The new house of the early 1700s was not any larger, still forty feet long by twenty wide. But to the front was attached an eight-foot "entry" or "porch" with an additional room above. Heat and light were now provided for the upstairs by larger end chimneys with both first-

Common Houses of Middlesex

THE POORER SORT

Weatherboarded walls & roofing

Plank door and window shutter

Dirt floor Earthfast studs

Lathe & plaster hood & chimney

Ladder to loft

16'

20'

FOUNDATION PIER CONSTRUCTION

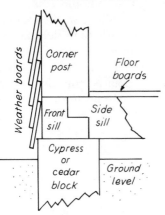

Weather boards

Corner post

Floor boards

Front sill

Side sill

Cypress or cedar block

Ground level

ONE STEP UP

stairs to loft

Brick chimney & fireplace, raised board floor, stairs, shingled roof, casement window

16'

24'

AMONG THE BEST

40'

Up

Hall

Inner room

20'

Porch

to kitchen house

Down

Outer chamber

Inner chamber

Porch room

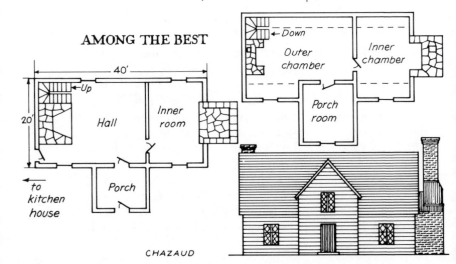

CHAZAUD

and second-floor fireplaces and by a "porch chamber" window, perhaps even dormer windows. And the hall no longer doubled as kitchen, a separate building being provided for cooking, another to serve as a dairy.

What is most striking about all of these houses—the glebe houses described and others that could be described—are their small size and the progression over time. The glebe, recall, is comparable to the home of an above-average planter; most other houses in the county were smaller. Indeed, the majority of the families of Middlesex, together with their possessions, crowded into spaces not much larger than a modern two-car garage. But the glebe was gradually enlarged and improved; sundry outbuildings came to surround it, and specific functions—cooking, for example—were removed from the house itself. At least on the level of the middling and better-than-middling planter, this was generally the case.

Beyond these two points, however, we must catch a mental image of the buildings. With their steep roofs, narrow casement windows, towering end chimneys, and grey, weathering look, they summon to mind the adjectives "gothic" and "medieval", and indeed just such have been attached to them by one scholar.[9] The adjectives flesh out our mind's eye view of the landscape of the early county: a winding dirt road, stump-pocked fields, rail fences, tiny buildings medieval and dilapidated in appearance, and the ever-present woods.

There are many ways to glimpse the people of early Middlesex. We can, in our imagination, knock on the door of one of the houses along the road and enter as visitors. If the house were that of Thomas Tuggle and the date 1668, we would find within Thomas himself, his wife Mary, Mary's eleven-year-old son by a previous marriage, John Burke, three of Thomas and Mary's own children—Mary (age seven), Thomas (four), one-year-old Anne—and William Steward, a newly arrived fourteen-year-old obliged to serve Tuggle for ten years. As visitors are likely to do, we might (still in our imagination) engage the older children in conversation. The talk would be constrained but revealing.

School? These particular children had none, although in a few years time there would be occasional schoolmasters offering one or two years of lessons in reading and ciphering to some of the county's boys. Sports? Games of a sort played now and again, yes, but of formal sports, none. Their day? For the most part, work—John Burke and William Steward in the fields beside Tuggle; and Mary minding the smaller children and helping her mother in the house and vegetable garden, perhaps even going with her to carry plants when the tobacco seedlings were being transplanted or picking worms from the leaves in season. Their futures? A modern American child would undoubtedly talk in terms of choices, even if it were no more than policeman versus fireman. But life for these children did not involve choice. John Burke would answer that he would be a planter, as his stepfather was and his father had been; Mary, that she would be a wife and mother. Aspirations? In a worldly sense, minimal. The children would not talk of traveling or of garnering great wealth or power or fame. Burke might talk of adding to the land he expected to inherit, while young Steward might talk of what his master had accomplished and aspire to do the same. For Tuggle, too, had arrived in Virginia as a servant, leased land on obtaining his freedom, and become a freeholder only in 1662 when he purchased the one hundred acres on which stood the house.

In whatever way they answered such questions about their futures and aspirations, however, the children would answer awkwardly. Life, in their context, was more a matter of being than of progressing. Time simply passed. It was not, as with us, a matter of perpetual revelation but of a cyclic repetition of what was already known. Winter gave way to spring and fall presaged winter again. Sons became fathers who begat sons, a way of thought epitomized by their very names: John Burke carried his father's and grandfather's first name; Mary, her mother's and grandmother's.[10] To these children, questions about their futures predicated on choice and change would make little sense.

Our imaginary conversation with the children of the Tuggle household underscores a fundamental and vital fact about the people of our county. They were, in the scholar's vernacular, more "traditional" in their outlook than "modern," more inclined to accept the world as it was and pass it unchanged through the generations than to expect each passing generation to change the world.[11] It is a point that we will have to keep in mind as we proceed, for it explains much of the lifestyle of the county. But we must keep in mind, too, that while changelessness was part of their mentality, the people of the county did, indeed, live in a milieu that was perpetually changing. It is an equally fundamental and vital point. The historian catches a glimpse of the first in a particular (albeit imaginary) conversation with children; he senses the second when he abandons the particular and becomes ubiquitous.

The Tuggle household of 1668 was one of eighty-three in the county that year, its seven members part of a population of 912. In the immediate background of every inhabitant was change. Fathers and mothers, masters and servants—all remembered and undoubtedly recounted childhoods lived elsewhere and the journeys that had brought them into the county. Over the years immediately ahead, still others would enter, an annual accretion of new faces to be remembered and new personalities to be learned. Continuing immigration, together with natural increase, constantly swept the population upward, the number of people in the county more than doubling by century's end, almost doubling again by the midpoint of the next century. The change implied by growth was not simply quantitative, however, but qualitative as well. The very type of people within the population changed over time.[12]

The families of 1668—the Tuggles on their hundred acres and the Chicheleys on their thousands—lived in a sea of servants. Tobacco profits were a matter of combining land and labor, and bound servants supplied a large part of the latter. Servants were not, of course, spread evenly through the population. Tuggle's one servant boy is to be contrasted with the forty-odd servants working Chicheley land at the same time. But in the aggregate, bound laborers amounted to roughly 45 percent of the population of 1668. Most (just over 38 percent of the total population) were white, preponderately male, and fifteen to twenty-five years old, recruited for their labor from the farms, villages, and city streets of old England. In the Chesapeake, their servitude was temporary. Depending upon the terms of their entry and to some extent their age, they would labor four, five, even as many as ten and twelve years and then, provided always that they lived, merge into the free population.[13] The rest were black, for the most part carried into the Chesapeake from the slave-based societies of the Caribbean. They, their children, and their children's children were increasingly bound for life to their masters.

In absolute numbers, 334 white servants and 65 blacks labored in Middlesex in 1668, the former outnumbering the latter by five to one. Thirty years later, however, the situation was vastly different. The number of families in the county had risen to 270, and the population to 1,771. Bound labor as a percentage of the population had declined to just under 30 percent, but it was largely black. At the turn of the century, black slaves, the majority imported directly from Africa, outnumbered white servants by four to one.[14]

Slavery would ultimately change the face of our county. For the moment, however, our concern is with white servitude, the dominant labor system through the 1680s. Because of its temporary nature, servitude had wide ramifications in the economy of the county. As bondsmen, the servants profited directly the individual families within which they labored and indirectly, by their labor on the principal export crop, the larger society of families. In all likelihood, the majority did no more than this. The conditions of their lives and, above all, the disease environment of the Chesapeake was such that only a minority survived.[15] But those who did moved into the free society with aspirations for a house and land and wife and children of their own. They had little in the way of capital, only the "freedom corn and clothes" that the law required their masters to give them.[16] But they knew the way of the land and of tobacco culture from their years of service and hence could take up land as sharecroppers or renters. With luck and hard work, at least some eventually amassed enough capital to buy their own land. A few others took a shortcut into the ranks of the landed by marrying the widows of freeholders and assuming control of the property.

There are two ways to look at this process. We could consider it solely from the standpoint of the former servants and note the extent of their opportunity to obtain land. Was it great or small? Did it change over time? And there is much to be said for this strategy.[17] By itself, however, it fails to encompass the whole of the system of which the freedmen were a part. For the former servants themselves constituted an opportunity for others. They sought land, and there were those in the society with land to rent and sell. The point is vital and requires elaboration.

Passing down the road from the northwestern border of the county to its end at Stingray in 1668, we noted where the population was located. Consider now the vacant land. Virtually none of it was unowned. Indeed, in the first flush of the entry into the county in the 1650s and through the early 1660s, up to 80 and 90 percent of the land had come to be claimed by someone, the last major original patent in Middlesex (1,100 acres) being granted in 1674 to George Hooper and John Richens. Only here and there in the tangle of patent boundaries were there still parcels to be claimed, more often than not by discerning and canny residents who could walk the woods to spot areas where boundary blazes failed to meet.[18] Some of this early-patented land would remain in the family of an original patentee and become one of the "great plantations" of the eighteenth century. Wormeley's Rosegill is both the largest and best example of such in Middlesex. But most would be conveyed and conveyed again as early speculators sold or—the most important aspect—as patentees and subsequent purchasers found that in order to develop one part of their holdings they had to rent or sell other parts.

The Nash family holding on Sunderland Creek is an example. On arriving from York County in the 1650s, Arthur Nash, an ex-servant, bought servants of his own and, in partnership with John Needles, made crops on other people's lands until he had enough to buy, purchasing 400 acres from Thomas Pattison in 1664. Arthur died shortly after, but a part of the land was rented out to support his minor son, John. In 1681 John came of age, cleared accounts with his guardian, Matthew Bentley, and took possession of the property. The 2,478 pounds of tobacco he collected from Bentley as the profit of fifteen years running the estate (less the cost of raising young John) was hardly enough to develop his own establishment; hence in 1683 Nash sold acreage to Richard Allen, a former servant of his father's. The next year, in return for title "to one able manservant" and an annual rent of one ear of corn, he signed a long-term lease for another part of the land with

Thomas Radley.[19] Still a third part he leased to Christopher Fisher, while in the early 1690s he sold off two small plots of 60 and 40 acres. Ultimately Nash would pass on a fully developed 240-acre plantation to his own children.

The "ancient Jamaica" patent of 1658, which gave its name to the far northwestern section of the county between the road and swamp, is still another example of land that was divided and resold. Originally patented by John Curtis as a speculation and conveyed by him to John Harris, the land (an estimated 1,200 acres) began to be subdivided at Harris's death. Four hundred acres fell to John and Penelope Richens as Harris's heirs, the rest being set aside to satisfy debts. Neighbor Nicholas Cocke, as executor of the estate, apparently paid the debts and held onto the land, selling 200 acres to Robert Porter in 1684. What was left, 646 acres by survey, passed to Nicholas's son Maurice and at Maurice's death in 1696 to Rice Jones, Maurice's sister's son, who in 1704 sold it to William and Robert Daniell, each of whom took half for himself.

Still a third example is the Lindsey patent of 700 acres along the Dragon, to the south and west of Jamaica Land. Patented by John Lindsey in the early 1670s, the land lay idle until conveyed to James Atwood in 1682. Atwood that same year sold 150 acres each to John Bristow and John Micham, 80 acres in 1683 to George Guest (who in turn sold 50 acres to Richard Reynolds and still ended up on resurvey with 100 acres!), and in 1686, 140 acres to Thomas Stapleton. At his death, Atwood left 100 developed acres to his son Richard.

In the far southeastern section of the county, Stingray Point itself was subjected to such subdivision. The whole point—an estimated 800 acres but subsequently proving to be 1,100—was patented by William Brocas in 1654, assigned by his heir, John Jackson, to Sir Henry Chicheley in 1657, and by Cuthbert Potter, as Chicheley's attorney, to William Bawdes in 1661, passing to Bawdes's daughter Mary at his death in 1665. Ultimately William Dudley came into control of the land by marriage to Mary and began selling: 300 acres to Thomas Alloman in 1686 and, all in 1690, 100 acres to Thomas Hill, 50 to Patrick Miller, another 50 to Richard Farrell, and 600 to John Ashburn. Ashburn's 600 acres were again divided when his heir sold off 100-acre plots in 1701 and 1703.

Servants entering the free population on the one hand and a steady process of subdivision on the other—the two phenomena link to form a single system that carried people into every corner of the county, filling in a land of empty patents. Freed servants rented or cropped to obtain the wherewithal to buy, then sold or rented part of what they bought to obtain the wherewithal to develop the rest. Fully three out of four purchasers noted above were freed servants and exemplify the system. So, too, does Thomas Tuggle himself. Finding an unpatented gore of 110 acres near his original 100, he took title to it in 1669 and promptly rented it to another ex-servant, Thomas Oliver, for five hundred pounds of tobacco and three bushels of corn a year plus every fourth hog raised by Oliver from six hogs that Tuggle supplied.[20] The arrangement provided Oliver with a start on the land (as Tuggle's own tenure as a renter had given him a start); the rent Tuggle now received repaid him the patenting costs and provided him the wherewithal to continue improving his original holding.

The decline of the servant body, setting in at least in Middlesex in the 1670s and quickening in the 1680s and 1690s, strained the system.[21] Freedmen buying land found it harder and harder to find still newer freedmen to rent or buy their excess; hence they found it harder to develop their holdings. Moreover, the cost of development itself increased as slaves began to replace servants, the purchase price of the former being two and three times the cost of buying a servant with four or more years to serve. Tuggle conceivably bought ten years of young Steward's labor for two thounds pounds of tobacco; a comparable black at century's end would have cost him five thousand.[22] The inability to develop their lands made the later freedmen far more vulnerable to failure than the earlier. At the same time, those with capital flourished. In the long run, blacks were cheaper since, for those able to purchase them, there was no need for a recurring outlay of capital to replace white laborers completing their terms. Indeed, given that the progeny of the black were also bound, the slave replaced himself. And those flourishing were on hand to buy the partially improved holdings of those failing, turning them into quarters to be worked by ever more black slaves. Stingray

Point again is an example. Subdivided by William Dudley in the late 1680s and early 1690s, it was in part reassembled as a single property by William Churchill, who bought out Alloman, Miller, and Farrell between 1699 and 1703.

All the while an inexorable demographic process was at work, ever changing the situation in the county. Men settling the land and taking wives begat children, some of whom, despite a high mortality rate, grew to maturity. One result of the process, when joined with the decline in the number of emigrants from England, was a steadily increasing proportion of native-born in the population. While in 1668 only some 19 percent of the white population had been born in the Chesapeake, that percentage rose to almost 55 percent by the turn of the century, to 77 percent by 1724, and to well over 90 percent by the half-century mark. In personal terms, the luck of the demographic lottery—the element of random chance that determines the fertility of a couple and the survival of its children—was Janus-like in effect. On the one side, young sons and daughters were an asset, additional hands for the fields and housework. But on the other, too many grown sons and daughters could spell disaster for a family's fortunes or for individual children.

John Nash is again a case in point. Having built a plantation of 240 acres, he was, when writing his will, faced with the problem of one plantation and four children, three strong sons and a daughter. To his wife he devised (as by law he was required) a widow's "third"—the "use," or income, of a third of the land during her lifetime. The livestock and slaves of the plantation he carefully distributed among all four children. To his eldest son, Arthur, went possession of the land itself, but Arthur was to take his brothers John and Henry "to live and labour" with him until they reached twenty-one and thereafter to allow each "a competency of living" from the land.[23] Young John died a year after his father. Arthur died the next year, leaving half of the 240 acres to his own wife, Anne, and half to his younger brother Henry, who thus began life with 120 acres.

Still, but for the death of John, Henry might have started with only 60 acres, the fate of the six children of Robert Chowning who shared equally his 350 acres. William Daniell

THE CHANGING AGE STRUCTURE OF
THE WHITE POPULATION

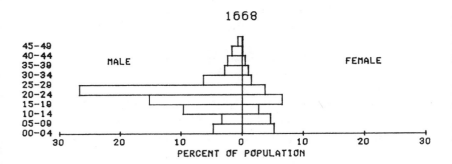

1668

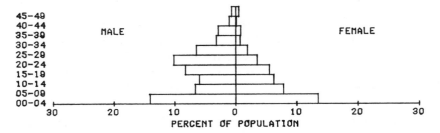

1687

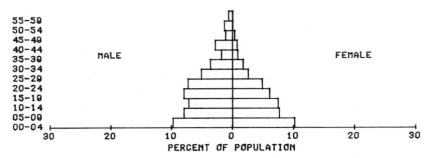

1704

is another example. Arriving in Middlesex in the early 1660s, Daniell amassed 600 acres, which, at his death in 1698, were divided roughly equally among four sons. One of the four, Robert, managed to rebuild to his father's level, amassing almost 750 acres before his own death, but he divided these acres among his own four sons. Of them, only one, another Robert, managed to add land to his inheritance, a 50-acre tract. Marrying twice, this Robert left eleven children, including six sons. The eldest received his father's original inheritance (190 acres). Another received the 50-acre addition. Four received nothing.

Let us return to the Tuggles, the family with which we started this discussion. Late in 1684 Thomas Tuggle died, his wife Mary having preceded him. By then William Steward was gone. Like that of so many other servant boys, Steward's life in the Chesapeake had been short. He died shortly after the date of our imaginary visit of 1668, aspirations unfulfilled. John Burke, too, was for the moment disappointed in his expectations. In writing his will, old Thomas had devised his 110-acre plot to his eldest son Thomas and his original 100 acres to his second son Henry, unborn at the time of our visit. To John Burke, married by then and with an infant son, went only the right to till a particular piece of tobacco ground on the home plantation until Henry "comes att age and no Longer." Tuggle seems to have anticipated his stepson's disappointment. Thomas junior was to head the family, caring for Henry and his unmarried sisters, Mary and Anne; and all four, plus John Burke and his family, were to live together in the Tuggle house "If they Can Live Contentedly together"; otherwise John was to build himself a separate fifteen-foot house on his tobacco land and live apart.[24] As it turned out, John knew (or learned) of an unclaimed gore of land tucked into the curls and swamps of Sunderland Creek. In a series of transactions in 1686, he sold 50 acres of what he thought was 170 in order to obtain the wherewithal (twelve hundred pounds of tobacco) to complete the survey and patenting of the gore, ending up with clear title to 141 acres. On these he would live out his life, fathering in all seven children by three wives before his death in 1699.

All aspects of the early Chesapeake system are exempli-

fied in the story of the Tuggles and John Burke—the progression from servant to renter to freeholder (Thomas senior),
the parceling among sons of what fathers accumulated and
the disappointment of some (the disposition of Thomas's land
and John Burke's failed expectations), and finally, the way of
financing a freehold by renting or selling part of it (old
Thomas's renting out of his 110-acre plot; Burke's sale of 50
acres to obtain title to 141). In this case, the system left its
participants happy. Indeed, in naming his own children, Burke
displayed no rancor toward the stepfather who had failed him,
only the sense of generational progression that we remarked
upon earlier: One son he named Thomas, a second John, and
a third for his half-brother Henry, the child's uncle.

We can, however, sense in the story the potentials for personal failure, pinpointing them by a series of "if" propositions. What if old Thomas had not been able to garner as a
renter the capital to buy his original land? What if he had not
found and been able to patent the gore and hence been forced
to divide 100 acres instead of 210? What if John Burke had
not found his gore or had been unable to figure a way to
obtain it, or had been unable to find a purchaser for the part
that allowed him title to the rest? Historians frequently speak
of "tensions within society" leading to this or that cataclysmic
event. What they are really pointing to is the aggregate of
such "if" propositions that circumscribes particular lives, the
degree of tension depending upon the frequency with which
people faced potentially adverse resolutions.

In the early fall of 1676, armed horsemen cantered along
the road. Tumult, riot, and rebellion had come to Virginia.

The troubles had begun far from our county. To the west,
from the Potomac to south of the James River, Indians and
English were still in contact (as they were not in Middlesex),
and the depredations of one upon the other provoked blood-
shed. The residents of the inland counties and Virginia's governor, Sir William Berkeley, disagreed as to the best way to
counter Indian assaults. Even in the lower counties—those
closest to the bay—there was discontent as levies to pay for
what proved to be an ineffective defense rose to a point where
a man relying on his own labor, possibly supporting a wife

and children, was obligated to pay between a quarter and a
half of his crop in county, vestry, and colony taxes. Virginians
along the freshes of the James River soon found a champion
in Nathaniel Bacon, a man "young, bold, active, of an inviting
Aspect, and powerful Elocution," who would search out and
kill Indians rather than pay for forts and garrisons to guard
against their raids.[25]

Bacon's defiance of the governor on Indian matters spiraled into mutiny during the summer of 1676, and then into
rebellion. Titling himself "Gen'l By the Consent of the People," Bacon labeled Berkeley "as one, who hath Traiterously
attempted, violated and Injured his Majesty's Interest,"
demanding in the name of the "Commons of Virginia" that
Sir William surrender himself and mandating confiscation of
the estates of all who supported him. At the same time, he
distributed an oath to be sworn to by the inhabitants. They
were to acknowledge the legality of all his doings and the ille-
gality of Berkeley's, oblige themselves "to oppose what Forces
shall be sent out of England by his Majesty against
mee. . . . Divulge what you shall heare at any time spoken
against mee . . . [and] keepe my secrets, and not discover them
to any person."[26]

Active warfare broke out when Berkeley, having abandoned the mainland counties for the Eastern Shore, recrossed
the Chesapeake to seize Jamestown, whereupon Bacon gave
up Indian chasing, beseiged the town, and ultimately forced
Berkeley to retire once again across the bay. Burning Jamestown on the night of September 19, Bacon crossed the York
River into Gloucester, both to impose his oath upon the
inhabitants and to counter a force of the governor's supporters moving down from the Potomac counties under Giles Brent.
No battle was fought, however. Brent's men abandoned him
when they heard the fate of Jamestown. The rebellion—led
by Joseph Ingram after Bacon succumbed to disease in October—became a matter of isolated skirmishes as the rebels for-
tified houses here and there along the York and James rivers
and the governor conducted a riverine campaign against them,
sending flying companies to drive the rebels from their
strongpoints or to force their surrender. By mid-January it
was all over, with Ingram surrendering January 2 and his

remaining captains following his example within the next two weeks or fleeing the colony.

It is impossible to say exactly how much of this turbulence spilled over into Middlesex. Certainly the affair disrupted the county. No courts met between May 1676 and March 1677. At some point, the early records of the vestry were defaced and pages ripped out. Certainly, too, Bacon's oath was administered in Middlesex. In the aftermath of the rebellion, William Dudley's widow petitioned for the restitution of tobacco seized from her husband as penalty for administering the oath, claiming that Dudley had been forced to the act and even then had done so "with a salvo to his allegiance to his Majesty."[27] But when? And where?

Certainly, too, armed men had been abroad in the county. In all likelihood, Brent's "army of the north" forded the Rappahannock upriver and moved down the county's main road, crossing to Gloucester and the battle that was never fought via the Dragon Bridge.[28] And in October or November, according to one account, there was a vague "riseing" of Middlesex men against the rebels, implying that for a time the Baconians were in control. But the loyalists "were no sooner got upon ther feet" than the rebels "resalves to bring them on their knees" again, Ingram sending his second in command "with a party of Horses, to do the worke."[29] Finally, there are tantalizing glimpses of personal confrontations: Minister John Shepherd "Compelled . . . to leave the Parish by meanes and Armed Force of Ill Disposed persons Then in Rebellion," presumably because of his loyalty to governor and king; Ralph Wormeley, Christopher Wormeley, Walter Whitaker, and John Burnham, all imprisoned by the rebels and their property "much worsted": Middlesex's Robert Beverley gaining renown as a commander of one of Berkeley's flying squadrons and eventually leading his horsemen to pacify the county; a letter from the governor, aboard ship on the York River, to Beverley, dated January 18: "Yesterday came on board to me, Boodle, and submitted himselfe, and promissed that, this day, his soldiers should lay downe their armes, upon which I gave him his pardon, and promissed his soldiers the like."[30] Robert Boodle and his troopers were Middlesex men and among the very last to surrender.

If events within the county are unknown, the nature of Middlesex's indigenous Baconians is not. A series of suits for damages identify at least some of them for us. In one, Christopher Wormeley brought action against the nineteen men of "Captain Boodle's troop," alleging that on the last day of October they had entered upon his plantation "with force and Armes," plundered his house of goods valued at 285*li* 6*s*, and, in camping on his tobacco ground, destroyed a crop worth another 150*li*. John Lewis of New Kent County lodged suits against a number of Middlesex men, but particularly Matthew Bentley as "Commander" of "Fourty or Fifty" men who had quartered themselves on his plantation, consuming "Three hoggs and two Sheepe . . . [and] a great quantaty of my Corne for themselves and horses," and then carried off a variety of supplies for Ingram's forces in Gloucester.[31] In all, twenty-four Middlesex rebels can be positively identified in these suits.

As we scan this list of Baconians in the light of what we know of their lives in the county, a number of things stand out. First, they were not idle, wandering men. Neither were they the brash young. In age, they ranged from twenty to forty, averaging thirty.[32] Two were native-born sons of Middlesex families, eleven others had arrived in the county in the 1660s or earlier, and another four are identifiable as residents as early as 1671. Only three cannot be placed in the county before the rebellion. Of the twenty-four, nine were married, and six of these had children.[33]

Secondly, more of the twenty-four than one would expect from simply a random sample of Middlesex men show in some way a tendency toward trouble making.[34] In 1672 George Anderton had been fined five hundred pounds of tobacco for fathering a bastard child; after the rebellion (1683), he would father another and, in 1687, stand trial for adultery. Robert Knight, although he rode as a Baconian, had been pilloried for refusing to fight Indians when drafted into a Middlesex contingent sent to the frontier. Jeremy Overy was obviously quick to take offense, for he had been plaintiff twice in suits for defamation. Andrew Ross, whose father-in-law and brother-in-law had both been to court on various occasions charged with assaults and swearing, was himself imprisoned on suspicion of felony in 1681. Two years later, Thomas Weatherby would be suspected of attempting to embezzle the estate of orphans left in his care. And still another of the group, George Hooper, had at one point attempted to reduce to servitude an orphan who had chosen him as a guardian.

Thirdly, all were enmeshed in what we have called the early Chesapeake system. Aggregated, they appear as a cross section, a slice of the population encompassing men at all points of the process, from newly freed servants working as tenants and croppers, through the newly landed and the successful, and on to native sons. Eight of the twenty-four can be identified as ex-servants, but that number is a minimum; servitude is a status difficult to establish from the record base; hence there were probably more than eight ex-servants in the group. Fifteen of the Baconians were tenants or sharecroppers at the time of the rebellion; seven of these would, after the rebellion, go on to obtain land of their own, six by purchase, one by marriage to the heiress to three hundred acres. Nine owned or controlled by virtue of marriage land of their own, ranging from John Guthridge's half-share in two hundred acres to Matthew Bentley's two thousand plus acres.

Finally, the Baconians were not unknown to each other prior to their participation in rebellion. The connections between them appear in a multiplicity of ways as one scans the records of the county. By way of example (and note that the names of known Baconians are italicized): *John Guthridge* had, before the rebellion, purchased land from Thomas Loe, *Andrew Ross's* father-in-law; Ross was a witness to a land conveyance in which *John Brewer* was involved; Brewer had purchased land from *Jeremy Overy*, who had in turn bought land from the former partner of *Richard Blewford's* father and was a legatee of Thomas Radley, *Barnard Reymey's* landlord and a neighbor and friend of *Matthew Bentley;* Brewer had also been a servant to Humphrey Owen, overseer with Nicholas Cocke of the estate of John Harris, whose principal legatee was *John Richens;* Richens, in partnership with his neighbor *George Hooper,* had patented eleven hundred acres in 1674; *John Brim* was another neighbor of Richens's and a close friend—Brim would name a son "Richens." The string of connections extends and doubles back upon itself: Brim dealt extensively with Thomas Crank, who also dealt extensively with *William Black-*

ford, who worked land adjoining that of *Matthew Bentley.*

Such interconnections should not surprise us. Riots and rebellions do not emerge from the air but are concocted by men who, in this society, perforce must meet and talk face-to-face. Indeed, Middlesex's small rebellion connects in just such direct fashion to the larger rebellion when we realize that Richard Lawrence—a close confederate of Bacon's, perhaps even, as contempories claimed, his tutelary genius—had sojourned in the county as a surveyor, that one of the properties he surveyed was that of John Richens, and that of all of the county's Baconians only Richens was truly punished. While the rest were pardoned or ignored, Richens was sent to the governor, tried, and banished from the colony.[35]

Aggregations such as we have been indulging in are informative but not particularly enlightening. They summarize the county Baconians as a rather ordinary group of Middlesex inhabitants, somewhat more prone to trouble than the rest. They do not tell us why these ordinary men took up arms, looted Christopher Wormeley's house, and rode off to join Ingram. To put it another way: If we imagine Richard Lawrence, in person or by letter, awakening John Richens to the Baconian cause developing in the south in 1676 and Richens, in his own hall, at church or court, even across a rail fence, haranguing his neighbors, urging action, we are still left with questions. Why did Richens listen to Lawrence? Why did these neighbors listen to Richens? And toward what end did they all act?

Lawrence himself offers a clue. Oxford-trained, a literary man, a leader in the larger events (as none of our Middlesex men were), he left an imprint on the historical record, and what we can learn of his personality might guide us to an understanding of our Baconians. Lawrence was, according to a not entirely unsympathetic contemporary, one who transformed personal frustration into political discontent. "My self have heard him," Thomas Matthew wrote, "Insinuate as if his fancy gave him prospect of finding (at one time or other,) some expedient not only to repair his great Losse, but therewith to See those abuses rectified that the Countrey was oppress'd with." And he goes on to write, "I know him to be a thinking Man, and tho' nicely honest, affable, and without

Blemish, in his Conversation and Dealings, yet did he manifest abundance of uneasiness in the Sense of his hard Usages, which might prompt him to Improve that Indian Quarrel to the Service of his Animosities."[36] Richens, too, had frustrations and "Animosities" to be served. His inheritance of four hundred acres had been under constant court challenge from Nicholas Cocke for sixteen years, while his ambitious partnership with George Hooper of 1674 was already failing in 1676. Neither Richens nor Hooper had the capital to develop the eleven hundred acres or the ability to wring capital for its development from the land itself.[37]

The lives of others among the Baconians we have identified display a similar potential for frustration. Robert Boodle and Matthew Bentley had each married a widow of a man of substantial estate and social position—in both cases the deceased had been vestrymen. Marriage gave Boodle and Bentley control of their predecessors' lands but not the social acceptance marked by office. It is not at all implausible that their leadership of Baconian troopers was a surrogate for the offices they did not hold.

For his part, Richard Blewford, a young man of twenty, native-born, could already sense an indifferent future, one not of his own making. His father had been an early entrant into the county, purchasing 217 acres in 1657 and, in partnership with another, 300 in 1663. But bad luck or a lack of ability or both had plagued him. In 1661 the county court declared the elder Blewford "a man not caapeable of an oath"; by 1676 he had lost all but ninety acres and was working those with his sons Richard and Thomas. Ultimately he would surrender all to a son-in-law who undertook to pay his debts, and he would die bankrupt, leaving his widow to the charity of others and Richard to make his way in the world as a renter.[38]

Henry Nichols, too, was native-born, his father the owner of nine hundred acres and well respected in the county. In 1676, at twenty-two, young Nichols was already landed, having inherited two hundred acres from William Pew. Henry's riding with Boodle's troop might well have been nothing more than an escapade inspired by a friend—the Blewford land was immediately adjoining Henry's two hundred acres and in the vicinity of the larger Nichols family holding. Or perhaps it was more. Had the elder Nichols already announced that Henry, the only son, would not be a singular heir, that his three sisters would share in the land? Such would eventually be the case. Did Richard Blewford's more obvious frustration come to define Henry's? Of course, we can only conjecture. The potential for Henry feeling a particular way can be demonstrated, but not the feeling itself.

Still, frustration seems a better key to Bacon's Rebellion, at least in Middlesex, than any other; and tensions seem best defined in terms of the frequency with which people faced potentially adverse resolutions to the "if" propositions of life. In the county, men and women sought to gain (or hold) for themselves and their families that comfortable constancy we sensed in imaginary conversation with the Tuggle children. But the world and their lives were inconstant. Turnings, some requiring conscious actions and decisions, others determined by situations, were myriad, and as many (perhaps more) led away from the goal as toward it. The rebellion—a chronic enigma to historians—seems in Middlesex neither a great cause nor a traumatic uprising of "losers" against "winners," oppressed against oppressors, but simply a venting of frustrations and a release of tension, precipitated by events unrelated to the county's doings and, in the end, negligible in effect.[39]

The rebellion ended in Middlesex as Captain Beverley led the governor's troopers into the county. The Baconians clattered homeward and quietly took up their lives, repairing ignored fences and preparing their seedbeds for another year's tobacco crop. They were neither hanged nor hounded for their actions. On the contrary, the remarkable thing is their immediate reacceptance into the society of the county. Captain Bentley was briefly jailed but released by Beverley. Both Boodle and Bentley were required by the county court to find securities—in effect, bail money—for their "abeareing" themselves "Peaceably and quiately towards the Kings Majestie and all his Leige People."[40] Richard Perrott, Jr., Richard Robinson, William Gordon, and Alexander Smith stood bond for the two. Perrott and Robinson were justices of the court, and all were large landholders. At the very next meeting of the justices, Captain Boodle was named a constable for the county.

Sued by Christopher Wormeley and John Lewis for trespass, the Baconians lost, but they appealed the jury verdicts to the colony's general court, finding securities among their non-Baconian neighbors for the prosecution of their appeals.[41] Minister John Shepherd, who had been harried from the county by the rebels, stood security for Baconian John Clarke.[42]

Only Richens was, at least for a while, unforgiven. Sent by the county court to the governor and banished, he was back in Middlesex by July, at which time he was arrested and imprisoned without bail, in part for violating his banishment, in part, too, for "uttering publiquely very Scandalous, and abusive Words of this Court and all the Members thereof. And giveing Such threatning Language to the Undersheriff of this County . . . Soe that he was in Dread of his life."[43] In September Richens was sent south to the governor again. There is no record of his reception, but in 1680 he was back in the county prosecuting his by then two-decades-long suit against Nicholas Cocke for the peaceable possession of his inheritance. In 1689 he would die on his land.

The trial of Christopher Wormeley's suit against the Baconians was held on Monday, September 3, 1677, a court day like any other in the early county. Middlesex had no courthouse at the time. The justices met at Richard Robinson's mid-county house, just off the main road between its junction with the church path and the cutoff to the Piankatank ferry, paying Robinson twelve hundred pounds of tobacco yearly "Howse Rent and Candle."[44] Hence it was toward Robinson's that men from all parts of the county moved that morning.

In the upper precinct, justices Richard Perrott and Abraham Weekes, neighbors sharing a neck of land on the Rappahannock between creeks bearing their names, might well have set out together, meeting John Burnham, another justice, and Thomas Haslewood at the Upper Chapel, then riding along the chapel path until it struck the main road. Haslewood was on his way to court to give an accounting of his guardianship of the orphans of William Thompson. At the road, they might have met John Jones coming down from above, on his way to submit a claim to the court for supplying

arms to soldiers dispatched from the county to join the gar-
rison at one of Berkeley's forts. Just beyond Mickleburrough's bridge, they might have met John Vause, another
justice, and Christopher Robinson, clerk of the court, riding
in from their lands on Rappahannock-side. All along their
route, the party would have fallen in with, or passed, the old
Baconians on their way to trial, fully half of whom (including
Matthew Bentley) were from the upper precinct.

Coming toward Robinson's from the other direction, justices Robert Beverley and his step son-in-law Francis Bridge
would certainly have ridden together. Bridge and his wife were
living at Beverley's. Traveling the lower precinct paths to strike
the main road, they might have been joined by Walter Whitaker, the sheriff of the county; John Mann, undersheriff;
and George Wooley, whose business at court this day involved
the estate of John Hilson, of which Wooley was both executor
and principal legatee. At the Lower Chapel, they might have
met Christopher Wormeley himself, both plaintiff and justice, whose plantation lay directly north along the Green Glade.

Middle precinct men had less distance to travel. Courthouse and home were one to justice Richard Robinson. William Daniell could ride in from his house near the Dragon
Bridge in half an hour. He was attending to prosecute a suit
against Thomas Radley. Erasmus Withers, heading to court
on the matter of an orphan being bound to him, and Captain
Boodle could come up from their lands along the ferry path
in about the same time. George Reeves, pursuing separate
suits against Daniel Bouton and John Allen, had only a mile
along the main road to come, as did Michael Musgrave, who
was suing William Wood for trespass.

On business or simply to share the excitement of court
day, the people of the county flocked to Robinson's. The
assemblage was primarily male, but women and occasionally
children were frequently before the court officially, while
women and children, at least those from the immediate vicinity, were undoubtedly on hand as onlookers. The county's
taverners, closing their ordinaries on court day, set up stalls
in the yard or along the road, selling their beer and hard cider.
A nearby field became an impromptu race course, for inevitably conversation about horses led to wagering. Milling in

the yard, our people met, talked, smoked, and read the pot-pourri of announcements attached to Robinson's door—intentions to leave the country (did John Ascough, departing for England, owe one money? would he carry letters with him?); proclamations by the governor: notices of stray horses, of distress sales, and of missing heirs; and the rules of the court:

Noe person presume to move the Court for anything, but by peticion.

Noe peticion bee presented to this Court but in a faire and legible hand, otherwise the peticion to bee rejected.

Noe person presume to speake to any busines in Court wherein hee is not onely called and concerned, [but] permitted by the Court.

Noe person presume to smoke tobaccoe or to be covered in the face of this Court upon the penaltie of lyeing in the stocks one houre or payeing 100 lb of tobaccoe.[45]

Stocks, together with the pillory, stood in the yard awaiting use.

All the while, inside, Robinson would be directing his servants as the hall was rearranged for the session: a table and chairs at one end for the justices; a jurors' bench to the side; and as much open space as possible for litigants, their spokesmen, and spectators to stand in. The spokesmen were sometimes attorneys in a real sense, but too often—despite the rules of the court—simply "busy and ignorant men who . . . pretend to assist their freind in his busines and to cleare the matter more plainly to the court although never desired or requested thereunto."[46] Finally, at ten in the morning, the justices entered to take their seats and the sheriff opened the proceedings by reading their commission from the governor:

To all to Whom these present shall come, Greetings. Know yee that I have assigned these gentlemen severally and every one of them justices to keep the peace for Middlesex County, charging them to keep all ordinances, statutes, and acts of assembly set forth for the conservation of the peace and the good rule and government of the people, to cause to come before them any or all such that shall threaten or assault any of his Majesties liege people either in their bodies or burning their houses to give good and sufficient securityes before you of their peace and good behavior, to hear and determine all

suites and controversies between party and party, as neare as may
bee according to the lawes of England and lawes and customes of
this countrye.[47]

The justices swearing to discharge their duty, the session began.

As the rules indicated, business was brought before the
court by petition—perhaps a request from an inhabitant for
payment for a service done the county or to be named executor to an estate; or from a group of inhabitants asking that
the justices order the clearing of a road or building of a bridge;
or from one inhabitant charging another with trespass, defamation, assault, or nonpayment of a debt. But petition was a
broad word in the context of the court's rules. A petition could
be in the form of a presentment submitted by the churchwarden on behalf of the vestry charging a servant girl with having
a bastard child or by the county's grand jury through its foreman charging that an ordinary keeper was selling liquor "at
greater rates than is set by Law" or that a cooper was making
hogsheads out of unseasoned wood. Petitions and presentments were submitted usually in advance of the session directly
to the clerk or to a single justice, either of whom was empowered to issue a writ to be delivered by the sheriff or subsheriff
commanding the presence of an opposite party.

At court the clerk took up the petitions in the order in
which they lay in a pile on the table, ostensibly the order in
which they were received, reading each in turn; and the sheriff summoned the parties involved. Petitions were put over,
nonsuited—that is, dismissed with costs of appearance awarded
to a defendant when the complainant or plaintiff was not present to press his suit—or resolved at the moment, the justices
approving or rejecting, awarding or denying damages and
costs, directing the sheriff to collect a fine here or inflict physical punishment there. Punishment was swift, an earlier court
having on hand one "Grasher a Neager [to] be a Beadle for
the Whipping of such delinquents as shall be found deserving." Yet leniency of a sort was not unknown; another court
ordered that "Elenor Jackson being very sick and having a
Soore brest hir punishment for having a bastard Childe is
Refered to the next Court."

When jurors were needed to make a finding of fact, the

sheriff simply selected the needed number from a panel of eligible males he had earlier commanded to attend court day, having care only that each one selected had no immediate interest in the case. The resulting panel would not appear impartial to modern eyes; among the jurors hearing the Baconian case at this session were Thomas Dudley, whose father had administered Bacon's oath in the county, and John Jones, whose brother stood attorney for the defendants. But then, among the justices sat the plaintiff, his brother-in-law Robert Beverley, and Beverley's son-in-law Bridge. And "fact" was a relative thing in this small society. What could be demonstrated in law and what was known to the county were two entirely different things, with the latter frequently the more important. The evidence against William Evans, charged with theft, was not such as to "touch his life," but the court nevertheless considered him to be a man of such "bad Character" and the circumstantial evidence against him so "pregnant" that it ordered him whipped in any event. Similarly, the evidence against John and Margaret Hardy offered "not sufficient ground" to proceed, "but for as Much as they appear to the Court to be people of bad Characters," they were remanded to the jail until they could give bond for five pounds sterling each "for their good behavior for one year and a day." Only occasionally was a matter beyond the jurisdiction of the court— when the sum involved was too large or the presentment involved such a "hanious Crime . . . against almighty God" or the king's majesty as to place the perpetrator in hazard of life and limb. Such matters were forwarded to the colony's general court.[48]

Case followed case to the figurative bar of justice. And always a constant coming and going, even of justices, as men traded places with each other, some crowding into court, others pushing outside to smoke, imbibe, relieve themselves against the fence, and talk. Court day! A once-a-month event in the life of the county.

This particular court day was as any other. In the myriad of petitions dealt with by the court lay one from Thomas Tuggle asking that, because of infirmity, he be made "levy free." The court approved it. Yet this court day was also exceptional. As the session opened, four men not of the court entered to sit with but slightly apart from the county's justices: Sir Henry Chicheley, Ralph Wormeley, Nicholas Spencer, and Richard Lee. Sir Henry and his stepson Wormeley were, of course, Middlesex men; Spencer and Lee were from Westmoreland County. But Chicheley was deputy governor of Virginia, and all four were members of his majesty's council of state for the colony; all had been declared, with Berkeley, traitors "against the cominality" by Bacon; and all had suffered Baconian depredation.[49]

Quite conceivably their mutual presence at court was merely coincidental. Spencer and Lee could well have been on their way to or from Westmoreland, breaking their journey at Rosegill. Chicheley, who had business unrelated to the Baconians to attend to at the court, might simply have invited the others to come along. It is equally conceivable, however, that their attendance was purposeful, that they suspected Baconian sympathies were rampant and intended to overawe with their presence the court, jury, and milling populace. Such suspicions might well have been to the point. Berkeley himself supposedly spoke of "not above five hundred persons untainted" by rebellion in all Virginia, while an underlying Baconian sympathy born from common frustrations and tensions could explain the ease with which the Middlesex Baconians slipped back into their normal lives.[50] In any event, the councillors sat through Chicheley's business—the first to be called—and the trial itself, but left immediately thereafter, perhaps simply to go to dinner at Rosegill, perhaps because their task was done when the jury brought in its verdict for Wormeley.

We remark the brief presence of the councillors at this September court to make a point. The rebellion had been born in the stiff, unbending characters of its major actors—Bacon and Berkeley—and carried along by the anxieties and frustrations of common Virginians. Passing, it left a residue of suspicion. But it by no means shattered what had come to exist in the county. Sir Thomas Grantham, a ship captain who had placed his vessel in the service of the governor, subsequently wrote of "the Ties we are under, from the Relation which we bear to Communities" and of being all "link'd together in society"; these "engage our Care" for the defense of "Particular

Beings" and our "Concern for their Welfare." The councillors sitting with but apart from the justices hark back to the rebellion; the otherwise ordinary court day epitomizes the ties and common concerns of the society that had emerged along the road, a society, moreover, that commanded allegiance if not always affection. "Concerning my Seeing England I give you many thankes," Alice Corbin, nee Eltonhead, relict Burnham, wrote about this time. Widowed once more when, in 1676, Henry Corbin was killed by Indians, Alice was responding to an invitation from an English brother-in-law to live with him. "But I have not any inclination to leave Virginia whilst I live, though I must confess the last years troubles both with in our selves and those with the Indians hath given but few people reason to fall in love with it, the differences with in our selves being far greater then those without. . . . God be praised [they] are now well composed."[51]

4. Family, Friends, Neighbors

The trees in the streets are old trees used to living with
  people.
Family-trees that remember your grandfather's name. . . .
He is not from Virginia, we never knew his grandfather.
— Stephen Vincent Benét, *John Brown's Body*

IT WAS ELIZABETH'S wedding
day, and a hundred or more people crowded in and about
the Montague house on the broad neck formed by Perrott's
Creek and the Rappahannock in the county's upper precinct.
Days had been spent getting ready. Pigs, chickens, geese, and
even a steer had been slaughtered, then boiled, stewed, hashed,
and roasted at the great fireplace—the copious "meats of all
kinds" upon which a passing traveler invited to the wedding
by the groom would later comment, "I am sure there would
have been enough for a regiment of five hundred soldiers."
Gowns and waistcoats, petticoats and bodices—the family's very
best, valuable enough to bequeath to children and grandchildren—had been carefully removed from chests, mended, and
pressed. The house was too small to hold the wedding guests;
hence tables and benches had been set up in the yard outside.
Neither did the tiny house hold enough of the trenchers, plat-
ters, spoons, noggins, and tankards needed for the tables.
During the days before the wedding, Elizabeth and her sister-
in-law Marie (more often called simply Mary) had bustled about
the neighborhood borrowing.

The wedding ceremony itself was in the late morning,

performed by the Reverend Mr. Shepherd, come up from his house in the middle precinct. (His fee was 250 pounds of tobacco.) The guests sat down to eat in stages, the "first table" at two. As they finished, Peter Montague, Elizabeth's brother, mixed the first batch of punch:

> Three jugs of beer.
> Three jugs of brandy.
> Three pounds of sugar.
> Some nutmegs and cinnamon.
> Mix well together and when the sugar is melted, drink.

Bride and groom drank first, lifting together the "silver drinking Cupe with two handles," which the groom's mother had brought with her to Virginia and which she would bequeath to her eldest daughter. Thereafter, as the guests made away with the punch, old Deco, a black servant of the groom's father, and Deco's "wife" Phillis mixed more. Dancing began to the music of a fiddle, was abandoned for the inevitable horse race, then began again. Elizabeth's departure with her new husband at dusk was marked by celebratory musket shots; the two would spend their wedding night at the home of the groom's father, less than half a mile away. The dancing and drinking continued, however. A few guests with homes nearby drifted off as the night deepened. Others gradually found places to sleep here and there—men and boys wherever they could outside; women, girls, and infants two, three, and four to a bed, in the house. Still others "caroused all night long."[1]

The marriage of Elizabeth Montague and Doodes Minor in 1671 was, for the neighborhood, an event, a coming together, in the same way that court day was an event for the whole county. Sitting amidst the merriment but blessed with the omniscience of the historian, a visitor might well have glanced around at the participants and guests, contemplating the relationships that linked them.[2]

Start with Elizabeth herself, a girl in her mid-teens, standing by the door to the house. To one side is her groom, to the other her brother Peter. Even before the wedding the two were brothers-in-law. Peter's wife, Mary, was Doodes's sister.

And even before they were brothers-in-law, Peter (and all the Montague children) had been close to the Minors. The senior Peter Montague and Doodes Minor—the latter an emigrant from Holland who had transposed his Dutch name, Mindoort Doodes, to create his English name—had known each other in Nansemond County as early as 1653 and had come up to the Rappahannock together in 1656. Montague had settled on the Southside, in what would become Middlesex, Minor on the Northside. Montague's wife (Elizabeth's mother) died soon after, followed by old Montague in 1659, leaving Peter and a stepmother, Cicely Thompson-Montague, to see the youngest children—Margaret, William, and Elizabeth—into maturity. Two older children were already married—Anne to neighbor John Jadwyn, Ellen to Cicely's son William Thomp-

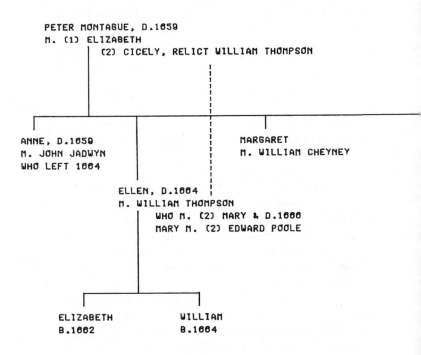

ELIZABETH (MONTAGUE) MINOR'S FAMILY 1671

PETER MONTAGUE, D.1659
M. (1) ELIZABETH
    (2) CICELY, RELICT WILLIAM THOMPSON

ANNE, D.1659
M. JOHN JADWYN
WHO LEFT 1664

ELLEN, D.1664
M. WILLIAM THOMPSON
    WHO M. (2) MARY & D.1666
    MARY M. (2) EDWARD POOLE

MARGARET
M. WILLIAM CHEYNEY

ELIZABETH
B.1662

WILLIAM
B.1664

son. The link to the Minors persisted, however. When, in 1665, old Doodes fell on hard times, Peter came to his assistance. Doodes sold 200 northside acres to Peter, who in turn leased them back to Doodes for a term of fifty-four years. By 1666 Peter and Mary Minor were married, and sometime after 1668 Doodes, his wife Mary Geret, and Doodes junior, moved to the Southside, renting from Peter a portion of the Montague family's 1,000 acres. Close by the river and separated from the mainland by a labyrinth of tidal creeks and swamps, the roughly 200 acres were known locally as "Montague's Island." Elizabeth and her husband would live on the island with the elder Minors until young Doodes was able to buy 650 acres from his brother-in-law Jadwyn.

The "family" at the wedding was, therefore, a close but

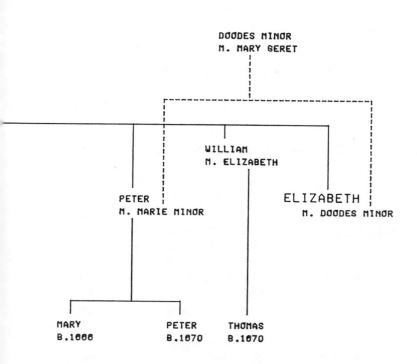

mixed affair. Old Doodes, representing the founding generation, was the patriarch, the father of the groom but also the
father-in-law and tenant of the bride's brother and guardian.
Doodes's wife, Mary Geret, had undoubtedly come across from
the island early on the wedding day to help her daughter, the
bride's sister-in-law and the matriarch of the Montague house.
(Stepmother Cicely had returned to England following Peter's
marriage and the death of her own son.) Peter and Mary's
children—Mary, five, and Peter, one—represented the generation to come.

Others of the family on hand for the wedding included
Elizabeth's brother, William, and his wife Elizabeth, still nurs-
ing her infant son, Thomas; Elizabeth's sister Margaret, childless, with her husband, William Cheyney; and Ellen (Montague)
Thompson's children—Elizabeth, nine, and William, seven—
in the company of Edward Poole, who had married their
father's second wife following the deaths of first Ellen, then
William Thompson. None of the family had far to come for
the celebration. William Montague was living on the five
hundred acres immediately adjoining Peter's, having taken
possession of his half of his father's land at the time of his
marriage. The Cheyneys lived as life tenants on one hundred
acres of John Jadwyn's land, leased to them when, after the
death of his Montague wife and their one child, Jadwyn
departed the county for Maryland. Poole, as guardian of the
Thompson orphans, lived on the three hundred acres adjoining the Cheyneys that had been left to the children by their
father.

Turn to the guests. Henry Corbin and his wife Alice might
well be on hand, the guests of "social standing" commented
upon by the passing traveler.[3] The Corbins were of a decid-
edly higher rank in the society than either the Montagues or
Minors. He was a member of Virginia's council of state and
she was an Eltonhead, related to the Wormeleys and Chicheleys. But old Montague had served as a member of the colony's assembly in his Nansemond days, briefly as a justice on
the Lancaster court in the 1650s, and, with Corbin, on the
vestry of the old Lancaster Parish. One can even imagine Master
Shepherd riding up from mid-county the day before, spending the night with the Corbins, then riding over to the

Montagues with them to perform the ceremony. His necessary return to mid-county would give them all an excuse to leave before the festivities turned to overly familiar carousing.

Certainly John Haslewood would be there, along with his brother Thomas and his sister-in-law and ward Mary Cole, who would soon marry Thomas Haslewood. Both the Haslewoods and Coles were near neighbors and long-term friends of the Montagues; Mary's stepfather, George Marsh, had witnessed old Peter Montague's will. Mary Cole and the Corbins conceivably chatted, for Alice Corbin's first husband, Rowland Burnham, and Mary's father, Francis, had been close—Cole was one of the two overseers named in Burnham's will. Nicholas Cocke would be there too, with his wife Jane, their son Maurice, daughter Jane, and Cocke's stepsons, Giles and Nicholas Curtis. Cocke, like Minor, was a Hollander. Richard and Margaret Perrott would be there, and their son Richard junior. In time, after old Doodes's death and when anticipating her own, Mary Geret Minor would ask Richard Perrott, Sr., and Nicholas Cocke to divide what property she had among her heirs. The Blazes would be on hand: William, his son James, and his daughters Rose and Mary. And Humphrey Jones. Jones was a close friend of the Cockes and Haslewoods, a vestryman and frequent churchwarden for the Upper Chapel. With him would be his wife, the former Eleanor Owen, relict Seager, her son Randolph Seager, and Humphrey's daughter by an earlier marriage, Mary Jones.

We have, of course, used our imagination in reconstructing Elizabeth's wedding. The relationships cited are real. Placing particular people on the scene, however, is simply the work of imagination guided by the knowledge of the existence of a relationship, either kinship or, in some fashion, friendship. And the whole exercise is designed to make a point. Even at this early date (1671) some of the people of the county were deeply embedded in a web or network of social relationships.[4]

In terms of kinship—that is, the five families to which our young bride was linked by ties of blood or marriage—Elizabeth was certainly atypical. Her father, Peter Montague, had arrived early during the settlement years, bringing with him

a wife and nearly grown children who soon married, providing Elizabeth with in-laws, nephews, and nieces. Most of those
arriving after the initial entry into the county were younger
than Peter, unmarried, more often than not servants with
indentures to work off, and sometimes freedmen who had
completed their servitude elsewhere. Marriage to a son or
daughter of the county, or to a widow or widower, might give
such an individual instant kin. But only over time, with the
maturing and marriage of children, would the union itself
contribute to the pool of relationships. As late as 1687, more
than half the families of the county had neither kin nor affinal
ties to any other of the county's families, 43 percent had ties
to between one and four families, and only a handful (4 percent) had ties to five or more. Still, Elizabeth's was the web of
relationships toward which all those persisting in the county
were inevitably and rapidly heading. By 1724 more than half
of the county's families would be linked to five or more other
families; the average household head would live in a milieu
of thirty-one relatives, ranging in kind from a sister's infant
children to a wife's aging uncle.

Kinship is only one aspect of the social bond, however.
Recall that we placed simple friends at Elizabeth's wedding—
Blazes, Haslewoods, Cockes, Joneses, Perrotts, and Corbins.
Given the nature of the remnant materials of this early Chesapeake society, our ability to discern friendships is limited.
Occasionally they are delineated in wills, letters, and other
documents. Thus in 1687 Margaret Perrott left minor bequests
to her "Loving Friend Mistress Mary Goodlaw" and her "loving friend Mistress Elizabeth Weekes."[5] But more often we
must infer friendship from a variety of reciprocal relationships spotted in the county records—men witnessing documents for each other or standing bond for one another in
suits at court.

The glimpse we obtain of friendship in this fashion is, we
stress, minimal. The gregarious Virginian is well documented
in literary materials. In a letter of the 1680s, we see Ralph
Wormeley "in company with another gentleman" teasing a
rattlesnake along the road with a posy of dittany tied to a
stick, then, "tired with skipping about after the snake," dropping into a neighbor's house "to refresh themselves." William

Byrd in 1686 wrote to an absent uncle of the "great misfortune amongst many . . . that wee are wholly deprived of ever haveing your good company in Virginia again, where wee have been so often merry together, and I must assure you its seldome the upland gange meets but wee remember your good health, though wee so often forget our owne. . . . All our friends here in health; B.B. is as you left her, and soe is Bumble B. Dumble B. Only Bradly and Hall quarrell who spins most cotton." A traveler during the same decade wrote that "when a man has fifty acres of ground, two men-servants, a maid and some cattle, neither he nor his wife do anything but visit among their neighbors." Taken by an acquaintance to visit "many houses" in cider-making time, the traveler complained that "everywhere we were required to drink so freely that even if there were twenty, all would drink to a stranger and he must pledge them all."[6] In contrast, our gauge of friendship catches individuals at a few relatively serious moments in their lives, when securities had to be found or a will or deed written, although conceivably friendships caught in such a manner were among the strongest and steadiest. Certainly, however, ours is a biased gauge, inflating the number of friends of a long-lived man active in affairs relative to those of a man dying young and intestate.

Limited as it is, our view of friendship is enough to put us on guard against presuming that the kinless axiomatically lived in isolation. Richard Allen shows us otherwise. Entering the county in 1662 as a servant to Arthur Nash, Allen completed his service in 1669, rented land for a while, was married by 1679 when his first child was born, and in 1683 purchased land from Nash's son John. Through the 1680s, we are unable to link Allen or his wife Anne to any kin in the county. Yet they were deeply ensconced in a web of relationships.

The tie to the Nashes, living a few hundred yards away, was clearly reciprocal. Allen had served old Arthur and bought his land from John, but he had stood security for John's sister Betty in her administration of her husband's estate; John, his wife Mary, and son Arthur would witness Allen's own will. Another neighbor, Thomas Chowning, witnessed Allen's deed from Nash. Thomas's father Robert had been an overseer of Arthur Nash's will. Allen himself would be named one of two

"friends" to look after the children of Thomas's brother, Robert junior, when they were orphaned by the death of Robert's
widow. For his part, Robert was close enough to John Nash
to call on him for security when assuming control of his sister
Catherine's inheritance in 1689. Allen in 1688 stood security
for neighbor William Nicholson, executor of the will of Edward
Bateman, who was the "trusty and well beloved freind" of John
Skeeres, who in turn stood security for Robert Chowning when
Robert was administering his father-in-law's estate. Bateman
would subsequently witness Robert's will. When Skeeres himself had to post bond, Richard Allen stood security, and Allen
was named executor in Skeeres's will, "to do what he thinketh
fitting for all things." Among Skeeres's heirs was George
Johnson, Jr., son of Allen's neighbor George; Allen and John
Nash were witnesses to the senior Johnson's will. To return to
Bateman: When he named his "friend" John Skeeres to serve
as his attorney, the document was witnessed by Mary Shippey,
a widow subsequently married to John Purvis, who, with
Skeeres, was a beneficiary of the estate of Alexander Crerar.
Mary was the godmother of the daughter of Nicholas Love,
who called Skeeres "friend" when charging him to execute his
will and raise his daughter, Frances. John Nash witnessed the
will. Skeeres later took guardianship of Love's other daughter, Lettice, who ultimately became a charge of Allen's when
Skeeres died.[7]

In all, this complex series suggests a network of friendships tying the Allens in the 1680s to at least nine other families, all living in the near vicinity of the Allen property just
above Mickleburrough's bridge on the main road. The hints
of the network lie in cold and scattered legal entries, but it
takes little in the way of imagination to envision what Byrd
called a "gange"—in this case, Chownings, Batemans, Skeereses,
and the rest—gathering in the Allens' hall for a night of
drinking and talking.

Friendship and kinship ties were clearly interwoven. For
one thing, formal relationships tended to follow prior friendships. Richard Allen's daughter Anne would eventually marry
John Nash's son Arthur; his daughter Catherine would marry
William Nicholson's nephew William Southward; Mary Shippey's daughter Lettice would marry Edward Bateman's son

Thomas; Allen himself, as a widower, would marry John Skeeres's stepdaughter Elizabeth Osbondistall; and after Allen's death his "then-wife" would marry William Davis, whose sister was wife to Robert Chowning's son Thomas. For her part, had Elizabeth Montague been endowed with prescience on her wedding day, she could have looked out at those we have placed on hand only as friends and seen in almost every case a future connection. She herself, after Doodes's death, would marry in turn two of them, Maurice Cocke and James Blaze.

For another, the same pattern of reciprocal relations by which we infer friendship frequently identifies a kin or affine as a friend, a phenomenon that increases dramatically over time. In 1687, 17 percent of all identifiable friendships between household heads in the county involved a tie by blood or marriage, a percentage rising to 64 by 1724. At the same time, however, the number of external households to which the average householder was linked by ties of friendship remained roughly constant, shifting from 2.5 in 1687 to 2.2 in 1724. Between the same years, the percentage of household heads tied by friendship to between 1 and 4 other households rose only slightly, from 67 percent to 73 percent, while the percentage related to 5 or more actually dropped from 15 to 14. Admittedly our measures are crude, but they seem to suggest the existence of an upper limit to the number of friends one could have in a society such as ours, and it is a limit constantly achieved—in the early years, when the likelihood of kin in the vicinity was relatively scant, more by friendship alone; in the later years, when the likelihood of nearby kin was greater, by a conjunction of kinship and friendship.

Let us return to our bride, Elizabeth. In the years after her marriage, she grew into womanhood. She bore children—at least five sons and a daughter—three of whom survived to maturity and had children of their own. Following Doodes's death, she remarried twice, outlived both husbands, and died in 1708. Her own marriages and those of her siblings, her children, and her nephews and nieces by blood and by marriage steadily expanded the web of kinship that surrounded her and strengthened it as kin married kin, doubling and tripling the strands that connected her to others. Indeed, by the early 1700s she would be related in one fashion or another to fully three out of every four households in her immediate vicinity.

Such networks as surrounded Elizabeth—in her case, largely definable in terms of kinship; in others, simple friendship; in still others, a mixture of kinship and friendship—were the warp and woof of Middlesex society, important to all, but particularly important to the women of the county. In their roles of mother and housewife, women tended to be tied to house, garden, and fields, in contrast to husbands, who traveled the roads and met and talked to others on their own or on county

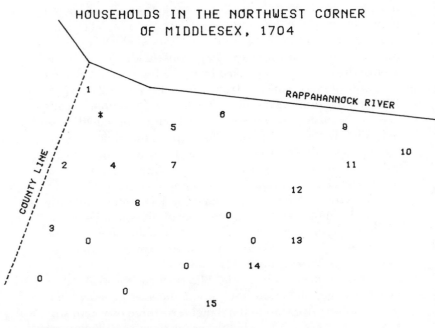

HOUSEHOLDS IN THE NORTHWEST CORNER OF MIDDLESEX, 1704

* ELIZABETH (MONTAGUE) MINOR–COCK–BLAZE
NUMBERS=HOUSEHOLDS RELATED TO ELIZABETH
ZEROES=UNRELATED HOUSEHOLDS

1/2 MILE

1) *Rice Jones* was Elizabeth's nephew by marriage. His mother, the former Jane Cocke, was the sister of Elizabeth's second husband, Maurice Cocke.

2) *Thomas Toseley* was the father of the first wife of Minor Minor, Elizabeth's son, and the maternal grandfather of Elizabeth's grandchildren through Minor.

business. Husbands had tobacco to sell and communal tasks to perform as jurors, assessors, surveyors of highways, and the like. They could, and did, gather in public houses, attend court and militia musters and the races. Women for the most part had but their pots, animals, and children to tend and the services at chapel or church to go to. Yet from a neighborhood of kin and friends, women received support and reciprocated in kind. Neighbors crowded to Elizabeth's wedding. Giving birth to her children, Elizabeth was surrounded by matrons of the vicinage. No stranger, but instead a mother-

3) *Charles Maderas's* mother Elizabeth had married Thomas Toseley and was the maternal grandmother of Elizabeth's grandchildren through Minor Minor. Charles was her grandchildren's uncle.

4) *John Parsons's* wife Mary was Elizabeth's niece by marriage. Mary's mother was the sister of Elizabeth's third husband, James Blaze. Mary had also been Elizabeth's ward after the death of James. And Mary was the stepdaughter of Elizabeth's daughter-in-law Alice, second wife of Minor Minor.

5) *Thomas Blewford's* wife Mary was the mother, by a previous marriage, of Elizabeth's daughter-in-law Alice, second wife of her son Minor. In 1707 Blewford's son Henry would marry Mary, widow of John Parsons. Thomas Blewford was also the guardian of Elizabeth's grandnephew, John Somers.

6) *John Hickey* was the stepfather of Elizabeth's grandniece and grandnephew, John and Elizabeth Somers, children of the daughter of Elizabeth's sister Ellen Thompson, having married the children's stepmother.

7) *Minor Minor* was Elizabeth's son.

8) *Garrett Minor* was Elizabeth's son.

9) *William Montague* was Elizabeth's brother.

10) *Rice Curtis* was Elizabeth's nephew by marriage. He was the son of her second husband Maurice Cocke's half-brother. He was also the stepfather of Peter and Thomas Montague, Elizabeth's grandnephews. Their father had been the son of Elizabeth's brother Peter and his wife Mary, sister of Elizabeth's first husband, Doodes Minor.

11) *Thomas Montague* was Elizabeth's nephew, son of her brother William.

12) *Penelope Warwick Cheyney* was the second wife of Elizabeth's brother-in-law William Cheyney, who had earlier been married to Elizabeth's sister Margaret. And Penelope's brother Thomas had married Mary Minor Montague, Elizabeth's sister-in-law (sister of her first husband Doodes Minor and wife of her brother Peter) after Peter Montague's death. Penelope's granddaughter, Penelope Warwick, would eventually marry Elizabeth's grandnephew, Thomas Montague.

13) *Philip Warwick* was the son of Penelope Cheyney, Elizabeth's brother-in-law's widow.

14) *Thomas Warwick* was another son of Penelope Cheyney. He was also the godson of Jane Cocke, mother of Elizabeth's second husband.

15) *David George* was the brother of Elizabeth's daughter-in-law Alice, second wife of her son Minor Minor. He was also the son of Mary, wife of Thomas Blewford (number 5 above).

in-law, a sister, or a brother's wife helped her from bed to birthing stool. And it would be Elizabeth who would help a son's or nephew's wife, a husband's niece. Friends and kinfolk visited her hall—and she theirs—the "many brabling women" who, the law complained at one time, "scandalize their neighbours for which their poore husbands are often brought into chargeable and vexatious suites."[8] Had Elizabeth, in her ultimate widowhood, cause to forward (or defend) an action at the county court, she could call upon any one of a dozen male heads of house to act for her. Finally, friends and kin would crowd around her deathbed, helping her devise a last testament, steadying her for what some Virginians called simply "Dissolution."[9]

Isolated vignettes indicate something of the way in which such networks lent support. In 1709, for example, Penelope Diatt consented to the sale of land by her third husband. (The sale conceivably could have divested her of dower rights; hence her consent was required.) Mary Brim, a neighbor and old friend—Mary's husband and Penelope's first husband had ridden together in Captain Boodle's troop during the rebellion—petitioned the court to stop the sale, complaining that Penelope, an "aged" women, had been forced to the act by her husband Thomas. As a consequence, the court dispatched two men to Penelope's to make sure that she had freely consented to the sale.[10] Dorothy Needles's appeal to Thomas Stapleton in a letter of 1705—and her extension of a kinship term—again exemplifies this type of situation. The letter, addressed to "Brother Stapleton," involved a family affair. Sometime earlier Dorothy had made a bargain with William Downing "that he should Learne my children two years" and "take Cyder for Learning them at 6d per Gallon." Downing, however, had reneged, and an action was pending between the two in county court. Would Thomas "be so kind" as to represent her before the court? "I hope you will do [this] for me." The note closed: "So with my Love I rest Yor Loveing Sister."[11] Dorothy and Thomas were not siblings; Dorothy was merely the widow of the brother of Thomas's deceased wife.

Depositions concerning a disputed will of 1681—in this case that of a man whose land, in the absence of a will, would have escheated—offer another glimpse. John Burnham had fallen ill on a trip upriver into Rappahannock County and had been brought home to die. Without wife or children, his death scene was nevertheless crowded.

Neighbor Elizabeth Weekes was an early visitor to the house, and when told that Burnham had but a little time left, she immediately "Sent her Man with a Letter . . . to Master [Henry] Creyke," the dying man's stepfather. The next day Creyke and his wife Alice (Burnham's mother) arrived, bringing along Abraham Kenyon, a visiting minister, and Mary Hanbury, a friend. Still other relatives and neighbors show themselves. Kenyon told the court of Leroy Griffin, husband of Burnham's half-sister, passing "through the Hall with paper in his hand to write the will" and of sitting by the hall fire with Brian Radford and a "Doctor Read" while the will was being prepared in the next room. Samuel Olney, a neighbor, hearing of Burnham's illness, "bids" his wife Jane "goe down and see whether . . . Burnham was Dead or alive." In Jane Olney's testimony, we spy Richard Gabriell, a servant but also something of a confidant of Madam Creyke's, sitting in a corner of the hall, and we see the crowded deathbed itself. Jane asked Mary Hanbury whether Burnham was conscious or not and was told that "when she [Mary] first came . . . he was not but when she went and sat downe on the Bedd side the Gentleman that sat on the other side of the Bedd asked Colonel Burnham whether he knew this Gentlewoman. Colonel Burnham replyed 'Yes, it's Mistress Mistress [sic] Handborough.' "[12]

Jane Olney's appearance at the Burnham house and what followed from it add still another and vital point to our understanding of the social webs in which individuals were embedded. The strands of their webs crossed yet at the same time respected a hierarchical layering of society. Burnham himself, Elizabeth Weekes, and the Creykes were all of a social rank considerably higher than that of the Olneys. (With Madam Creyke, we run into Alice Eltonhead again, now enjoying her third marriage.) Elizabeth and the Creykes visited the dying man to lend him support. But Jane's visit was more in the nature of a duty call. She did not go of her own accord, recall, but only at the bidding of her husband. And, as it turned out, she soon came to wish she had not made the visit at all. Madam Creyke subsequently brought suit against Jane, summoning her to the Weekes's house to give bond before Justice Weekes for an appearance at court. Madam and Jane talked privately in the orchard. Jane to the court:

[I] Asked, "Madam, I pray Madam, why are you in such Anger and bitterness against me?"

Mistress Creyke replyed, "Jane, not I. But you meddle with Dick the Taylor my Servant . . . and threaten to take away his Eares."

"Truly Madam, Not I if I can help it."

"Yes," said Mistress Creyke. "Dick has taken his Oath that he did not hold Colonel Burnham's hand when he made his mark to his Will."

"Truly Madam I shall not meddle with Richard nor any that belongs to you if you please to give me . . . my Bond [back]."

And Mistress Creyke immediately replied, "Provided thou wilt not appear against Richard Gabriell at Court."[13]

It is, however, where a support network is demonstrably absent that its importance is most clearly suggested.

The situation of Sarah Williamson was the very antithesis of that of Elizabeth Montague, the latter comfortable amidst kin and friends in the northwestern corner of the county, the former emerging as a near-hysterical harridan in an isolated corner of the mid-peninsula.

Sarah's problems began to surface in 1679, shortly after the birth of her twelfth child, Margaret. By then she was probably in her early forties and had been the wife of Andrew Williamson for more than twenty years. She and Andrew made their first appearance in Middlesex in 1663, Andrew being listed on the tithable roster for one person that year. Probably a former servant, Andrew had earlier lived in Gloucester County, south of the Piankatank. Who Sarah was, or where she had come from, we do not know. Certainly she had no relations in Middlesex. In 1663, however, Sarah and Andrew were long married and the parents of three young sons, Andrew, Augustine, and Robert. A fourth, James was on the way.

At first Sarah and Andrew lived along the main road, renting land adjoining that which Richard Robinson would sell to the parish for a glebe. In 1675 Andrew bought his own land—four hundred acres for seventeen thousand pounds tobacco—and the Williamsons moved to a house on the path from the main road to the Piankatank ferry. Travelers frequently passed by along the path, and Robinson's house—the courthouse—was but a mile or so away. Yet the pattern of land-holding was such as to isolate the Williamsons' land, and Sarah. To the north and northeast lay only the vast backlands of Wormeley's Rappahannock-facing Rosegill, and to the east and southeast lay the large holdings of George Reeves and Augustine Cant, both men of stature in the county who, for the most part, worked their land with servants and itinerant sharecroppers. To the northwest was Richard Robinson's land. And to the west and southwest was Butcher land, now in the hands of Captain Boodle of Bacon's Rebellion fame, he having married Martha, the widow of William Butcher. Directly south, between the Williamsons and the Piankatank, lay the establishment of Erasmus Withers, a prominent planter-merchant, and the last remnant of William Brocas's once vast holdings. The latter was empty in 1675, but in 1681 would be occupied by Oswald Cary, a young merchant who entered the county and married Brocas's grandniece Ann Jackson. In this cul-de-sac, Sarah's immediate neighbors, with one exception, fell into two unhelpful groups: those of higher social status, on whom she might make duty calls (as Jane Olney made hers), and unmarried males. The one exception would become her first victim.

What was Sarah's life like? She was, it seems, forever pregnant, for children arrived regularly: Mary (1669), Thomas (1670), Sarah (1671), Rebecca (ca. 1673), Arbella (about the time of the move onto the new land), Charles (ca. 1677), Charity (ca. 1678), Margaret (1679). And defying averages, all lived, at least through 1682 when, following Andrew's death, Sarah's custody of them was recognized by the court. Andrew himself was illiterate—he could not sign his name—but over the years he served the county occasionally as juror, appraiser of estates, and assessor of crop damages in cases of trespass. His entries in the early tithable lists range upward to four persons; yet the extra hands seem to have been renters and lodgers rather than servants. He probably rented out part of his land and certainly part of his house; in 1679 John Wright's "chest" containing his possessions was in the Williamson house and Williamson lent Wright bedding to use while in prison for debt. Thomas Twiddy was apparently another of Williamson's sometime lodgers, as was David Hume.

Andrew and Sarah had few if any close ties in the county. Andrew's will indicates as much. It was witnessed by three men, Richard Robinson, Thomas Wharton, and Thomas Hucklescot. Robinson, a planter-merchant, court justice, vestryman, and significant landholder, was (relative to Andrew) a powerful and knowledgeable neighbor but hardly a supportive friend. The social distance between them was too great. Hucklescot, at the time of Andrew's will making, was Robinson's bookkeeper; Wharton, an attorney with old ties to Robinson and none to Andrew. Andrew's will, moreover, mentions no friends; his bequests include only a division of his land between his eldest sons, with Andrew junior getting the house and surrounding land, Augustine "the part upwards towards the plantacion of Richard Robinson." The remainder of his estate was "to be Equally Devided betweene my dear wife and children." He named only the two eldest boys as executors.[14]

Neither does Sarah, as a widow, display female friends. She was asked to witness no one's will. The only time she was mentioned in a will other than that of her husband was in 1684 when Alexander Crerar, a bachelor, forgave her a debt of 150 pounds of tobacco. When she needed someone to stand security for her in 1682, Augustine Cant and Oswald Cary did so. Both were well above Sarah in social standing. Cant, moreover, was a bachelor; Cary's wife was young and childless. In 1685 Sarah needed security again. Once more, Augustine Cant stood up, this time with Philip May, an attorney long associated with Cant. Even Sarah's grown sons, who seem to have lived with her in their father's house, failed to provide her with companions (daughters-in-law). Andrew never married. Augustine would not marry until 1692; James not until 1697. Only Robert married earlier (1682), but he found wife and land in the upper part of the county and seems to have divorced himself from the family. In brief, nothing ties Sarah to a supportive network.

At this point, we must make an imaginative leap. From

1679 through 1685, Sarah exhibited a pattern of behavior that can only be categorized as hysterical animosity. There is no other series of cases like it in the Middlesex records. She was not—as another Middlesex woman was—declared "Craised and not in her right Sences."[15] Yet the first outbreak corresponds to the birth of her last child—was the twelfth simply the last straw?—while the latter date corresponds to the beginning of the breakup of nearby lands and the entrance into the immediate area of women of equivalent status. We cannot but sense Sarah's outbreak as a direct consequence of her isolation.

In September of 1679, Sarah and Andrew (he as responsible in law for her actions) were sued by John and Barbara Allen; and in October, Sarah was found guilty by a jury of slandering Barbara. Barbara Allen was the only woman approaching Sarah's status in the vicinity—an ordinary planter's wife. The Allens had been renting, probably from Cant, since 1668; their sole child, Erasmus, had been born in 1671. Why Sarah slandered Barbara, or even what she said, is unknown. But their situations (despite equivalent status) were widely different. Barbara was younger and had one child to Sarah's twelve and servants to help her. In any event, the jury sentenced Sarah to pay fifteen hundred pounds of tobacco or "be Ducked" and Andrew made "Choyce to pay."[16]

Less than a year after her verbal assault on Barbara Allen, Sarah was in court again. In July 1680 another jury found her guilty of "an assault made upon" John Powell, probably a sharecropper on Reeves's land. The assault could not have amounted to much, for the damages were assessed at only five pounds of tobacco, but it may well have been involved with the next entry in the court records: Phebe Pharnell made oath that she went in "feare of her life" by reason of threats made by Sarah and her daughter, little Sarah, that they "will beate wound or Kill her." Phebe was, at the time, twenty-two years old and had for five years been a servant of Reeves's. Again, we do not know why Sarah threatened her or why she dragged her nine-year-old daughter into the business. It may well have had something to do with Phebe's affair with Edward Wilkeson, a former Reeves servant and now a leaser of nearby land. Just the year before, Wilkeson had sued Andrew Williamson, though Andrew had obtained a nonsuit against him. Whatever the cause or course of the argument—conceivably Sarah and her daughter were berating Phebe, Powell attempted to intervene, and Sarah turned her wrath on him—Andrew again had to come to Sarah's rescue, posting a twenty-pound bond to guarantee her good behavior and that of little Sarah.[17]

For the next five years, at least so far as the court was concerned, Sarah stayed out of trouble. But in 1685, by then a widow, she stood before the justices once again. Young Dr. Thomas Stapleton had married into the county and purchased from Augustine Williamson the two hundred acres he had inherited from his father. In April 1685, however, Augustine refused, in court, to acknowledge the sale, although he was obliged to do so by an earlier contract for purchase. In July, Stapleton was ordered by the court to return to Sarah a horse "forceably taken" by him from her property. Stapleton then moved to stop Augustine from selling his land to someone else, and in September he obtained a jury award of the horse, while Sarah, in return, obtained an injunction in chancery for an equity hearing on the matter. The bitter brouhaha climaxed on December 1 at Richard Robinson's. Two witnesses were later to testify that while Robinson, Stapleton, and some others were talking in Robinson's entryway, Sarah arrived. Spying Stapleton, she shouted, "Ah you Rouge [sic] have you gott him," then grabbed Stapleton by the hair "and with a Glaziers Knife [did] make twoe Stabs at him." Carpenter Robert Gillum intervened, "tooke her in his armes and carried her away lest futher mischief might ensue." In the aftermath, Stapleton brought suit against Sarah for assault and battery, asking one thousand pounds tobacco in damages, and a jury was empaneled. Unfortunately, the verdict is blank in the records; we do not know the upshot. Unfortunately, too, we do not know whether the "him" Sarah referred to was her horse, her son, or quite possibly Robinson himself. For it is not at all inconceivable that Sarah (like Andrew before her) had sought out Robinson as a prominent neighbor, intending to solicit his support in her troubles, only to find her enemy already ensconced at Robinson's side. Did she mean, "Ah you Rogue, have you got him, my only friend, leaving me friendless"? Such a feeling of deprivation could easily have led her to pick up a nearby knife and make her assault. All is,

of course, supposition. Our only reality is the absence of a
network of friends or kinfolk surrounding Sarah and, in turn,
her singular behavior.[18]

The family in its own house was at the base of our Chesapeake society. In its ideal form, the family in its house involved
a connubial couple, their minor children, and any servants of
the house.[19] Reality, of course, departed from the ideal.
Households consisting of a single male, or of two males living
together, were not unusual, particularly in the early years of
settlement when there was an imbalance in the number of
men and women—too many of the former, largely ex-servants, and too few of the latter. Elizabeth Montague and Doodes
Minor lived for a while with Doodes's parents on Montague's
Island, forming a two-generation household, which was
uncommon but not at all unique. Only when Doodes could
afford his own land did the couple set up independently. And
at her death the "family" in Elizabeth's house (exclusive of
servants) consisted only of Elizabeth—an aged widow—and
her ward, the niece of her deceased third husband.

For the most part, variations from the ideal flowed naturally from the essentially pulsating or cyclical character of family
life, itself a function of the passage of time. The Williamsons
illustrate such natural variations. In the beginning of their
marriage, Sarah and Andrew were but two—a couple. The
nuclear ideal was matched when children arrived. With old
Andrew's death, Sarah's family was a matter of a widow, grown
sons, and minor children, all housed together. Then, gradually, the family shrank. Children died (Andrew, unmarried,
in 1689, leaving his patrimony to his brother Augustine). Others
moved away, sometimes completely (as Robert did in 1682),
sometimes simply to their own houses elsewhere on the land
(James and Charles, each of whom bought land from Augustine), and sometimes to land just down the road (Sarah, who
married carpenter John Hipkins in 1687). In the early 1690s,
the Williamson family on Piankatank path included Augustine, his wife and child, old Sarah, and two of Augustine's
sisters, Charity and Margaret. In the normal course of events,
the last two would have married away, Sarah would have died,
and the family (Augustine's now) would again match the ideal.[20]

Other variations stemmed from the strategies resorted to when the death of parents left minor children parentless. Mortality along Chesapeake Bay was high, and parents tended to die young, leaving children behind. In this at least Elizabeth Montague was typical. Losing her parents early in childhood, she was raised in a household headed for a while by a stepmother, then by her brother. Almost half (48 percent) of the children born in the county through 1689 lost one or both parents by their ninth birthday, and almost two-thirds (61 percent) by their thirteenth. And the phenomenon of parental loss was a continuing one. Of Middlesex's children born 1690 through 1709, 43 percent lost at least one parent by age nine and 60 percent by age thirteen, percentages roughly matched among those born 1710 through 1749 (45 percent and 57 percent). The passage of time brought no surcease from parental loss, at least in Middlesex, no diminution of a fearsome mortality rate.[21]

Children losing one parent generally remained with the surviving parent, who more often than not remarried, endowing them with a stepparent, sometimes stepbrothers and sisters, and at least the potential for half-siblings.[22] Orphanhood, a condition in which 20 percent of the children born from 1650 to 1689 found themselves before their thirteenth birthday, 37 percent before their eighteenth, required other arrangements.[23] The county court had general oversight of the children. On its own, or at the request of a child of fourteen or older, it could specify custody and guardianship. But the wishes of parents expressed in their wills were, by law, paramount. Tobias Mickleburrough provided that his minor son by a first marriage "remain and abide" with his second wife (the child's stepmother), "provided shee deals well with him"; otherwise the designated overseers of the will were to "remove and place him where in their discression they shall see most Convenient." Frequently wills designated that orphaned children were to be put into the charge of an elder brother or stepbrother, sometimes even an elder sister or stepsister. James Dudley, for example, survived three wives and was survived by five children: in writing his will, he charged his eldest son (born to Dudley's second wife) with the care of his two youngest children (born of the third marriage). Thomas

Stiff, leaving two grown children and two minor children (ages nine and seven), named his eldest son executor "and required him to take care" of the two minors. William Daniell survived two wives and was survived by children ranging in age from thirty-four to four; in his will, he stipulated that his three youngest daughters remain on the plantation bequeathed to his eldest son, William, "till they are marryed." Thomas Kidd provided that his four "smallest" (ranging in age from eight to eleven) remain upon the land left to them and be brought up by his daughters, Frances, twenty-two, and Mary, eighteen. Thomas Toseley, in writing his will, assumed that his two minor children would remain with their mother, his second wife, but provided that, should she die, the two sons of his wife's first marriage (in other words, not Toseley's sons at all) "manage and looke after My Children and their Estates."[24]

Children were left in the care of uncles as well. When, for example, James Blaze died in February 1701, two young nieces were living with him—Agatha Vause, who had lost her father at age two and remained with her mother through two remarriages before being orphaned, and Mary Osborne, age two when her mother died, twelve at the death of her father. Blaze's then-wife—our Elizabeth—undertook to raise the two. On occasion godparents took their godchildren into their homes, or, as in the case of the widow of Minister John Shepherd, the godchild of a deceased spouse. Richard Robinson, Minister Shepherd's godson, was thirteen when his mother died, eighteen when his father died, and was living with Mistress Shepherd at age nineteen (1694) when he testified in her behalf in a suit against Francis Dodson. Even simple friends were relied upon. Anne Chowning, widow of Robert Chowning and mother of seven children ages fifteen through four, made no other arrangement than to ask friends Richard Allen and Richard Shurley "to Act and doe" for the children "for the best Advantage." Such designated overseers seem to have been expected to take the children in and act as guardians in the absence of kin. And in a society in which orphans were so common and where wives and husbands could reasonably expect that their own children might require accommodation, the widow Chowning's trust in her friends seems not undue. Edwin Connoway foresaw no problems when he interceded on behalf of the orphans of Elias Edmonds. Their estate was being rapidly dissipated by bad management (or so he thought); hence he suggested to one of the justices of the court new managerial arrangements. In anticipation of objection, he added that "you will say who will keep the Children upon those terms. I answer I will find those that shall keep them and give them better Education than those in whose Custody they are."[25]

Connoway's letter points up a very real problem associated with the death of parents in this society, although not one to be overstated. The children were often heirs and heiresses of property and personalty large and small, and those to whose charge the minors fell—widows and guardians—had control of inheritances until the children came of age or, in the case of a girl, married.[26] To both the father of the children and the society at large, the central concern was to effect the transfer of the property from the testator, through the minority of the child, to the mature adult in as nearly intact a condition as possible. A multitiered system for handling estates—in some cases, fathers named executors and overseers as well as guardians to watch after their children's estates—was one defense mechanism. Beyond that, fathers sought to protect their children's inheritances by prescribing and proscribing, in their wills, the actions of those who would have charge of the children. Thus James Blaze stipulated that his wife Elizabeth was to have the use of his plantation during her lifetime, but she was "neither to sell nor Give Aney of the timber," cutting only "for hur owne ocashon to build with." "If she Cannott Keep Hands upon the plantation In the Ingan necke and Keepe the Houseing in Repare Shee may Lease it and Like wise to Keepe the plantation In Repare wheare on I nowe Live." James Dudley required designated overseers of his will, in the event his wife remarried, "to take good and Sufficient Security for the Money left to my Dear Children and also to see that none of my lands above any new tobacco be cleared which I have given to my Son James nor no timber be cut off of it further then what is Necessary for repaireing the houses and for tobacco Caske for the said Plantacon."[27] The justices of the county court, for their part, required performance bonds of most guardians and administrators; set aside special court days for "Orphans' Court," when the guardians were to bring in accounts for auditing; and acted promptly to protect the estates of orphans when malfeasance was called to their attention. And in the colony legislature, the same sorts of men—fathers and justices—passed one after the other general laws to protect and preserve the estates of orphans.

All of this is testimony to the realization that great opportunity existed to despoil the parentless. And, indeed, examples of spoliation or attempted spoliation can be found. In 1664 the children of Oliver Seager and Humphrey Owen sought the assistance of the court against Humphrey Jones, who had assumed their guardianship by virtue of marrying their common mother Eleanor. In response to their assertion that Jones was claiming (as part of Eleanor's dower) a goodly portion of their estates, the court empaneled "a Jury of the ablest and neerest inhabitants" to make a just division. When, in 1681, Henry, Edwin, and Martha Thacker went to court to obtain a guardian other than their mother's new husband (William Stanard), it was obviously because the children—or at least Henry, the eldest at eighteen—suspected that their new stepfather would act against their interest. In 1686 Henry, on behalf of himself and the other children, brought suit against Stanard for his mishandling of their estates, and Stanard fled the county. In 1683 the county court acted quickly to preserve the estate of John Gore and George Ransom from spoliation by John Ascough, who had married the mother of the children and was "about Selling all his [and their] estate" prior to sailing for England. The court ordered that all of Ascough's property, and the children's, be forestopped "from any Sale or Alienacon untill the said Orphts. estates be well Secured." And in 1706 the court moved to protect the children of the deceased Richard Stevens. His "considerable personall estate" was "likely to be Imbezelled away" by the "ill Management and Riotous Liveing" of the widow Sarah "and the orphans of the said deceased thereby ruined"; hence the court placed the estate in the hands of the county sheriff.[28]

But given the extensiveness of parental loss and the number of children whose estates were vulnerable, the number of assaults upon the estates of orphans seems relatively few. Most men involved with the estates were like Edwin Connoway—scrupulously attentive in the welfare of the Edmonds children when, in 1654, he questioned the management of their estate—or like Henry Corbin's English brother, who wrote following Henry's death in 1676 that "it must now bee our care, as it was his, so to gett an estate, that wee improve it all we can for his children," or like Robert Carter, one of the five overseers of the estate of Ralph Wormeley just after the turn of the century. Every page of the extant Wormeley estate record testifies to Carter's concern for the young heirs to the largest fortune in Middlesex.[29] One suspects that care and scrupulosity in such matters were in effect products of the situation: What men did for the children of others, they could hope other men would do for theirs.

The combined phenomena of parental loss and the remarriage of surviving parents tended over time to result in ever more mixed and complex families in Middlesex. Were we, for example, to drop into the household of George and Mary Keeble in the 1660s, we would find a familiar nuclear unit: mother, father, children. In the 1680s, however, visiting the family of Robert and Katherine Beverley, we would find the Keeble children and the children of Mary Keeble and her second husband, Robert Beverley, of Theophilus and Katherine Hone, and of Katherine Hone and Robert Beverley—an array of step- and half-siblings ranging from the newly born to those in the early twenties. Beverley himself would be the natural father of some, the stepfather of others, and simply the guardian of still others. Just about any other household in Middlesex would display much the same progression.

From the standpoint of children, parents were ephemeral. A father might give way to a stepfather, an uncle, a brother, or simply a friend of the deceased father; a mother might well be replaced by an aunt, an elder sister, or a father's "now-wife," to use the wording frequently found in conveyances and wills. The children themselves would run a wide gamut of ages and be related to each other in a variety of ways. Viewing such families, we could easily leap to the conclusion that childhood in this Chesapeake society was a matter of disruption and trauma and that family attachments were consequently weak. How could it be otherwise when the family as we think of it—the union of mother, father, children—was so fragile? We need only point to Agatha Vause: By the time she was ten, she had lost a father, two stepfathers, a mother, and her guardian uncle.

The leap, however, would neglect the hints of familial affection that are found among the sparse remnants of this past society. We have already—in describing Thomas Tuggle's family—remarked on the familial orientation of children's names. First and second sons and daughters tended to carry on the names of grandparents and parents.[30] Beyond that, the expressions of a planter living to the south, on the James River, can be applied to Middlesex. In 1685, William Byrd wrote to his father-in-law in England to report on his family: "My wife (I thanke God) is well and fair for another [child]: in the mean time little Molly (who thrives apace) diverts us." Middlesex's own Christopher Wormeley, in his 1698 will, asked that he be buried "in my own Garden and Betwixt my first wife Frances, and my last wife Margrett." Middlesex's Long brothers, Joshua and Thomas, in 1704 sold the hundred acres left to them by their father, but reserved to themselves "a certain Spott . . . twenty foot square Lying in the orchard it being the place where their father and mother were buryed . . . for a burying place to them and their heirs." In George Ransom's 1675 will, we catch a hint of that whimsy that proceeds from the love of a parent toward a child, Ransom leaving his daughter Elizabeth a "Jack in the box." And in 1708, "for the filiall Love and Affection that I bear to my Father Ringing Gardner and out of desire that he may live by me," William Gardner leased to the elder Gardner sixty acres of land.[31]

The leap would ignore, too, the consequences of the commonplace. To some extent at least, trauma and disruption are to be associated with departures from the normative. But death and parental loss were the norm in this society and for its children. To use the symbolism of Johann Sebastian Bach, death was a singing watchman in their world, teaching them from an early age that life was transitory. A planter of nearby Stafford County, referring back to his childhood, put the matter succinctly in a letter to his mother: "Before I was ten years old as I am sure you very well remember, I look'd upon this life here as but going to an Inn, no permanent being."[32]

Above all, such a leap would neglect the very essence of this Chesapeake society. The family within its own house was basic, true, but the boundary between the immediate family (so paramount in our twentieth century) and a larger collectivity of kin and friends—the collective family of the neighborhood—was slim, permeable. And if the former was fragile, the latter was not. In this situation, stability for children as well as for adults lay not so much in the transitory family of the household but in the permanent network of friends and relations within which the family was embedded. Instability and insecurity lay in being apart from a network.

Rooted in families, the web of relationships and friendships that, in sum, made up this society spiraled upward and outward—an expanding helix. Families were linked to other families by ties of kinship and friendship to form neighborhoods. Neighborhoods were linked as their men came together for periodic militia musters and as families gathered for services at the Mother Church and its two chapels, forming rough geographic divisions within the county—reflections of the three parts that had joined to form Christ Church Parish in 1667 and the county itself in 1668. And the three divisions were themselves linked through the institutions of county court and court day to form a single social unit.[33]

The neighborhood is the most amorphous of these levels. For one thing, it was not structured around any central (or nodal) point, but around the individual houses of its members—the neighbors gathering here for a wedding and there for a childbirth, across the road where a householder lay sick, and perhaps in the same house for a funeral a few days later and, some months later, for the auction of the deceased's personal property. Public houses and stores such as Mickleburrough's—more a room in the Mickleburroughs' house than a store in our sense—or Kemp's down on the Piankatank, tapped the trade of a neighborhood but did not really define it. Events, not places, were central.

In addition, we can measure the neighborhoods only in terms of individuals. When, on a map, we plot the locations of Elizabeth Montague's kin or Richard Allen's friends, or the kin and friends of almost any householder, they form relatively tight clusters two to three miles across with only occasional outliers. When we plot marriage "runs"—how far apart the parties to a marriage lived—we find that 36 percent of all marriages in a five-year span at the turn of the century were between persons living within a half mile of each other, and 95 percent between persons living no more than five miles apart. In a few instances, auction records allow us to identify buyers, at one sale sixteen; all of them lived within three miles of the deceased, and at least seven were related to him and to each other.[34] The distances suggest the effective limits to neighborhoods in a society constrained to foot and horse for mobility, a limit exemplified in negative fashion by Mabel Hackney. Mabel was the only daughter of William and Elizabeth Hackney, whose land lay in the southeastern part of the county a mile or so below the Lower Chapel. She was, it seems, a willful girl, attracted to (or by) a neighbor, Francis Dodson. Dodson, however, already had a wife and child. With Mabel he fathered another, a son baptized as John Hackney Dodson. Yet another was on the way when Mabel's father managed to find a proper husband for her, marrying her off in 1687 (six months pregnant) to Nicholas Paine. Putting distance between Mabel and Dodson—removing her from the neighborhood—was clearly on Hackney's mind. Paine's land was in the county's upper parts, fourteen miles away.[35]

Now and again the records offer us a glimpse of a neighborhood working together toward a common goal. Thus in 1699 eight householders, all residents of the extreme southeastern tip of the county—Stingray Point—petitioned the county court to have "the Antient Road" connecting them to the rest of the county cleared "for [their] better Conveniency." An anonymous traveler of a decade earlier, although confining his observations to "Gentlemen," hinted at the existence of an even more direct form of common endeavor. In the hot Virginia summer, fresh meat could not be kept "above a few days," he wrote; hence "half a dozen or eigth [sic] gentlemen" join together to kill a steer "every week, by turns and send everyman a portion of it."[36]

Far more often, however, the records speak of the neighborhoods as recognized (and used) by the larger society simply for the familiarity of their members with each others' lands

and business. Processioning—the quadrennial circumambu-
lation of property boundaries and renewal of boundary
markers—was a neighborhood affair. "Two intelligent honest
freeholders" of the vicinity appointed by the vestry were in
charge, but that they led an array of neighbors on their walk-
about and relied upon a collective memory of the lines, at
least in the early years, is clear from the original statute: "If it
shall happen any difference be present that cannot be by the
neighbors themselves decided . . . two . . . surveyors shall in
the presence of the neighbour-hood lay out the land in con-
troversie."[37] Disputes were frequently referred for resolution
to "the ablest and neerest inhabitants" empaneled as a special
jury (1664), to "an Able Jury of the Neighbourhood . . . that
are noe wayes Concerned by Affinity Consanguinity or Intrest"
(1693), or to "three honest house-keepers of the neighbourhood, who are no ways related to the party injured, nor interested concerning the trespass" (1705).[38] The inventory and
appraisal of estates were for the most part placed by the county
court in the hands of neighbors of the deceased. Surveyors of
highways were chosen on a neighborhood basis, the extent of
the road or path a surveyor was charged with maintaining
being invariably defined as two or three miles either side of
his own house.

    Christ Church and its chapels defined a level of life half-
way between the neighborhood and the county. In this regard,
the creation of a single parish in the 1660s and the early terminology of "mother church" and "chapels" is deluding for it
implies a hierarchy, with the chapels subsidiary to the church.
Such might well have been in the minds of the prominent
mid-peninsula householders who seem to have inspired the
creation of the parish, but it was never the case in fact. Loy-
alties to the old independent parishes persisted. Henry Corbin, for example, although a vestryman of the whole parish,
lavished his attention on the Upper Chapel, in 1669 building
a pew in the chancel and a stable nearby for his use. In 1681
his widow and her then-husband, "out of . . . pious zeal and
love to the Church," gave the Upper Chapel a silver trencher
with the Corbin coat of arms engraved on the brim and Henry's name on the bottom, together with a damask tablecloth
and napkins for the communion table.[39] Even when memo-

ries of Lancaster and Piankatank parishes had faded—simply
names from the early pages of the vestry book—each family
of the county looked upon one structure or the other as its
particular church.

Indeed, the terminology itself changed. The phrase
"mother church" disappeared almost immediately and was
replaced by "Christ Church" and "the Greate Church," which
in turn gave way to an innocuous "the Middle Church." Similarly, the designation "chapel" gradually was replaced by
"church"—"the Lower Church," "the Upper Church." Which
of the churches one took as one's own depended largely on
location, but also to an extent on preference. The Middle
Church—situated in the center of Rosegill—seems to have been
shunned by some, for there were families that eschewed a
shorter trip through Wormeley land to travel a longer distance to one of the others, particularly the Upper Church.[40]
The phenomenon hints at a dislike for the manorial attitudes
displayed by the Wormeleys of Rosegill, which in due course
we will consider.

The orientation of the parishioners toward particular
churches rather than toward the whole was reflected in the
organization of the parish, which tended to be more federal
than centric. The three geographic areas of the parish defined
by church attendance were very early recognized as distinct
"precincts." The parish vestry inevitably consisted of members drawn from all three precincts, and on occasion a matter
particular to one was delegated to the "Gentlemen of the Vestry in those parts" or the "Gentlemen of the Vestry in that
Precinq."[41] The minister was required to conduct his services
at each of the three churches in turn. For the intervening
Sabbaths, each had its "Distinct" lay reader, described in 1689
as "a Man of good Sober life and Conversation" who was to
"Duely . . . Read Divine Service, and a Homily and also heare
the Children The Catechisme of the Church of England." The
readers doubled as clerks, keeping "punctually an accompt of
the Burialls Christnings and Marriages In Theire Respective
Precinq." Initially they did the duty of sexton as well, each
looking "after the Church under his Charge Keeping of it
Cleane and Decent."[42] Each precinct, too, until the 1720s, had
its own churchwarden, an adminstrative officer charged not

only with church affairs (general oversight of the church building itself, in most years collecting the minister's salary from the parishioners), but with a variety of social tasks ranging from the enforcement of laws against immorality, bastardy, and sabbath breaking to overseeing the care of the otherwise uncared-for sick and indigent within his precinct.

In this federal arrangement, the Middle Church was superior only because it was, indeed, in the middle of the parish and hence the most convenient location for general meetings of the vestry, a fact testily pronounced in the midst of an interprecinct squabble. When a "rump" vestry tried to move the meetings elsewhere, the full vestry "ordered . . . that for the Future The Vestry be Summoned unto, and Sett in the Middle Church of the Parish And There and no where Else to Dispatch all Parish business."[43] The clerk of the Middle Church generally served as clerk to the vestry as well, keeping the minutes of its meetings and the periodic accountings of parish expenditures.[44] One single register of births, baptisms, marriages, and deaths was kept by the clerk of the middle precinct; regulations of 1689 specified that the clerks of the upper and lower precincts "make . . . True and Timely Returne" of their own registers to him, while in 1701 and 1702 all of the records were transcribed into two volumes—a register and a parish book—especially purchased for the purpose. Thereafter it became a matter of keeping the books physically within the walls of the Middle Church as various clerks, even the minister, persisted in carrying them off to their houses and the vestry ordered them back.

To their own particular church, then, the families of the various neighborhoods came on a Sabbath. What in the way of religion, or how much of religion, they imbibed it is difficult to say.[45] From 1668 on, the parish was never long without a minister.[46] One (Samuel Gray, serving the parish from 1693 to 1698) verged on the scandalous and was ultimately dismissed by the vestry. Another (Deuel Pead, 1683 to 1690) was so scrupulous that he offered monthly Saturday afternoon sermons as preparation for Sunday communion. Still another (Bartholomew Yates, 1703 to 1734) clearly had the respect of at least the vestrymen, who, from 1721, when another parish tried to entice him away, paid him four thousand pounds of tobacco more than the sixteen thousand pounds prescribed by law. In 1726 they described him to the Bishop of London as a man of "pious life and Conversation" who had "given us the great advantage of good example, and by his excellent discourses, and advices taught us our Duty both to God and Man."[47] And the regular purchases of sacramental wine recorded in the records of the vestry lend substance to the claim in 1724 of 230 communicants, roughly a third of the white, adult population of the parish.[48]

It was, however, the face-to-face contact at the services that was socially important, a necessary addition to lives lived in the neighborhoods. A traveler of the mid-1680s sets the scene for us: A graying frame building in the woods, as dilapidated as the houses, with an array of plank benches surrounding it; the families straggling in, some on foot, some riding, striking up conversations with each other. What struck the traveler most was the smoking. "When everyone has arrived the minister and all the others smoke before going in. The preaching over, they do the same thing before parting. They have seats for that purpose. It was here I saw that everybody smokes, men, women, girls and boys from the age of seven years." What most strikes us is the social scene. Ninety years later the church might be brick, but the scene itself might be exactly the same, another visitor writing of "the three grand divisions of time at the Church on Sundays, Viz., before Service giving and receiving letters of business, reading Advertisements [on the church door], consulting about the price of Tobacco, Grain etc. and settling either the lineage, Age, or qualities of favourite Horses. . . . In the Church at Service, prayrs read over in haste, a Sermon seldom under and never over twenty minutes, but always made up of sound morality. . . . After Service is over three quarters of an hour spent in strolling round the Church among the Crowd."[49]

County court and court day set the limit to the social horizons of most in Middlesex. Some, as we shall see, had contacts beyond court day—the few who, by virtue of wealth, connections, and political office, lived on a scale higher than the county. For the moment, however, our concern is with the many.

The court bounded the society as nothing else did. At the

extremes of the county, where contacts were not blocked by geographic features—the mile-wide Rappahannock or the dense tangle of the Dragon Swamp—neighborhoods could span the artificial political and ecclesiastic boundaries of the county and parish. Thus in the far northwest, Joneses, Humphreys, Seagers, and even Elizabeth Montague had kin and friends across the line in Essex County. In the southeastern part of the county, the narrow Piankatank was a permeable social boundary. On occasion Gloucester men and women came across to services at the Lower Chapel, even bringing their children to be baptized there. What kept the county society one was the existence of the court as an administrative and judicial heart. To it or its officers—notably sheriff and clerk— one turned for a good road (as the householders of Stingray did in 1699), for the adjudication of disputes, for the king's justice, and to establish clear title to land by recording a conveyance or will. And because these things were vital to their lives, the men and sometimes the women of the county— including the Joneses, Humphreys, and Seagers on the periphery—were regularly drawn inward, to the county's center: the courthouse on court day. We followed them in for the trial of the Baconians in 1677. There is no need to redraw the scene, only to recall it as a larger version of the churchyard on a Sabbath, as a place where once a month, year in and year out, men and to an extent women from all the various neighborhoods and precincts came together. The formal functions of the event can be discerned in the court records themselves—in the findings of juries and the various orders of the justices. But for the all-important informal function we must again resort to imagination.

Consider the plight of William Hackney, that upright, moral, stern man, aghast at the behavior of his daughter Mabel, yet unable to control her. We easily envision the stormy scenes in the Hackney house, perhaps a confrontation with Dodson—Hackney warning him to tend to his own wife and leave Mabel alone—and Hackney's conclusion that the only solution was to marry Mabel away from the neighborhood. But knowledge of marriageability was one of those items that traveled the circuit of neighborhood and precinct. Hackney wanted a distant husband for Mabel. How did he find one? Let us conjecture: Hackney's neighbor, John Nichols, had a daughter who had married John Bristow, who had subsequently bought land in the upper precinct and moved away. Did neighbors Hackney and Nichols talk? Did Nichols carry the story to Bristow at a chance meeting on court day? Did Bristow, at a loss for a marriageable male in his own upper precinct neighborhood, make inquiries around the Upper Chapel yard on a Sabbath and ultimately learn that Nicholas Paine was in search of a wife? The sequence of conversations is not suggested to explain how Mabel really came to marry Paine— we can never know for sure—but to conjecture how the levels of our county society might have worked to link its people as one.

5. Strata

The heavens themselves, the planets, and this centre,
Observe degree, priority, and place,
Insisture, course, proportion, season, form,
Office, and custom, in all line of order; . . .
. . . How could communities,
Degrees in schools, and brotherhoods in cities,
Peaceful commerce from dividable shores,
The primogenity and due of birth,
Prerogative of age, crowns, sceptres, laurels,
But by degree, stand in authentic place?

— Shakespeare, *Troilus and Cressida*

HERE AND THERE in passing we
have already glimpsed the hierarchical ordering of Middlesex
society: Henry Corbin's stature among the men of old Lancaster parish met to engage a minister; the councillors sitting
with but apart from the county court at the trial of the Baconians; Sarah Williamson's isolation, at least in part a function
of the social distance that separated her from others in her
immediate vicinity; and the confrontation between Alice
(Eltonhead) Burnham-Corbin-Creyke and Jane Olney. "[I]
asked, 'Madam, I pray Madam, why are you in such Anger
and bitterness against me?' Mistress Creyke replyed, 'Jane, not
I. But you meddle with Dick the Taylor. . . . ' " Looking up
from her station in life, Mistress Olney spoke to "Madam"
Creyke; looking downward from hers, Mistress Creyke spoke
to "Jane."

There is no question that ours was quite consciously a layered society. Law, custom, and even public architecture
acknowledged social differentiation. Whether one was fined
or whipped for an offense was dependent upon status.[1]

Orphans of one sort of family were treated differently from orphans of another sort. Thus Elizabeth (Armistead) Wormeley-Churchill's son Armistead was placed in the minister's house to learn Latin and Greek; Henry Gore was apprenticed to Christopher Robinson to learn the "Office of Clerke" and serve "in all lawfull Imployments, Common workeing at the house in tending Corne and Tobaccoe excepted"; the minor child of William Baldwin, "being Cast on the Parish," was simply bound out a servant to Henry Pickett.[2] When a courthouse was eventually built in Middlesex (1704–6), it would be a rectangular building with a great double door at one end and a raised platform guarded by a real, not metaphoric, "bar of justice" at the other. Entering by the door, the generality perforce moved forward—approached—to stand as suppliants before the seated and elevated gentlemen justices.[3]

One sat in church according to one's status, and someone pushing into a place to which he or she was not entitled sent reverberations through society. "Take but degree away, untune that string, / And hark what discord follows," Shakespeare had written for his Southwark audiences. Our Virginians would well have understood. To them Richard Price's crowding into a chapel seat reserved for a county justice was an act "tending to the dishonor of God Almighty, the contempt of his Majesty and Mynisters, offence of the congregacion, scandall to religion, and evill example of others."[4] The very children imbibed the notion of status and place, if not with their mother's milk then in the course of growing up. Devereux Jarratt's recollection of his early-eighteenth-century childhood in nearby New Kent County is applicable to our Middlesex. "We were," he wrote, "accustomed to look upon, what were called *gentle folks*, as beings of a superior order. For my part, I was quite shy of *them*, and kept off at a humble distance."[5]

The existence of a layered or hierarchical society acknowledged, the problem of delineating the layers and the relationship of one to the other remains. It is not an uncomplicated matter.

The bound laborer was the mudsill of our county society. In the seventeenth century, bound laborers were predominantly white and servant; in the eighteenth century, black and slave. The latter we reserve for separate consideration. Our concern for the moment is with the former.

By any standards, the lot of the servants was hard and the amenities of their lives few. They worked from sunup to sundown, some as artisans, most in the fields. They slept in sheds and lofts. Their clothes were coarse linen and woolen shirts tied at the waist and overhanging loose trousers or skirts. The mainstay of their diet (as reported by one traveler) was "an excellent but somewhat indigestible soup" made of corn, which was sometimes augmented by cornbread, occasionally by meat.[6] They were prey to disease, particularly during their first six months to a year in the Chesapeake; yet they had minimal recourse to even the poor medical assistance of the times; hence only a minority lived to the end of their service and joined the ranks of the free. Individually they were vulnerable to the unscrupulous and cruel. Collectively they were feared. Their attempts at collaborative action—few and feeble as they were—moved into folk memory to be recalled in panic as great conspiracies when occasion seemed to warrant it.[7]

As a group, moreover, the servants were denigrated by those of higher status. They were referred to as "filth and scum"—the women among them as "prostitutes" and "shameless creatures"; the men as "the boldest and most insolent young scoundrels in all England" or, alternatively, "such poor miserable Wretches, as not being able to get Bread at home, are forced to submit to be Servants."[8] And yet all knew that the servants were essential to the society as a whole and to its individual members. When, during the last decades of the century, fewer and fewer were being recruited from England for the Chesapeake, the leaders of the society bemoaned the fact, blamed the region's poor reputation, and sought to improve its image in pamphlets.[9] In Middlesex, as we noted in another context, the loss of his one male servant (a runaway) cost Peter Montague "the whole loss of the Last Cropp." His was not the only such instance. When Edward Goffe's manservant, George Bowden, ran away in the spring of 1701, Goffe "could not gett his Cornefield hoed"; when, during the summer, Bowden ran away again, "there was such a Glutt of horne Wormes" attacking the tobacco that Goffe alone "Could not destroy them" and the crop was all but lost.[10]

The very statute that defined the basic rights of servants—to "competent dyett, clothing, and lodging," "moderate" punishment not "beyond the meritt of their offences," freedom to complain to the nearest county court justice of "harsh and bad usage"—was founded not on justice but on necessity. "The barbarous usage of some servants by cruell masters bring soe much scandall and infamy to the country in generall," the preamble to the law noted, "that people who would willingly adventure themselves hither, are through feare thereof diverted . . . and the well seating [of] his majesties country very much obstructed."[11] The statute underscores a truism. Servitude in the Chesapeake was a condition defined and limited by the law, the marketplace, and the vicissitudes of human nature. Indeed, most of what we know of the day-to-day lives of the servants we know by virtue of the laws passed to protect them and the various bargains they struck with their masters as recorded by the county courts. All of these suggest the complexities of the relationship between the bound laborers and those for whom they labored.

Consider, for example, an act of the Virginia Assembly of 1662. An earlier act had established that female servants giving birth to bastards were to serve their masters an additional two years—a matter of both punishment for the immorality and compensation for the loss of labor. As a result, however, "some dissolute masters have gotten their maides with child," then claimed the benefit of the extra service. Clearly female servants were considered vulnerable to sexual and economic harrassment, and hence they must be protected. But how? The assembly considered freeing the woman caught in such a situation, then dropped the notion. "If a woman got with child by her master should be freed from that service it might probably induce such loose persons to lay all their bastards to their masters." In this the assembly was acknowledging that the women were not all that vulnerable, that some at least were quite capable of using sex and the law to their own advantage. The assembly's solution was to vest the additional service in a person other than the master, the law specifying that a churchwarden of the parish sell the two years (later reduced to one), with the proceeds of the sale going to support the parish. We see the operation of the law thirty-odd years later in Middlesex, when Jane Floyd was put to one year of service to Matthew Kemp "for her offence in haveing a bastard begotton by her Master," with Kemp paying the parish five hundred pounds of tobacco for her service. About the same time, however, we glimpse the use of sex by a female servant against her master. Whatever her contretemps with Henry Thacker, Jane Craddock sought sweet and, in the small society along the road, effective revenge: She left his house to "Spread up and down the County a most Notorious and Scandalous Story of him in that he attempted to ravish her." Ultimately Thacker prosecuted her as a runaway, but took pains to have the court question her about her tales. (If she had been free, he could—and probably would—have sued her for defamation, but servants could not be sued.) Upon examination the court declared the story "utterly false and that She onely invented it to bring him into disgrace."[12]

Consider, again, the matter of flight—the runaway servant. His labor being the property of another, a servant's flight was considered a deprivation of property. The master or a justice of the court might administer "moderate corporall punishment" by way of dissuading the recovered servant from running away again. The servant's hair might be cut short so that, should he (or she) prove a recidivist, he might be the more easily recovered. But the thrust of the law was compensation. At least double the time the servant was away was added to the term of servitude in order "to repair the damages susteyned by the master." If "the time of their running away was in the crop or the charge of recovering them extraordinary," the court could assess a longer period of additional service, one "proportionable to the damage the master . . . hath susteyned."[13]

Clearly the law was reflecting a significant problem: men and women abandoning their work to pursue an "idle course" or to follow the main chance and "procure entertainment with others for wages or shares." In either event, they were diminishing their proper master's ability to tend a labor-intensive crop—hence damaging him.[14] The law was also implying that servants were coerced back to their proper labor. Certainly in many cases they were. But servants also used flight as a bargaining chip with their masters. Thus, in 1662 Edward Dale and runaway Thomas Knight appeared in Lancaster County Court, Dale to signify that he was "contented not onely to remitt" Knight's "sevrall offences . . . for the tyme past but alsoe to give hym . . . one yere of his full tyme . . . provided always he noe more [runs] away." In 1680 John Burdon compounded his five-year absence from Robert Beverley's service by agreeing to serve him for six years "either as Gang leader Overseer or otherwise as a good and faithfull Servant ought to doe without departeing from or neglecting his Service . . . and without wasteing purloyneing imbeazelling or . . . looseing any his Masters Goods or Stock." Beverley, moreover, agreed to pay Burdon fifty shillings sterling a year for the first two years, three pounds the third and fourth, four pounds the fifth, and six pounds the last. Should Burdon absent himself again, the agreement would be canceled and Beverley would claim ten years' service for the original misdeed. Richard Robinson's servant Ann is another example. Ann ran away forty times in the 1680s and compounded her "escape time" by agreeing in 1689 to serve three years; subsequently she was allowed to marry John Marter, another Robinson servant, following which John and Ann compounded their joint service for one year.[15]

Finally, consider the phenomenon of servants suing their masters, keeping always in mind that the court in which such suits were heard was an assemblage of masters. John Merryman's abuse of his servants ("one mayd servant and two boyes") was such that in 1661 the Lancaster court ordered him to sell their services to another. In the interim, the servants were to "follow their busines as they ought to doe, otherwise their said Master to geve them moderate correccon." For his part, Merryman was not to put them "to doe any kind of Labour after day light shutt in." James Bonner's regularly encouraging Gregory Gibbs to "good service" by promising him "one yere of hys time hee came in for" was construed to be a valid contract by the court when testified to after Bonner's death. Gibbs was given his year in a suit against the estate.[16] Servants whose indentures specified that they were to labor as artisans and not in the fields, or who, having completed an indenture, agreed to stay on for wages under particular conditions—as Robert Clark did when he agreed to remain with Robert Beverley so long as he was not put to "workeing in the ground, carryeing or fetching of railes or loggs or the like things"— found such agreements enforceable in court. Also the court would intervene on behalf of the sick and lame. Thus Henry Nichols was ordered to "speedily endeavour the cure of Mary Blake . . . otherwise this Court will sett the said Mary free." In this case, it turned out that Mary had indentured herself to Peter Harris in return for a cure; Harris had sold her service to Nichols "before the cure was perfected." "It nowe appearing . . . that the said Mary is in a very bad condicion and in no probable way for her cure," she was declared "free and at her owne disposall," and Harris was ordered to repay Nichols what he had paid for her, plus all court costs.[17]

The point in all of this is that servitude and masterdom were not dichotomous states with the servant completely powerless and the master all powerful. Jane Craddock could indeed embarrass Henry Thacker in the county. John Burdon could bargain with Robert Beverley, promising what Beverley needed to make his crop: "A good and faithful Servant." And the county court was conscientious in adjudicating between the parties in the system.

In the end, however, bargaining and adjudication were not enough. Ours was a cruel society. Ralph Wormeley could tease a snake along the road; hares and foxes were hunted by chasing the creatures into hollow trees, then setting fire to the bases; wolves caught live in pits were hauled out and killed by being "drag'd at a Horse's Tail"; in Jamestown (and later Williamsburg), crowds trooped to public executions, turning hideous death into an occasion for merriment.[18] In the countryside, cruelty could, it seems, be a way in which those in the next layer up in the society separated themselves from the servants beneath them. Events in the house of Henry and Ann Davis in January 1696 are a case in point.

The Davises were free, but little other than that fact separated their condition from that of the servants about them. In the mid-1690s, they tended rented ground in the county's upper precinct, probably along the path that led from the Upper Church to the main road. Their house, we know, had two rooms and a loft. Into it were crowded the Davises themselves; Rose Gates, a thirteen-year-old orphan placed in their

charge by the county court; four-year-old Alice, Henry's illegitimate daughter by Mary Carey; John Marter, a boarder;
and Marter's servants—Sarah Gambrell, probably in her late
teens, and a young boy, Tom. Were we to sit down to supper
in this complex household, we undoubtedly would find ourselves with that excellent but indigestible corn soup and cornbread that the traveler described as the servants' diet. For with
the Davises, we are among the poorest of the poor.

It is not enough, however, to call the Davises poor and let
it go at that. They were failures. Henry, like so many others,
had entered the county as a servant. By 1678 he was free and
renting land from the Montagues. In that year he was a witness to Mary Minor's will. In January 1679 he bought one
hundred acres adjoining Nicholas Paine's land, and in June
he married Ann West, whose brother Nicholas, a small planter
(two hundred acres) who did a bit of tailoring on the side,
lived nearby. Conceivably Ann and her brother were native-
born, but we know nothing of their parentage.

The succession from servitude to renter to married landholder was a common one in early Middlesex. It was the path
by which one after the other of the county's families became
established. In this case, however, by virtue of bad luck, bad
judgment, or bad character, the path led nowhere. By 1683
Davis was deep in debt, confessing a judgment of 1,500 pounds
of sweetscented tobacco. In May 1685 he sold his land to James
Ingram. A year later he was back where he had started, a
renter on Montague land. His marriage was no more productive. At least two children were born to Ann—Alice in 1682
and Henry in 1686—but they (and any others) died in infancy
or early childhood. As renters, the couple floated from one
patch of ground to another. They were not friendless, although
their friends were not always of the most savory sort. Walter
White, a former servant of William Cheyney's, was in and out
of their house. There are no details, but in March 1690 White
and Henry were codefendants in a suit brought by Thomas
Stapleton; and in November Ann and White were accused of
theft by Joseph Carter. A jury found them innocent. By then
the Davises were on what passed for welfare in the county. In
1691 the vestry paid Henry 150 pounds tobacco for cleaning
the Upper Chapel yard—a form of poor relief. The same year

the county court, taking into account Henry's "Age and Lameness," determined that he was "not able to get his Livelyhood"; hence it exempted him from levies.[19] Age and lameness did not prevent him from fathering a bastard daughter on Mary Carey, a former servant of Maurice Cocke's; Alice was baptized at the Upper Chapel in January 1692. Two other appearances before the county court deserve notice, both involving vague suits for slander. In the first (April 1692), Henry brought suit against Jacob Booseley, obtaining a judgment for 100 pounds tobacco. In the second, a year later, Booseley and his wife Elizabeth initiated but failed to prosecute a suit for slander against Ann.

As in the case of Sarah Williamson, we have only our informed imagination to guide us when we consider the various motives behind events in the Davis household in January 1696. Ann is the central figure. In her mid-thirties and childless, she was nevertheless the surrogate mother of her husband's four-year-old bastard. (Mary Carey apparently died in childbirth or shortly thereafter.) Devoid of all but the essentials of life, she could look up and down the road and see relative prosperity, including that of her brother Nicholas. Into her house came John Marter. An ex-servant, Marter had worked as a free laborer for a while and amassed the wherewithal to obtain two servants of his own, one of whom—Sarah Gambrell—was young, quite possibly pretty, and certainly had the promise of life ahead of her rather than, as with Ann, behind her.[20]

Depositions presented to the court tell the story of what happened. In Marter's words: Ann "did use at Sundred and divers times to beat and abuse the body of Sarah Gambrell but about three weekes since did unmercifully beate hir with an Iron about fourteene Inches Long and also upon the Eleaventh of this Instent did beat [her] three times . . . and . . . Sarah dyed the same day." Robert George told of going to the Davis house and meeting Sarah, who begged "for Gods sake to bring hir . . . a peece of Bread for shee was almost Starved." The next day, passing by on the road, "he heard one Cry out and he also heard the Sound of Severall Strookes." Entering he "saw Nobody but William Pryor and John Marter but heard Several Strookes Given and a great Cry in the Next

Roome and at last saw Ann Davis and Sarah Gambrell Come out." Pryor testified that the day Sarah died "Ann Davis did beat the said Sarah . . . three Severall times (Vizt) first with a Switch Secondly with a Shoemakers Sterrup thirdly with a paire of flatt Leather Spanells." William Norcott told of "Mauling . . . Railes by the Road about a Quarter of mille from the house," when Sarah approached him saying "shee was Verey Cold"; Norcott "bade her Warme hir Selfe" by his fire, and while she was doing so "a little boy Tom Called hir Severall times. At Last shee went into the house and presently" Norcott "heard a great Cry as if Some body was Murthering and the next day the said Sarah Gambrell Dyed." William Provert, a servant himself, told of going by the Davis house and seeing Sarah "upon hir hands and Knees in the Snow." When he asked John Marter "to fetch hir In," Marter replyed that Provert "might Fetch hir in [himself] if he would." Returning to the house later, Provert found Sarah lying "dead upon the Chest." He asked Marter "whether hir death would not Stick upon his Conscience and the said Marter made answer that the Money or Tobaccos . . . Sarah Cost him troubled him more."[21]

Ann's cruelty toward Sarah is, of course, the striking element of this scene. It was exceptional in its result, and eventually Ann would pay the price of murder and be hanged in Jamestown.[22] But equally striking is the indifference displayed by so many. Henry Davis is a mute specter. He must have been a witness to events; perhaps by making advances toward Sarah, he even precipitated them. But he did not try to stay his wife's hand. Sarah was Marter's property—almost the entirety of his capital—and in the end he bemoaned his monetary loss. But he did not attempt to protect either his property or Sarah as an individual. Norcott shared his fire with Sarah, but he did not rush toward the house when he heard the sounds of murder. George was drawn into the house by those sounds, but he simply listened with Pryor and Marter to the cries coming from the next room. Only Provert tried to intervene, and only he spoke of Sarah's death as a matter of conscience. To Ann and Henry Davis, and to Marter, George, Pryor, and Norcott, it seems that Sarah was simply a servant. Her very wretchedness defined their own condition—poverty-stricken but free—as something of worth. They were, in a curious way, compelled by their own plight to ignore hers. Only to Provert was Sarah a person deserving of protection and, in the end, a tear.

As we move from the poorest of Middlesex's free families to the county's "middling sort," another act of violence attracts our attention. The date was Thursday, September 13, 1711; the place an ordinary at mid-county. Earlier that day the middle precinct militia had met for muster and training exercises. The exercises completed, the men had begun impromptu horse races. And from the races the flow of the crowd was toward the tavern. Benjamin Davis—no relation to Henry—was one of the crowd, drifting from muster to races to ordinary. He would be one of the protagonists in the drama to come. The other would be George Wortham, captain of the militia company.

We have already met Davis.[23] Born in the county in 1680, he had lost his mother, a Pritchard from Gloucester, as an infant and his father at age eight. With his older brother John, he was bound out to Oswald Cary. Cary died within a few years, and when his widow married Randolph Seager in July 1691, the boys were bound to him. Then Seager died (1694), and once again remarriage by the widow brought another master, the Reverend Samuel Gray, the parish minister. In 1696 brother John reached his majority and left Gray's service to take up a hundred acres left to him by his and Benjamin's father. Benjamin, at nineteen, sought his own freedom, but was compelled by the court to remain with Gray until 1702. For a few years we lose sight of him. Perhaps he worked for wages or rented. But in December 1706 he married the widow of Sarah Williamson's son Charles. With the marriage, Benjamin gained a two-year-old stepson, land to work for himself (Williamson's hundred acres), and a black slave couple and their infant boy. The next year he served as a grand juror, to our knowledge his first public service. Regular jury duty followed, and in December 1708 he was named by the county court a surveyor of highways, being charged with the care of the roads "from Turkes Ferry [on the Piankatank] to the Courthouse" and on to the Middle Church.[24]

Marriage and public service were the high points of Da-

vis's life. Then the tide turned against him. One of the blacks—
the female—died. Rather than himself and two blacks to do
the work of the plantation, Davis perforce made do with himself and one. At the same time, he had more mouths to feed.
To his wife, stepson, and the young black—not yet old enough
to work—were added two daughters born in 1707 and 1709.
Debts piled up, primarily to William Churchill, from whom
Davis obtained the necessities he could not produce himself
and to whom he paid over his tobacco. The crop never covered the cost of purchases. The final accounting would come
after Davis's death. Charles Williamson's estate, which Davis
had come to control by marriage, had amounted to the
hundred acres and personal property valued at 117*li* current
money of Virginia. Following Davis's death, his debts were
such that they could only be met by the sale at public auction
not only of his own personal possessions, but also of those
properly belonging to his wife and Williamson's son, including the two remaining blacks. When the tally was balanced,
the widow was left with the land and 5*li*.

   Benjamin Davis, a freeholder and minor officeholder, was
a cut above Henry Davis, albeit failing in the economic race.
For his part, George Wortham was a cut above Benjamin.
Wortham, too, was Middlesex-born (1673) and he was the third
of four sons and ultimately the only survivor of the eight children of John and Mary Wortham. Father John had moved
into what would become the the middle precinct in 1657, taking up four hundred acres on the Piankatank side of the main
road just below the cutoff to the Dragon crossing. A lay reader
at Christ Church, he was called upon frequently for jury duty,
as an appraiser of estates, and to serve as constable. In 1684
he was co-opted onto the vestry. That same year he took a
seat among the justices of the county court. Young George
came into his father's land gradually. Following John's death
in 1693, George took possession of the undeveloped land away
from the road, building his house there while a stepmother
lived on in the original "manor Plantation" of one hundred
acres. When she died (by November 1695), George took over
the old house, repaired and refitted it as a new courthouse,
and leased it, along with a prison that he built nearby, to the
county for a ten-year term, collecting five thousand pounds

of tobacco. By then he was married and a father; before his death, he would marry twice and father eleven children in all. His first public service had followed closely upon his father's death and proceeded apace: petit jury duty from 1693 onward, appraising estates from 1695, surveyor of highways in 1696, constable in 1701, a jury foreman for the first time in 1703, a seat among the justices in 1704, sheriff of the county in 1708. His personal fortune seems to have proceeded apace as well. In 1699 he attempted to add to his land a thirty-three-acre tract that would have given him frontage on the Piankatank. At the auction of Benjamin Davis's goods, Wortham would purchase the young black boy to add to his own stock of labor.

Davis and Wortham, two men of the county, were neighbors—their houses were no more than a mile and a half apart. Their argument that Thursday in 1711 began in mid-afternoon. Wortham, as captain of the company, exercised his troopers and then, done with the muster, "went to running of Races."[25] The captain was among the winners and bought cider for the men, who urged him "to stay and drink part with them." It was inevitably a bluff, hearty occasion in the yard in front of the ordinary. At one point, Wortham drew Davis aside. Undoubtedly the captain knew of Davis's worsening finances. He offered Benjamin the position of overseer on his own plantation. We do not know what Davis replied, only that the two had "some discourse" about the matter. The general talk drifted to the cause célèbre of the neighborhood at the moment: William Matthews, then languishing in the nearby jail. Matthews had some years before been an ordinary keeper, but had fallen into debt and lost his license. Since then he had been in and out of trouble, the most recent involving a suit with Wortham over a protested bill, Wortham claiming a debt of eight pounds, seven shillings and sixpence. Only a few days earlier, Wortham had obtained an attachment of a mare belonging to Matthews, had seized the mare, and had placed it with his own animals. Matthews had stolen it back again and had been committed to the jail by Justice Christopher Robinson to await trial for theft.

Had Matthews really "Stole his Mare or no?" one of the troopers now asked Wortham.

Indeed he had, George replied.

No! Davis interjected. Matthews was "an honest man and took his [own] Mare where he Could find her." He—Wortham—"had done the thing that was unfaire for that he had attached a mans Mare that he had noe more right to then himselfe."

Once started, argument escalated.

"Matthews did what any honest man would do and what I would have done myself!"

"Ah, Davis, do not trouble your head about it. It is no concern of yours. Be pacifyed!"

"Nay, not for a rogue and knave like yourself!"

Gradually the onlookers pushed between the participants, separating them. Richard Paffit drew Wortham into the ordinary itself to "Smoake a pipe and drink a pot and then they should be free of Davis' noise." But after a while, Davis and some others followed. Sitting apart from Wortham and Paffit, Davis continued ranting.

"If I had but four men of my own mind I would break the prison door open and lett him out."

When he raised no response from his prey, Davis rose, crossed the room, and demanded the prison key. Somehow Wortham (or the others) managed to quiet Davis and return him to his seat. It was only for a moment.

"Who was such a blockhead to put that man there?" Davis asked the room in general. Rising, he approached Wortham again. "Was it such a pupey as you, or do you know who?"

"Mr. Christopher Robinson committed him."

"Then Mr. Christopher Robinson is a blockhead and a pupey, and all the Justices are fooles and do not know their Duty."

Wortham was by this time obviously angered. He "bid [Davis] hold his tongue." When Davis persisted, Wortham, too, resorted to epithets. Here the record fails us. The witnesses conveniently forgot what Wortham said. "Captain Wortham Said Some word (which this deponent Saith he hath forgott) which disturbed Benjamin Davis who repeated it Severall times after. Whereupon Captain Wortham said 'Sure, Benjamin, it is not Come to that, that I must be afraid to Speak for you?' and with that bid him hold his tongue and talk noe more of it." The argument continued, but on a level so personal as to defy our understanding. Davis, said Wortham, was too much like his Gloucester Uncle Pritchard. (All we know of Pritchard is that he owed Davis a cow and calf but never delivered them.) [26]

"If I am like my Uncle Pritchard I will stand by my Uncle Pritchard till I dye."

Wortham had touched a sensitive area! He raised his cane as if to hold Davis away. Davis struck at the cane with his sheathed sword, then drew the sword from its scabbard and cut at the cane again. Wortham backed away toward and through the open door and into the yard, defending himself with the cane until it was finally swept from his hand, then drawing his own sword and offering it toward his attacker.

"Stand off, Davis. I have a sword as well."

Witness William Cheshire—he would subsequently marry Davis's widow—tells the rest of it: "Davis Still endeavouring to get a blow at [Wortham] followed him very close up and at last turned from him and came towards me . . . saying in a crying tone that he was a dead man and [he] opening his Shirt to look at Something I saw blood." Two hours later Davis died. He had run himself upon Wortham's outstretched sword. [27]

The "duel" was certainly a drunken brawl. One of the witnesses would later confess that he could not "be positive in [his testimony] because he was Something in drink." Indeed, the hard cider had been running for at least three hours! But the duel is also a window through which we glimpse personalities and tensions in the middle layer of Middlesex's free society, just as the murder of Sarah Gambrell offers us a glimpse of the lowest level. At the root of the duel was status. Benjamin was in danger of losing the status he had, so much so, it seems, as to be affronted by the offer of employment as an overseer. He lashed out at Wortham (who had made the offer) in behalf of a man in prison who could just as easily have been himself.

Status is the operative word here. By it we mean very simply an individual's position in some sort of normative hierarchy that in sum makes up the society within which one lives. We take the definition from our sister disciplines, sociology and anthropology. But to put the point in down-to-earth (albeit pristine and exaggerated) terms: If two people met in a given situation in Middlesex, the behavior of each toward the other would inevitably be guided by each one's individual assessment of his or her own status relative to the status of the other. If the situation was the classic one of meeting across two ends of a narrow footbridge, each would look for particular attributes in the other, scale those attributes according to a set of rules that both understood, and arrive at the same decision as to who was to precede whom. Sociologists have isolated those attributes that might be used in this very general social process: sex, age, wealth and its accoutrements (a fine house, fine clothes, in brief, appearances), political authority, ethnicity, education, occupation, and family connection or kinship.[28] But which did our Middlesex people actually use? And weighted how? In some societies—those marked by what is called "status consistency"—one party need only spy signs of greater wealth at the other end of the footbridge in order to assume greater power, higher family connections, better education, and a more prestigious occupation, and hence give way. In others—marked by "status inconsistency"—an individual might be from a socially esteemed family yet be politically powerless or be highly educated yet be penniless; and status claims on the one hand and deference on the other will vary according to the particulars of the situation. Historians too often have assumed the former prevailed in the early Chesapeake, writing of "the integration of economic wealth, social status, and political power."[29] But did it?

The most important imprimatur of status among the men of Middlesex that we have is the degree to which they served the public.[30] Vestry and county court were to all intents and purposes self-selected boards. The vestry was openly so. When one vestryman died, the remainder selected a successor, and appointment was for life. The members of the county court were, technically, commissioned by the governor of the colony, as was the sheriff. The justices served at the gubernatorial pleasure—he could commission others in their places; the sheriff served a one-year term. Yet almost invariably justices, once appointed, served for life or until they themselves stepped down, and the governor chose new justices upon the nomination of sitting justices. The sheriff's office, for the most part, rotated among the justices. With the exception of burgesses elected by the freeholders to represent the county in the colony's legislature,[31] all other public service was performed by individuals selected in one way or another by members of the vestry and court. And there were many tasks to be done, from service on petit juries (which determined the facts at issue before the court) and processioning and appraising estates, through grand jury duty, clerking, seeing to the condition of the roads (surveyors of highways), and carrying out the diverse duties assigned to the constables and to an undersheriff, to the work of the justices and vestrymen themselves. In the single year 1700, for example, eighty-four individuals—slightly more than a third of the number of heads-of-family then residing in the county—were active in 175 county and parish posts.[32] The intention of those making the selections was to get the public's business done as expeditiously as possible; hence, it can be argued, they selected those who were known to have the skills, sagaciousness, trustworthiness, and stature needed for the work—in other words, those who had particular status (or standing) in the society of the community.

In the lives that we have already touched upon, there are important clues to this selection process, hence to status. Henry Davis died the year after the murder of Sarah Gambrell, still a renter. What possessions he had seem to have been silently taken up by his then-landlord and principal creditor, Henry Perrott. No inventory remains of Davis's estate, and Perrott was awarded 150 pounds of tobacco by the county court for burying him in a pauper's grave. But we have a sense of what Davis might have owned from the inventory of John Bodgam who, like Davis, had begun life in the Chesapeake as a servant and ended it (in 1701) as a renter: a cow and calf and two steers; in one room of his house, a bed and some blankets; in the other, another bed, a table, a chest—all described as "olde"—an iron pot, a frying pan, some pewter dishes, two "milk trays," and two pails. In all, Bodgam's possessions were worth 1,362 pounds of tobacco, or roughly nine pounds, ten shillings current money.[33] With the exception of Davis's being paid by the parish to clean the Upper Chapel yard—a form of welfare, as we have said—neither Davis nor Bodgam was ever charged with a public task.

Recall the lives of Benjamin Davis and the two Worthams. Davis was charged with no public service to our knowledge until after his marriage, that is to say, until he was a settled householder in control of land. George Wortham began his public career only after the death of his father, when he came into land of his own. Definite career paths are suggested. Both Worthams seem to have risen through an ascending hierarchy of positions. John Wortham served successively as juror, appraiser, and constable before being selected for the vestry and court. George Wortham served, in order, as juror, appraiser, surveyor of highways, constable, and justice. Davis was a constable only after he had served as a grand and petit juror. The Worthams, finally, were almost constantly employed in one office or another. Davis was last called upon in 1708, the point at which we judge his fortunes turned for the worse.

What is indicated in a few cases is confirmed when we consider many. The possession of land and wealth were clearly vital elements in the selection process. Those without land—itinerant tenants and sharecroppers, hired laborers—were virtually excluded from public tasks. Until the turn of the century, colony statute was vague on the point of who could serve the public. Aliens, atheists, Catholics, Jews, felons, those residing in the county less than three years, and the immoral in general were barred from public service.[34] But even before colony law restricted jury duty and the like to "freeholders," few who did not own or hold long-term leases to property were selected in Middlesex.[35] Among the eighty-four men active in 1700, for example, only three came from this bottommost level of free society, one serving as a sexton, two as appraisers.

But the relationship of land and wealth to public service involved more than simply the exclusion of the landless. When we tabulate the careers of all those doing the public's work in the county, we discern—although imperfectly—the ordering of positions suggested by the careers of Davis and Wortham. County men generally began their public service as petit jurors and appraisers and rose, if they rose at all, from there. When we break down the highest office achieved into levels and compute for each level the median number of acres controlled by incumbents and the median appraised value of their

personal property, a clear correlation emerges. Those achieving positions as justices, vestrymen, sheriffs, churchwardens,
coroners, and burgesses—the highest level offices—controlled at the high point of their lives an average of 828 acres
and left estates valued on average at 615*li* current. Those
achieving only the lowest level offices controlled on average
180 acres and left estates appraised at 85*li*.

But there is still more to this matter of public office (and
status). The ranges of values in our analysis suggest as much.
For there were men who controlled upward of one thousand
acres and left estates of six hundred pounds and more who
never rose in public service beyond the lowest level, and men
of one hundred or two hundred acres and estates to match
who rose to the highest. Brief sketches of Middlesex families—some of which we have met in passing—and the offices
held by their members are equally suggestive.

The Seagers. We noticed the first Seager—Oliver—when
we looked at the initial entry into the county. Illiterate, probably an ex-servant, he acquired land at the cliffs in the uppermost part of the county in 1650. At his death in 1659, he left
a widow, Eleanor, and three children. Eleanor remarried within
the year, outlived her second husband, Humphrey Owen, then
married widower Humphrey Jones, a sequence of marriages
that provided the one Seager child to survive, Oliver's son
Randolph, with an elaborate network of step-relationships, a
network that was cemented in 1679 when he married his stepsister, Mary Jones. That same year Randolph seems to have
taken control of his father's land and begun his public service,
serving frequently as a juror, estate appraiser, constable, and
surveyor of highways. In 1690 he was named to the vestry.
Thereafter—but never before—he was referred to as "Mister
Seager." By 1692 he was a justice of the peace, sitting on the
county court. At his death, he was in control of at least four
properties—his father's in his own right; that of his second
wife, Ann (Jackson) Cary; and two held in trust for the children of his stepfather Jones. His personal estate in money
and tobacco was worth, in 1694, 660*li* current.

Early deaths like Randolph Seager's—he was only in his
mid-thirties—and the subsequent scattering of property and
children among executors and guardians were common

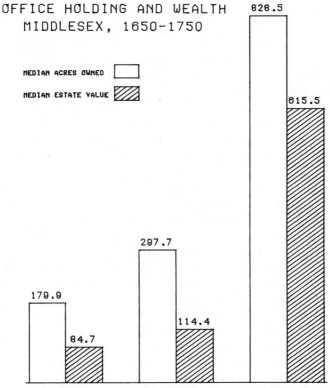

OFFICE HOLDING AND WEALTH
MIDDLESEX, 1650-1750

MEDIAN ACRES OWNED
MEDIAN ESTATE VALUE

828.5

615.5

297.7

179.9

114.4

84.7

LEVEL 1   LEVEL 2   LEVEL 3

THE PLOT DEPICTS FOR OFFICE HOLDERS
GROUPED BY THE HIGHEST OFFICE HELD: THE
MEDIAN OF ESTATE EVALUATIONS FOLLOWING
DEATH ADJUSTED AS DESCRIBED IN THE
EXPLICATUS (N=208) AND OF THE GREATEST
NUMBER OF ACRES OWNED OR LEASED AT ANY
POINT IN TIME DURING A SUBJECT'S
LIFETIME (N=726).

LEVEL 1 OFFICES INCLUDE GRAND- AND
PETIT JUROR, APPRAISER, PATROLLER,
TOBACCO COUNTER, PROCESSIONER.

LEVEL 2: READER, VESTRY CLERK, BAILIFF,
CONSTABLE, UNDERSHERIFF, SURVEYOR OF
HIGHWAYS, DEPUTY CLERK, LEVY COLLECTOR,
AUDITOR, VIEWER OF TOBACCO, TOBACCO
WAREHOUSE OFFICER.

LEVEL 3: CLERK OF COURT, VESTRYMAN,
CHURCHWARDEN, JUSTICE, CORONER,
SHERIFF, KING'S ATTORNEY, BURGESS.

A FOURTH LEVEL ENCOMPASSING THOSE WHO
ACHIEVED COLONY-WIDE OFFICE (N=20) IS
OMITTED. THE MEDIAN ACRES OWNED BY THIS
GROUP WAS 2,225; THE MEDIAN ESTATE
WAS 2,386 POUNDS CURRENT MONEY.

enough occurrences in the county. Oliver, Randolph's eldest, nine years old when his father died, was raised by storekeeper and planter Tobias Mickleburrough. His younger brother, John, spent a few years with neighbor Thomas Loe; then, when his sister Winifred married carpenter Thomas Hipkins, he went to live with them, Hipkins promising the court to "Learn" the boy "to Read and Write and teach him the trade of a Carpenter."[36] Both sons came into middling-sized estates upon reaching their majority, and both began to undertake public service. For his part, John regularly served on juries and as an estate appraiser, tobacco inspector, processioner, and twice as constable—but nothing higher. And he was never referred to as "mister." In contrast, Oliver, after serving several times as juryman, was named to the county court at the relatively early age of twenty-two and to the vestry seven years later; he served frequently as county sheriff and throughout his adult years was "Mister Seager." Clearly the difference between the brothers was not family. Neither was it occupation. Both were simply "planters"—there is no evidence that John practiced the trade taught him by his sister's husband. Was it wealth? Both were landed, and both had above average personal property at their deaths—John's estate was appraised at 379*li*, and Oliver's at 626. Was a form of social primogeniture in operation? Oliver, the more prominent, was after all the elder. Or was it something more subtle? For much of their adult lives, both brothers were unmarried. Oliver would take a wife at thirty-six; John never. But John seems to have lived without benefit of ceremony with the widow Nichols, acknowledging her illegitimate daughter Jane as his own in 1720. Did the liaison somehow lower John in the esteem of his neighbors?

Another family: Like the Seagers, the Perrotts made their appearance in the county early. Richard Perrott, the first of that name in Middlesex, arrived from York in 1650 with his wife Sarah. But unlike the first Seager, the first Perrott arrived with considerable means and status (as measured by public position). He was a member of the Lancaster court in 1655, a vestryman in 1657, sheriff that same year, a frequent churchwarden, and at least twice "president" of the county court. Perrott's only child—another Richard—was born in February 1651, "the first Man Child that was gott and borne In Rappahanock River of English parents," according to the parish register.[37] At twenty-one young Richard assumed control of eight hundred acres he had inherited at age nine from his half-brother Thomas Dale; at twenty-two he married a widow, Sarah (Curtis) Halfhide, and he received additional land as a gift from his father; at twenty-three, having served only once as an appraiser, he was named to the county court and shortly after to the vestry. He was, in brief, a young man of a well-reputed county family, with considerable substance of his own, and with a promising future.

Yet Richard was not, apparently, a prudent man. In 1678 he forfeited all personal property, servants, and cattle in lieu of paying a bill of 112*li* sterling; that same year, he was sued by minister John Shepherd, who wanted the salary Richard, as sheriff, had collected from the county but neglected to pass on. Six years later, young Perrott's downfall was completed when he defaulted on a bill and lost most of his land to Robert Beverley. Only with the help of his father did he manage to hold on to some acres. The disaster was immediately reflected in Perrott's public service. For a while, he remained, technically, a member of the court, but he never again sat with his fellow justices. For five years, he refrained from appearing at meetings of the vestry, after which time he made appearances only now and again. And for a long period of time, he was called upon to do no public work for the county, reappearing in the records only toward the end of his life as an occasional appraiser, auditor, and juror. The fall of the father was reflected in the careers of his children. Richard's eldest son, Henry, heir to his grandfather's land—the founder passed over his prodigal son when making his will—served on juries and grand juries, as an appraiser, and twice as surveyor of highways. Yet he was never named to either court or vestry. When he died he left 830 acres, some 232*li* in personal property, no will, and a long-term battle between his widow and younger brothers over the disposition of his estate.

Let us switch to the Haslewoods. George Haslewood was born in Middlesex in 1661, the son of Captain John Haslewood and Frances Cole, she the daughter of a vestryman who had died three years earlier leaving her a substantial estate. George's father John was himself landed and served on the vestry and county court. He had increased his estate by marrying, after Frances's death, Elizabeth Moone, daughter and heir of Abraham and Ann Moone and stepdaughter of both John Curtis and Richard Robinson. Then he had increased it again by marrying, after Elizabeth died, the widow of John Carter. George, for his part, upon coming of age, married Ann Robinson, daughter of court and vestry member Richard Robinson and his wife, the former Ann Moone Curtis, obtaining not just a wife but a sizable wedding settlement, plus control of her six hundred acres, plus within a year control of another eight hundred acres accruing to her. George Haslewood was, in sum, very much akin to young Richard Perrott at this age—a well-connected and well-to-do young man, one consistently referred to as "Mister Haslewood" in the records. Yet he was named only twice to appraise estates in the county and once to a term as constable. The latter was apparently disastrous. The court had to issue a warrant to compel him to take the oath of office and then heard a complaint against him that, as constable, he neglected his duties. He was never again selected to do the work of the public.

But the Haslewoods are even more interesting in their implications. George's uncle Thomas and cousin Thomas are cases in point. Uncle Thomas was Captain John Haslewood's brother and married to Captain John's wife's sister, an heiress in her own right. While Captain John served on court and vestry, Uncle Thomas served occasionally as juror, twice as estate appraiser, and once as constable—nothing more. His son Thomas—George's cousin—inherited land from both his father and mother and began public service as a juror and estate appraiser shortly after reaching his majority, but during the rest of his life was asked to assume no higher office and never was accorded the honorific title "mister." When Thomas died, he left a personal estate valued at some 356*li*. His nephew by marriage—Humphrey Jones—died about the same time, leaving personalty valued at 418*li*. Humphrey had been a member of the court.

We offer one more sketch: William Provert, the conscionable witness to the death of Sarah Gambrell. A few years after the murder, free of his service, Provert married, taking as wife a parish child, Hannah, the illegitimate daughter of a

servant of Richard Perrott the elder. Hannah had been bound
as an infant to Nicholas West (Ann Davis's brother), but West,
too, seems to have been a man of conscience, treating the waif
more like a daughter than like a servant and at his death leaving her one heifer and half of a two hundred–acre patent—
seventy-six acres by subsequent survey. Provert and Hannah
lived on the land after their marriage.

William Provert—illiterate, an ex-servant with a parish child
for a wife, holding but seventy-six acres of land—was clearly
of a different kind from the Seagers, Perrotts, Haslewoods,
and Worthams. He seems even a cut below Benjamin Davis.
What of his public service? In 1703 he served on his first petit
jury and in both 1705 and 1706 was a grand juror. In December 1708 he was named a surveyor of highways, a giant step
in office holding for a man in his circumstances. When he
died in January 1710, he left a personal estate valued at 5,913
pounds tobacco, amounting to slightly over thirty-five pounds
current money, and, to read between the lines of later admin-
istrator's accounts, virtually no debts. But Provert stands out
in the records in another way, too. While "sue and be sued"
seems the personal motto of most men in this litigious society,
Provert, with two exceptions, appeared in court only to give
testimony or claim witness fees for so doing or to serve as
security for someone else's appearance. Both of the suits against
him were dismissed out-of-hand.

What are we to make of this mélange? Here are instances
of wealth with and without office, of office with and without
wealth, of individuals embedded in identical kinship networks but with disparate rankings in terms of office held, and
of men rising and falling. To us the mélange suggests that in
this middle layer of county society—one demarcated on its
lower boundary by men like William Provert and Benjamin
Davis, the latter in danger of slipping into the layer below,
and by George Wortham on its upper—individuals were sorted
out according to a complex set of variables. Some of those
variables like wealth, we easily isolate statistically. Others seem
almost incorporeal.[38]

Wealth was indeed a factor—but not simply the possession
of eight hundred acres as against three hundred. The operation of wealth in this middle layer was far more subtle. Land

and house and tools and furniture seem to have proclaimed to the society that a man could take care of himself and his family, could meet his debts, could even, perhaps, come to the aid of a neighbor by posting bond for him in court or taking in his orphaned children. Such solvency raised a man's esteem in the society, gave him status; a demonstrable lack of solvency—Richard Perrott, Jr., is our case in point—diminished a man's esteem.

Family, quasi-familial relationships such as guardianships and godparentage and even friendships seem to have had a particular meaning for status as well. Recognition flowed from such relationships, recognition of the "I knew your father, hence I know you" kind. And an initial and tentative assignment of a degree of solvency followed such recognition. Moreover, relationships implied a form of social underwriting, the existence of resources of a particular kind and degree that lay behind the individual and upon which he could draw. Again, Richard Perrott, Jr., is our case in point. Recognition as the son of his father brought him to the county court at a young age. His downfall, when it came, was not absolute, as it was for others—some in his situation even fled the county and their debts—for he could call upon the resources of his father to maintain himself and his children to some extent.

Finally, personal qualities counted. One had to have the skill and willingness to do the public's work. George Haslewood seems to have lacked one or the other. William Provert apparently had both, and more. Provert is undoubedly our most curious case. Relatively impecunious, without relations, and his wife, as we said, a parish child, he was nevertheless entrusted by his betters with a variety of tasks. We can presume the trust was well placed, for he was called upon not once but frequently. But what called him to the attention of his neighbors in the first place? What marked him as a man to be esteemed in any way? As so often, we cannot know for sure, yet in that one instance—when he testified as to the death of Sarah Gambrell—he gives us evidence of himself as a man of conscience, of character; and in the absence of anything else, we can assume his neighbors took note of it as well.

Let us return for a moment to the scene of the duel. Mister George Wortham, militia captain, vestryman, gentleman

justice of the county court, and sometime sheriff, sits drinking with his men. We cannot make too much of the scene.
There were layers within layers in this society. Wortham is to
be located at the top of the middle layer; his men (including
Davis) occupied positions well downward from him. His
drinking with them was a bit of noblesse oblige on his part.
Wortham had, recall, bought the first round for the men, and
he drank with them only at their urging. Nevertheless, it is
hard to imagine a Wormeley, master of Rosegill, drinking with
the likes of Benjamin Davis. For when we enter Rosegill as
visitors, we are entering the very highest layer of our society,
one separated by a chasm from the layers beneath.

Rosegill was that vast tract of land stretching four miles
along the Rappahannock in the middle precinct of the county.
In the original patents, the land (thirty-two hundred acres)
extended a mile inland; but successive acquisitions had doubled the Wormeley holding by the turn of the century, and
Rosegill extended to and across the main road. A narrow cor-
ridor of Wormeley land joined Rosegill itself to a tract along
the Piankatank that included the best landing on the upper
reaches of that river. Still another Wormeley tract lay on both
sides of the road leading to the Dragon Bridge. Persons crossing the bridge perforce passed over Wormeley land to do so.

Rosegill was not one plantation but many. In 1701, when
the death of the second Ralph Wormeley led to an inventory
of the property, there were ten separate farms or quarters,
each with its own group of blacks and English servants.[39] In
all, eighty-five black slaves, two Indians, and eight white servants labored for Wormeley; 439 cows, steers, bulls, heifers,
and calves grazed his fields, plus 86 sheep, an undetermined
number of horses, and uncounted (and uncountable) pigs
running free in the woods. Other farms were worked by tenants, although how many we do not know.

The "home house" or "great house" was the capital of this
establishment. Either phrase is a misnomer, for the "home
house" was in reality a farm itself and boasted many buildings, not just one. In another context, we quoted a traveler
who, in the mid-1680s, referred to it as "a rather large village"
on the windswept point where Rosegill Creek entered the
Rappahannock.[40] At the time, there were at least two resi-
dences on the property, either one as large as any in the county.

By 1701 they were in all likelihood joined in some fashion to form one structure containing ten rooms and seven fireplaces.[41] Nearby stood a separate kitchen constructed in the 1690s; a dairy house; one, possibly two storehouses; a barn; a smithy; a tannery yard; a dock; and the ruins of a small battery erected and equipped earlier by the colony government to command passage of the Rappahannock. Either at the home house or on the headwaters of Rosegill Creek, near the glebe, was a Wormeley gristmill.[42] Among the ten rooms of the residence was a "parlor" (in 1687 a visitor noted its "very accurate clock"; in 1701 the clock was "out of kelter"), five "chambers," a "nursery," "the old Nursery," and two "closets," one for "Esquire" Wormeley, the other for his wife.[43] "Closet" carried the old meaning of the word: a room for privacy or retirement. In Madam Wormeley's closet were 150-odd books, a number of chairs, a desk, a brass warming pan, and a "Large Crimson sattin quilt"; in the master's closet were even more books, his desk, and an assortment of riding equipage.

Inventories suggest the distance between social layers in Middlesex. Bodgam's summed to between 9 and 10*li* current. Provert's personal estate was appraised at just over 35*li*. Davis's goods sold at auction for roughly 75. We do not have George Wortham's inventory, but one for an individual of roughly equivalent stature (Humphrey Jones) amounted to 418*li*. Ralph Wormeley's 1701 inventory—incomplete at that for it does not include personal possessions on his properties in York and Rappahannock counties—summed to 2,861*li* 6*s*, three hundred times as much as Bodgam's, eighty-one times as much as Provert's, thirty-eight times the value of Davis's goods, and seven times the value of Jones's. By aggregating many inventories, we gain a sense of the relative size of the layers of society and, again, the distance between them. Roughly a third of the families of Middlesex at the turn of the century were at Bodgam's level; as a group they owned less than 2 percent of the personal property in the county. Sixty percent of the families lay in the layer delineated by Benjamin Davis and Wortham and owned 36 percent of the personalty. No family matched the Wormeleys. It was by far the wealthiest. And only a handful came even close. As a group, the top 8 percent of the families (including the Wormeleys) owned 62 percent of the personal property of the county.

Such measurements, however, lack the subtleness of reality. They only hint at the gulf between the extremes of our society. Appearances are provocative. Consider the size of the Wormeley house and compare it to Henry Davis's two rooms and loft. Think of Madam Wormeley's "Crimson sattin quilt" and Bodgam's "olde blankets." Imagine either Bodgam or Henry Davis trudging along the road, afoot, dressed much like servants in loose, dull brown shirts and pants. A Worme-

PERSONAL PROPERTY OF MIDDLESEX
FAMILIES, CA. 1700

61.8%

THE WIDTH OF THE BARS IS PROPORTIONATE
TO THE PERCENT OF TOTAL POPULATION FREE,
MALE, HEAD-OF-HOUSE IN THE GROUP, THE
HEIGHT TO THE PERCENT OF ALL PERSONALTY
IN THE COUNTY OWNED BY EACH GROUP.
BASED ON INVENTORY EVALUATIONS ADJUSTED
AS DESCRIBED UNDER "WEALTH" IN THE
EXPLICATUS.

36.4%

1.8%

BOTTOM 32.2%   TOP 7.9%
            MIDDLE 59.9% OF HOUSEHOLD HEADS

ley canters by, his saddle crimson velvet, his pistols stuck in silk-fringed holsters, his broadcloth saddle blanket worth more and of better condition than the walker's very clothing.

Still we have not fathomed the chasm. Awareness of space, could we express it numerically, might serve as a gauge. A Bodgam or Henry Davis conceivably remembered English boyhoods and the trip to America, but other than those memories their world—and the world of the vast majority of those

born in Middlesex—was limited to their fields, neighborhoods, and precincts, with once in a while a walk along the
road to court day. Ralph Wormeley had been born on the
York River and sent to England after the death of his father,
matriculating at Oriel College, Oxford, in 1665. In Virginia
he traveled regularly to view his various properties outside
the county and as a member of the government. He was a
member of Virginia's council of state and served as secretary
of state for the colony, collector of customs for the Rappahannock district, colonel of militia, and trustee of Virginia's College of William and Mary. Where he had not traveled, he could
visit in his mind, his books carrying him across time and space.
He could, on an evening, live with the Cavaliers in Lambert
Wood's *Life and Reign of King Charles,* travel to *Barbados* with
Richard Ligon, speculate upon the habitability of the moon
with John Wilkins, or ponder with John Selden *The Privileges
of the Baronage of England.*[44] The last might well have intrigued
him for, as we will see, Wormeleys tended to think in baronial
terms. Men of Bodgam's and Davis's sort were for the most
part illiterate.[45]

Space is germane in another way. When we are with a
Wormeley, we are at a level of society that was at one and the
same time a part of the county and exceeded the county, one
that included in the 1670s Wormeleys, Beverleys, Smiths,
Burnhams, and Corbins, and added Robinsons, Churchills and
Grymeses in the 1680s and 1690s and Berkeleys in the eighteenth century. To one historian, the heads of such families
constituted "The first gentlemen of Virginia"; to another "the
One Hundred."[46] To us they are simply the cosmopolitan few
in our innately provincial (that is to say, county) society, set
off by wealth and, more importantly, by the wide sphere of
their activities. With lands and estates within and without the
county measured in the thousands of acres and thousands of
pounds sterling, they ranked head and shoulders above any
purely county family—Worthams, Seagers, Joneses, for
example. In the seventeenth century, they dealt economically
with county families, buying tobacco and selling goods out of
England from their "stores." But they were also deeply involved
in transatlantic trading networks that effected the vital
exchange of Virginia tobacco for English goods. They tended

to marry across county lines, while others married almost exclusively within; and they sent their children beyond the county for education and sought husbands and wives for them in families of equivalent rank anywhere in Virginia.[47] They coveted and some carried off political offices beyond the county, but they and their sons seldom served the county in any position below that of justice or vestryman. In brief, they were families of high status within their county of residence, but their status did not derive from within the county as much as it did from their activities outside of it.

Our problem, however, is not their position within a Virginia-wide elite but their relationship to the county itself. Recall the trial of Middlesex Baconians. Here the gentlemen of the moment seem to have been openly confronting the county, attempting (perhaps successfully) to bend the countymen to their will. The suits went against the Baconians; county sentiment probably ran the other way. In the years immediately after, the gentlemen attempted to manipulate the county in their own interest. At issue was their control of the colony, challenged in the aftermath of Bacon's Rebellion by the imposition of greater royal control. But as presented to counties such as Middlesex, the issue was the price of tobacco and the necessity of raising it by lowering production—'stinting the crop' as it was called.

Prior to Bacon's Rebellion, what we have called the cosmopolitan few were Virginia's effective and unchallenged rulers, gravitating around the person of Governor Berkeley as friends, advisors, and members of his council and of the colony's legislative assembly. In the abstract, of course, ultimate political authority rested in a monarch and government in England. But that was a distant arena even to Berkeley, a Whitehall courtier as a young man but in 1676 a Virginian of thirty-three years residence. London was of little import in the day-to-day government of the colony; Berkeley and his friends—frequently called by historians the "Green Spring Faction," after the governor's plantation near Jamestown— were what counted. When a Bacon or an Ingram or a Lawrence inveighed against Virginia's "French Despotick Methods," they had in mind the monopolization of high office by this faction.

Clustered around Berkeley, loyal to him and the king's commission that he bore, leading the governor's troops against Bacon in the name of the king, the faction in the end fell victim to a curious irony. In the aftermath of the rebellion, king and government in London turned against Berkeley and his supporters, not by way of condoning Bacon and rebellion, but in condemnation of a government that had failed to keep the king's peace. Berkeley was recalled to England in disgrace, his reputation—and that of his friends—besmirched. Even the hard-won victory over the Baconians was denigrated as "noe more than [a] sculking out to surprize small Guards of Rebells by night, and Plundering People without distinction of parties." Deprived of influence on the executive, the faction sniped at Berkeley's successors from the vantage point of Virginia's general assembly, postulating themselves as guardians of Virginia's liberties. Herbert Jeffreys, one of Berkeley's successors, was, in the eyes of the faction, a "pitiful Little Fellow with a Perriwig"; he, in turn, thought of them as engrossers, profiteers, a "Crossgrained faction" that valued "the Power and Laws of a few Ignorant Planters met in Assembly . . . of greater Authority than his most Sacred Majesty."[48]

The men and women of Middlesex had little to gain or lose from the high-stakes game that was being played. And yet they were drawn into it. Sometime in the fall of 1681 a petition began circulating through the county "about moving" the then-governor to call an assembly to pass legislation limiting the crop to be planted the next year. "Signed by a greate many of the Inhabitants and men of Best abilaty in the County," the petition was presented to the justices of the court on December 5. It was clearly an extraordinary meeting of the court, "the People earnestly pressing and thronging into the Courte howse [still Robinson's home] until it was full and a greate many remaineing at the dores and Windowes Impatiently expecting the Courtes answer to it." The justices had the petition read to the assembled crowd, then asked "if they all Consented to and desired what was Conteyned in" it, and "the People Unanimously answered" affirmatively. Thereupon the court adopted the petition as its own and dispatched four of its members "without delay" to attend on the governor and present the people's demands.[49]

Actually, the delegation did not have far to go. In the temporary absence of the governor, the acting chief executive was none other than Middlesex's own Sir Henry Chicheley. The delegation simply trooped across to Rosegill, where Chicheley was living, to present its petition. Similar petitions arrived from other counties, and Chicheley acquiesced, calling for an assembly to meet in session the following spring. By then, however, he had received instructions from London barring such a session. The assembly met for a desultory week in late April, then was dissolved. In May sporadic rioting broke out in a number of counties (including Middlesex), as a generality informed and excited by the petitioning and disappointed in the outcome went about enforcing a "stint" of its own by cutting down the growing tobacco plants.

Historians, borrowing from contemporaries, have made Middlesex's Robert Beverley the near-exclusive author of these events. "Allegedly, at least, he and a number of London merchants were particularly eager to decrease Virginia tobacco production in order to raise the price of what they had in storage." Beverley was " 'the premier Ministre' . . . anxious for an assembly-authorized cessation of tobacco planting to raise the price of the staple." As leader of "country partisans" seeking to "assert assembly authority," he "organized popular petitions," prevailed on " 'the easiness of an inclining Governor,' " and persuaded Chicheley to call the assembly. He orchestrated the riots. And, following the suppression of the rioters by Virginians more amenable to crown authority, specifically the members of the governor's council, he was arrested, held "incommunicado" under tight guard, and ultimately deprived of his offices.[50] In the microcosm of Middlesex, the affair appears quite differently.

We do not know who inspired the initial petition. Quite possibly it was, indeed, Beverley. Beverley was present among the justices who, in December 1681, received it and presented it to the people for their acclamation. But so, too, were Major General Robert Smith, Matthew Kemp, and Ralph Wormeley. Smith would, during the riots, arrest Beverley at the behest of the council; Kemp's father would lead militiamen into Gloucester to suppress the plant-cutting rioters there; Wormeley was both a member of the governor's council and Chicheley's stepson. Beverley was among those who carried the petition to the governor, but so too was Christopher Wormeley. And, of course, Chicheley received the petition at Rosegill, his stepson's home.

When we probe a bit, we readily see the close relationships between all of these participants. Smith's wife was Ralph Wormeley's first cousin, and her daughter (Smith's stepdaughter) was Wormeley's then-wife and Chicheley's stepdaughter-in-law. Smith's only son, Robert, and Robert Beverley, that very year, served as securities for Christopher Wormeley as sheriff of Middlesex. Christopher Wormeley and Beverley were related in that both of their wives were Armisteads from Gloucester. Smith's major business dealings were with merchant Francis Bridge, Beverley's stepson-in-law. Kemp and Dame Anne Kemp Skipwith would witness Smith's will, and the Lady Anne was (like Smith) a customer of Bridge's.

Moreover, when we examine Beverley's imprisonment we are struck by two anomalies. First, he was hardly held "incommunicado." There is extant a set of instructions from William Fitzhugh of Stafford County to his agent, dated during Beverley's incarceration, that begins: "First to Majr. Beverley there's two letters, and two bills drawn for him to sign. . . ." Beverley was quite obviously going about his business. Secondly, he, his captor (Smith), and his jailer, the captain of the ship *Duke of York*, seem to have enjoyed a curious rapport. When ordered by the council to read Beverley's letters, ostensibly to gain evidence against him, Smith wrote to the captain: "I would desire you to shew this order to Major Beverley that he may prevent my looking into any of his letters, which I desire not to doe."[51]

What all this seems to add up to is a game of realpolitik being played by the cosmopolitan gentlemen of Middlesex (and quite possibly of Virginia in general). Individually, their motives were undoubtedly diverse. Collectively, they were one. They more than others—with their broad view of the world—knew the relationship between the size of the tobacco crop arriving annually in England and tobacco prices. On and off over the years they had been arguing for a production stint. By forcing such a stint in the face of royal opposition, they would be reasserting their mastery over Virginia's affairs, a mastery sadly buffeted in the aftermath of Bacon's Rebellion. In 1681—following a bumper crop in 1680[52] and with one of their own in the gubernatorial chair—they appealed to the vox populi in order to legitimate their action and, when the game failed and an excited generality took to rioting and plant cutting, threw Beverley (very gently) to the wolves. Thereafter they seem to have made their peace with royalization. In 1686 and 1687, London's governor, Lord Howard of Effingham, would be residing as Wormeley's tenant in the "most comfortable" house at Rosegill. In 1688 Wormeley would be president of the council of state.[53]

It is, however, the populism of this affair that is important to us.[54] In 1677, we have suggested, the cosmopolitan gentlemen sought to subdue the county, marching into the court to sit as awesome spectators to the trial of the Baconians. In 1681, by resorting to the petition, they sought to draw the county into their political life, or at least to use an authority perceived as latent in the local community in their behalf. In both instances, the county court was the point at which the local society and the wider society of cosmopolitan gentlemen intersected.

Too many times visitors to the early Chesapeake (that is to say, other historians) have seen what is only most apparent: the poverty of the Henry Davises and the Bodgams on the one hand and the wealth of the Wormeleys on the other. They have thought in terms of an oligarchy of prominent gentlemen ruling the powerless through county court and vestry. We see something different: a complex layering of society, with court and vestry as bits of societal rabbeting joining the first gentlemen of the province to the county families among whom they lived.

The juxtaposition is particularly clear in 1677 and 1681, when events were extraordinary. But the rabbeting was a permanent part of the social structure. For men oriented solely to the county—Worthams and Joneses and Seagers—court and vestry were the apex of public careers. They worked their way up to their seats and took status from the positions. The cosmopolitan gentlemen, if they took seats on court or vestry at all, did so as a matter of right. Notably their appointments were not preceded by any period of testing in lesser offices. Equally notable is the fact that when they were named to court or vestry they sat only sporadically, leaving the month-to-month business of the county to the more county-oriented, lesser gentlemen who were all but constant in attendance.[55] The consequence of their sitting, moreover, was not the accrual of status to themselves—they had plenty of that—but the imparting of status to court and vestry, a status necessary to these bodies if they were to do the work of administering and adjudicating within a status-minded society.

Sitting at the pinnacle of the local society, insisting upon the accoutrements of their high status—recall the rules of the court quoted earlier: "Noe person presume . . . to be covered in the face of this Court"—the county-oriented among the justices (and vestrymen) nevertheless looked up to men of status greater than theirs. Indeed, the gentlemen justices and vestrymen collectively deferred to the cosmopolitan gentlemen living in the county, or at least handled them very gingerly. When, for example, the Middlesex court was called upon by a higher authority to supply information that only a Wormeley could supply, the justices did not, as they did so many times with lesser figures, simply order that the person in question appear before them. Instead, they dispatched the sheriff to "waite on the Honorable Coll Wormeley and acquaint him that they have adjorned the further Consideration of [that] matter" until such and such day at the court house "where they request his Honor will favour them with his presence."[56]

And the nuances of the case of Anne Webb, a servant girl presented to the court for having a bastard child, are clear enough. Anne "confest" the father to be one Daniel Hughes, a Wormeley overseer, and offered to give security for her fine. But in the small society of the county, it seems to have been common enough knowledge who the real father was and that what we can bluntly call a "fix" was on. The justices did not challenge Anne's confession directly, but debated instead whether she should be required to name the father under oath and eventually decided affirmatively. Poor Anne! Was she awed by her surroundings and the lengthy discussion of the penalties imposed by both man and God upon false swearers? Be that as it may, she could not swear the lie and blurted out the name: "John Wormeley." In this instance, a Wormeley was not above the law as administered by the justices, but it seems to have required a stratagem on the part of the justices to apply the law to one.[57]

6. "The Negro Road"

Everye white will have its blacke,
And everye sweete its sowre.

— Thomas Percy,
Reliques of Ancient English Poetry

THERE WAS ANOTHER ROAD in Middlesex, "the negro road," referred to only once, in a conveyance of land from Thomas Kidd to Thomas Hackett in 1716. The conveyance locates the road southwest of Mickleburrough's bridge, between the main road and the Dragon and, at least at this point, running toward the swamp.[1] But we cannot say exactly where it lay or what it connected. In any event, it was a reality, undoubtedly a path between two relatively large holdings of blacks and most frequently traveled by blacks. It is equally a metaphor. Toward the end of the seventeenth century, Middlesex (and the Chesapeake as a whole) took "the negro road."

From the very first years of settlement, there were blacks on the peninsula between the Rappahannock and Piankatank. The 1655 inventory of the estate of William Brocas listed eleven. The appraisers do not seem to have thought much of them. Gumbye and Gratia were described as "old"; Samia "full of the pox"; Deoge "very old . . . bedriden and full of diseases and blinde"; Mundina "a Negro Woman that hath been a mother of many Children"; Katherine "diseased": Marya "old"; and her six-year-old son "with one eye." Doodes Minor's Deco had been purchased in Nansemond County in 1656 and carried into Middlesex; by 1663 Minor had found him a wife,

Phillis, and by the time of Elizabeth Montague's wedding (1671) the couple had at least three children. The blacks in these early years were, however, a small minority in an overwhelmingly white labor force; the arrival of new blacks in the Chesapeake (and in Middlesex) happened only occasionally. Francis Cole, when writing his will in 1658, could only stipulate that "in case negroes do come this year" two were to be purchased, one for each of his two daughters. Thirteen years later, Governor Berkeley reported that "not above two or three ships of negroes" had arrived "in seven years."[2]

Blacks began arriving in significant numbers in the 1680s, concomitant with the decline in the number of new white servants. The records are scant, but in 1679 we glimpse two Virginia-bound slavers stopping at Barbados, the *Blossom* with 244 blacks, the *Swallow* with 179. In June 1681, understanding that "there are some Negro Ships expected into York now every day," Stafford County's William Fitzhugh wrote to Middlesex's Ralph Wormeley asking that "if you intend to buy any for yours self, and it be not too much trouble . . . [you] secure me five or six." (Five years later, Fitzhugh would have 29 blacks.) In 1683 the then-governor reported that "Blacks can make [tobacco] cheaper than Whites" and urged that action be taken by the government in England so as "to have Blacks as cheape as possible in Virginia." William Byrd, the very next year, expressed his fear that blacks "will bring our people much in debt, and occasion them to bee carelesse what tobacco they make." Still the blacks came.[3]

In 1685 Middlesex's Christopher Robinson was one of three agents charged with taking delivery of 200 Gambian blacks shipped by the Royal African Company aboard the ship *Speedwell;* in 1687 Robinson, William Churchill (also of Middlesex), and Dudley Digges of Gloucester were the agents to receive 220 blacks from a second run. A traveler in the mid-1680s wrote of the governor and council "sitting in judgment" at Wormeley's Rosegill on an illegal slaver and of a "ship loaded with negroes" wrecked on the Eastern Shore.[4] In 1689, according to another traveler, "in most parishes, the substantiall planters" had "negro slaves." When war broke out between England and France in the 1690s, the flow slackened, provoking complaints from Virginians that with "no supplies of Blacks . . . and the Whites in their service growing out of their times and becoming free, their Plantations are falne under a great Scarcity of hands, so that they have not sufficient for the management of them." When the occasional ship did arrive, "there were as many buyers as negros."[5] The Chesapeake, Virginia, and Middlesex were in turn committed; and in the first decades of the eighteenth century, successive waves of new blacks disgorged from the slave ships, the most significant for Middlesex in 1705 and 1706.[6]

In the county, black slaves came to exceed white servants in the labor force sometime between 1687 (when blacks constituted just 8 percent of the total population) and 1699 (by which time blacks constituted 22 percent).[7] Like the servants who had dominated earlier, the blacks were spread unevenly among the county's households. At the turn of the century, a majority were owned by major planters. Ralph Wormeley's holdings alone embraced just under 20 percent of the county's black population. But roughly a fifth of the male heads of household owned at least one.[8] The placement of the blacks on the land and in the society as a whole was, consequently, diverse.

When, in 1701, appraisers took inventory of Wormeley's estate, they found a few blacks at the home house—craftsmen like "Jack the Carpenter" and "Robin the Cooper," and domestics like "Frank," the "cook wench," and "Jersey," a maid. But most were located on the quarters into which Rosegill was divided. At "old Crumwells quarter," the appraisers found Crumwell himself, an "old" black who, to judge from the value placed on him, we take to have been past fifty; another "old man" of about the same age; an "old woman named Franck"; and young Crumwell, a boy in his early teens, perhaps Crumwell's son. At "the Pine Quarter," they jotted down the names and values of thirteen blacks ranging from "old Jack" and "his wife" Doll, through Will and his "wife" Betty, to a "Sucking Child named Samuel." At "the hogg house quarter," were "old Sarah"; three men (Jemmy, Ralph, and Gunner); three women (Betty, Sarah, Martha); a girl, Kate, probably in her late teens; and "one Sucking Child named Jenny."

There was no need for the appraisers to note the structures in which the blacks were housed. They did, however, specify the cattle and the cooking utensils found at each quarter—at Crumwell's "1 Iron pot and two pestells" for grinding corn, and and at the Pine Quarter "1 Iron pot[,] hookes and 1 pestell."[9] The demonstrable presence of more than one couple at a quarter (Jack and Doll, and Will and Betty at the Pine Quarter), and of utensils for one fireplace and the association with each quarter of particular livestock suggests a general pattern. Most of Wormeley's blacks were spread about Rosegill in small, mixed households consisting of one, two, and three couples, children, and a varying number of uncoupled adults, all living close to the cattle and fields they were to tend. Presumably a white overseer lived at each quarter and directed the labor of the blacks. An incident at the Hog House Quarter in 1691 suggests as much, although, as we shall see, such was not necessarily the case.[10]

Rosegill, by virtue of its very size, was not typical of the county holdings. It was unusual, too, in the absence of any significant number of blacks about the home house, perhaps a function of rudimentary specialization. The drudgery of crops and cattle was consigned to the scattered quarters, while the immediate vicinity of the great house was reserved for the business of the plantation and for crafts. Another form of specialization is hinted at by the presence only at the Pine Quarter of cart wheels and "draught oxen"; the wheels and oxen were undoubtedly utilized anywhere they were needed on Rosegill. Rosegill's quarter system, however, was that of every large holding of land and blacks. The inventory of Edmund Berkeley's estate is a case in point; although because it was made in 1719, it reflects a demographically more mature population.[11] At the home plantation were twenty-two adult blacks (fourteen males, eight females) and fifteen children; an additional forty-six blacks were spread over three quarters, with an average of nine adults and six children on each. At two the cooking utensils listed indicate two households; at the third only one.[12]

Quarter blacks—the majority of those owned by a Wormeley or a Berkeley—lived and labored apart from the white master and his family; they were, too, as apart from white society as the condition of slavery allowed. When we consider smaller and smaller holdings, however, we find more and more of the blacks tucked into the physical and social structure of the society in close proximity to white families.

In 1701 nine of Robert Dudley's blacks (four men, two women, and three children) plus two white servants (a "man" and a "boy") were living at Dudley's "Dwelling Plantacion." An aspiring man, Dudley was, just before his death, beginning the process of opening up quarters on his 950 acres. To one of them he had sent a mulatto woman, "1 Iron pot with pot hookes," and "1 old fryin pan." Six of John Vivion's blacks (a man, a woman, a teenager, and three children) were listed at his 181-acre home plantation in 1705; at an "upper plantation" of 100 acres were an adult black male; a teenage black girl; and Andrew Terry, "a Man Servant," presumably acting as a working overseer.[13] Dudley's and Vivion's home blacks were probably housed collectively in one of the outbuildings scattered about their homesteads—Dudley's laboring under the direction of his adult servant; Vivion's under the master's own supervision.

Moving to the smallest level of operation—to John Mactyre's single black, for example—the distance between black and white shrinks still more. Indeed, one scene suggests that it all but disappeared. Following a trail of tobacco leaves leading away from a broken hogshead in 1702, Robert George and Constable John Southern were led to Mactyre's barn, where they found John and his "Negroe Dick" busily packing purloined leaves into one of Mactyre's own hogsheads.[14]

The advent of large-scale black slavery everywhere in the Chesapeake at the end of the seventeenth century poses significant problems for historians. They have, for one thing, long puzzled over, even wrangled about, the reason for the shift from white to black labor. Was it a matter of supply—a changing economy in England making fewer servants available for the Chesapeake, while a changing system in the African trade made blacks available in greater numbers? Or of demand—Chesapeake planters sensing greater stability and efficiency in a slave system? What part did the course of tobacco prices play? Or the cost differential between white servitude and black slavery?[15] More recently historians have begun pondering the blacks themselves—their resistance to and acceptance of enslavement, their adoption of white ways and retention of African ways, and somehow their formation of an Anglo-African culture or life-style. Writers tease the scantest of sources in an effort to find the origins of this last in the welter of languages and customs that came from Africa and the diverse situations in which the blacks found themselves, from "Negroe Dick" working side by side with his master and probably sleeping in his master's loft, to Jack and his wife Doll living well apart from the whites on Wormeley's Pine Quarter.[16] The "negro road" is itself evidence that a black culture, even community, was in the making in Middlesex. By such paths, blacks from scattered homelots and quarters made and kept contact with each other.

Yet visitors to a single county cannot see enough to address either of these problems. We can only accept that there was, indeed, a shift from white to black labor and acknowledge that there was a process underway that would ultimately create an Afro-American subculture. We sense its evolution in a conversation recorded by a visitor to another time and place. This visitor could actually converse with "an old African." He asked whether the black had known any English before his arrival in the white man's country:

"Engreesh! Whi'side me go l'arn um?"
"You know no English at all when you come to Bakra Country?"
" 'T all 't all!"
"Who teach you when you come?"
"Who l'arn me? Eh-eh! No me matty?"
"How he learn you? Gi'e you book and so?"
"Book! Youse'f too! A-we nation got book . . .?"
"What fashion you learn?"
"Da Uncle me a lib wit' he se'f l'arn me. Uncle a say, 'Bwoy, tekky this crabash—de crabash dey a he hand—go dip watah. Watah—watah da ting inside da barrel O'So Uncle do, sotay me a ketch wan-wan Engreesh."
"So all of you catch Bakra talk, little by little?"
"Ah! Same thing! Matty a l'arn matty, matty a l'arn matty. You no see da fashion pickny a l'arn fo' talk—when he papa a talk he a watch he papa mout?"[17]

It is not at all difficult to imagine the learning described taking place everywhere in our county from the 1680s on: arriving Africans learning about a new life from blacks who had already learned, ultimately native-born slave children picking up naturally and making their own sole culture the black culture being fashioned. That said, however, we turn back to the dominant element in Middlesex—the white—to probe for the effects of slavery upon its society. For the conjunction of African and English inevitably forced change upon both. Note how even in the brief conversation above the language of the questioner shifts subtly but steadily toward that of the black.

When we make the turn back to Middlesex's dominant element, the first thing that strikes us is an ambivalence. It pervades the scene as, in the mind, we wander through early Middlesex. Walking the road to the Mother Church through Rosegill, we spy in the distance one of the quarters, perhaps the Hog House, a ramshackle structure much like any poor farmer's house in the county. A group of blacks bend to their labor in a stump-laden field. There is a wisp of smoke from the chimney, and we imagine old Sarah heating corn soup for a common meal. A horseman comes into view, Wormeley himself, riding over from the great house to see how the work progresses, perhaps to check the condition of a sick slave.

The idyllic scene of our imagination is given substance when we remember entries from William Byrd's diary: "In the evening we took a walk about the plantation. My people made an end of planting the corn field"; "I . . . went to view my plantation. The people were all planting. . . . Everything was in good order"; "I went with the women to take a walk about the plantation. My sick people grew better, thank God. . . . Negro Sue was taken sick at the quarters and I caused her to be bled." The scene is made even firmer in the mind when we remember his letter to the Earl of Orrery: "I have a large family," Byrd wrote, including in the word "family" his "people," his slaves. "Like one of the patriarchs, I have my flocks and my herds, my bondmen, and bond-women, and every soart of trades amongst my own servants, so that I live in a kind of independance on every one. . . . I must take care to keep all my people to their duty, to set all the springs in motion, and to make every one draw his equal share to carry the machine forward. But then tis an amusement in this silent country."[18]

The silence ends suddenly. The idyllic image disappears

and another forms as, in depositions given to the Middlesex court, we hear the crash of a black foot against the door of the overseer's room at Wormeley's Hog House Quarter, see the lock broken, and hear overseer James Douglas testify before the county's justices that "two shirts, one pair of Britches and a Gunn" were stolen and that the gun was later found in the possession of Lawrence, a runaway Wormeley slave. We note the justices' finding: Lawrence committed "as a fellon to this County Goale [sic]." The penalty, we know, is hanging.[19]

With somewhat less of an application of imagination, we see the same ambivalence in an incident involving the Reverend Samuel Gray, the minister at Christ Church in the 1690s. An "unfortunate accident" had occurred at the glebe and Gray's "Mulatto boy Jack" was dead—"an unfortunate Chance which I would not Should have happened *in my family* for three times his price," Gray wrote in reporting the event to a neighboring justice. "But it is past Cure and such Accidents will happen now and then." What sort of accident? The lengthy depositions describing the incident in detail are clear. Jack was a recovered runaway and the good parson, along with Thomas Williamson and Gray's "Negroe Peter," had literally beaten him to death. Jack was "family" to Gray, just as Byrd's "people" were "family." Yet Jack was also the object of furious violence. Tied to a mulberry tree, he had been whipped about the head, chest, and abdomen until the lash itself had broken. "With that Mr. Gray said the Lash did Noe good and made a new one and bade me Carry it [back to the tree.] With that he followed me with the Branding Iron in his hand. . . . And as soon as Mr. Gray Came the boy Cryed 'pray Master Lett me down'; . . . with that the said Mr. Gray stept up and gave him two or three knocks with the Branding Iron about the head . . . then sat him selfe down and bidd the Negroe Whipp him" some more.[20]

The incorporation of the blacks within the concept of "family" was, it can be argued, a way to rationalize slavery, to define in gentle terms a role for masters that otherwise would have been only ugly exploitation. Construed as familial dependents, as children, the slaves were properly protected, nurtured, guided, and even disciplined by the father of the house (the owner); in return, the father properly commanded obedience, respect, and the produce of the child's (read slave's) labor.[21]

The Virginians had not far to search when such rationalization was needed. "Family" in this extended sense was an integral part of the premodern mentality of England and Virginia. The apprentice moved from a "family" of origin (mother and father) to a "family" of labor (master and mistress). Thus in 1689 Middlesex's William Holly was apprenticed to Andrew Williamson for a term of sixteen and a half years: "His [Master's] secrets [William was to] keep close; his Commandments Lawful and honest Every whare he shall gladly doe; hurt to his said master he shall not doe or suffer to be done. . . . The goods of his said master he shall not Inordinately waste nor them to any body lend. At dice or any other Unlawfull game he shall not play whereby his master Incur any hurt. Fornication in the house of his said master or elsewhere he shall not committ. Matrimony he shall not Contract. Public houses or ordinaries he shall not frequent. His own proper goods or any other during the said term without the special license of his said master he shall not merchandize. From the service of his said master day nor night he shall not absent." In return, William's master would supply him "Apparell diett and Lodging and all other necessaries meete and convenient" and teach him "to read the Bible or cause him to be Taught."[22]

White servitude in the Chesapeake was based generally upon the principles of apprenticeship, and to some extent at least the servant was construed as "family." The names by which people referred to each other illustrate as much. Recall again that snippet of conversation between Alice Creyke and Jane Olney—one of the very few preserved in the historical record—and that the subject of conversation was Richard Gabriell, Creyke's servant:

[I] Asked, "Madam, I pray Madam, why are you in such Anger and bitterness against me?"

Mistress Creyke replyed, "Jane, not I. But you meddle with Dick the Taylor my Servant. . . ."

"Truly Madam, Not I if I can help it. . . .

". . . I shall not meddle with Richard nor any that belongs to you. . . ."

Their different *social* positions clearly determined the forms of address—Mistress Olney speaking to "Madam"; Madam speaking to "Jane." But the *familial* position of Gabriell relative to the speakers was also determinative. He was Madam's servant and a dependent within her family; hence Madam referred to "Dick". He was a person apart from the Olney family; hence Jane referred to "Richard."[23] When the entering blacks were assigned names, the same rule was applied. Overwhelmingly they were given diminutive or, more properly, familial forms of common English names—Jack, Will, Tom; Bess, Moll, Kate.[24] But, of course, because the slave had no existence apart from the family, he or she was never accorded anything but a familial name. To everyone and on every occasion a particular slave would be simply "Madam Creyke's Jack."

If the incorporation of the blacks as "family" can be seen as simply an extension of the notion of the familial servant, we must nevertheless stipulate a difference. The latter—the familial servant—was never in the Chesapeake as openly and self-consciously, even boastfully, asserted among men of rank like Byrd as was the familial black. Byrd, although the irony escaped him, characterized himself as well as others when, at a later date, he complained that the blacks "blow up the pride, and ruin the industry of our white people, who seing a rank of poor creatures below them, detest work for fear it should make them look like slaves."[25]

It can be argued, moreover, that the violence directed toward the black, exemplified by the beating to death of Gray's Jack, was simply an extension to a new sort of laborer of things done earlier to servants. After all, Ann Davis had murdered Sarah Gambrell. But, again, there was a difference. If the blacks served to "blow up the pride" of the whites, as Byrd said, they also engendered in them suspicion, distrust, even fear, and these seem to have lurked behind the violence in such a way that they did not earlier.

Historian Winthrop D. Jordan has resorted to the psychology of color to suggest an explanation for what seems an almost innate horror of blacks on the part of whites in the seventeenth and early eighteenth centuries. Long before

English and Africans confronted each other, the English associated blackness with ugliness, heathenism, and evil. Jordan
quotes George Best (1578), whose evil dreams

> . . . hale me from my sleepe like forked Devils
> Midnight, thou AEthiope, Empresse of Black Souls, Thou gen
>   eral
> Bawde to the whole world.[26]

Such repugnance, Jordan suggests, touched all aspects of whiteblack relations. Perhaps. The language of the laws against
miscegenation—"that abominable mixture and spurious
issue"—hints at something of the sort, and it is no great leap
to envision violence in terms of a lashing out against what is
seen as abhorrent.[27] But perhaps it was even more a matter
of the arrival of this strange and alien type in larger and larger
numbers. Byrd is, again, perspicacious: "Another unhappy
effect of many Negros, is the necessity of being severe. Numbers make them insolent, and then foul means must do, what
fair will not. . . . These base tempers require to be rid with a
tort rein, or they will be apt to throw their rider."[28]

In their time, the white servants had been denigrated;
periodically they had been suspected of conspiracies. Yet they
were familiar in appearance and—a few Irish servants
excepted—they spoke English and knew English ways. The
blacks, more and more arriving directly from Africa from the
1680s on, had none of these qualities. What did these strange
beings talk about in their quarters? What did their drums say
at night (for notably the drums came with the Africans)? What
went on when blacks took to "the negro road" to gather at
one quarter or another? What did the runaways, lurking forever around the edges of the quarters, intend?

We are, of course, placing questions into the minds of our
Virginians, but not arbitrarily. The laws of the colony suggest
their paramountcy. "The frequent meeting of considerable
numbers of negroe slaves under pretence of feasts and burialls is judged of dangerous consquence" (1680). "Noe master
or Overseer Shall at any time . . . permitt . . . any Negro or
Slave not properly belonging to him or them, to Remaine or
be upon his or theire Plantation above the space of foure hours"
(1682). And (1691) the assembly expresses its concern that

many times Negroes and other slaves "lie hid and lurk in obscure places killing hoggs and committing other injuries to the inhabitants." In Middlesex there was a particular fear of slaves living isolated without white supervision, a county petition to the Virginia legislature in 1700 "praying that Negroes be not kept att Quarters without Overseers." Patrollers took to the roads, militiamen in squads of five charged with visiting "all negro quarters and other places suspected of entertaining unlawful assemblies" and authorized to "take up" those assembling "or any other, strolling about from one plantation to another, without a pass from his or her master, mistress, or overseer." Special commissions were issued to county justices allowing them to try blacks accused of felonies, something never done with white labor when it had predominated; accused felons, including servants, had always been sent to Jamestown for trial before the general court. Now, however (1692), local trials and "a speedy prosecution of negroes and other slaves for capital offenses" were considered "absolutely necessarie" in order "that others being detered by the condign punishment inflicted on such offenders, may vigorously proceed in their labours and be affrighted to commit the like crimes and offences."[29]

And yet, despite the clamour of the laws, relatively few blacks ever came before the court in Middlesex, far fewer in proportion to their numbers than did white servants. Between 1676 and 1690, a period when white labor still dominated, servants were accused at court of 104 misdeeds of various kinds, roughly 24 misdeeds per thousand servants per year. Between 1711 and 1725, a period of slave labor, slaves stood before the justices only 54 times, a rate of approximately 3.5 appearances per thousand slaves and exaggerated at that for thirty-four of the offending slaves were the property of one person, Christopher Robinson, a man whose temperament either brought out the worst in his laborers or precluded his controlling them, or both.[30] At first glance, the disparate rates might seem to indicate that the blacks were a more placid labor force. Closer scrutiny shows something else.

That few slaves were brought before the justices as runaways—in all only seventeen in the period through 1725—is eminently logical. In the case of runaway servants, the primary function of the court was to recompense the master for his loss by adding time to the servant's term; punishing the runaway was only secondary. But how could the court wring compensation from a slave who already owed a life of service to his master? In the case of a servant girl having a bastard child, the court functioned to compensate the master for the loss of that girl's labor, make arrangements for the child that, if at all possible, would ensure that it not become a public charge, and, finally, punish the immorality of the offender. But, again, how could the court seek compensation from a slave "wench"? And the public was already spared the cost of the child for the law made it, too, a slave.

Slavery, in effect, made irrelevant many of the functions of the court. It is, then, no wonder that the slave so seldom appeared before it. Slaves still misbehaved. They drank and malingered; they stole from their masters and from each other; they argued and arguments led to assaults; they left their quarters to lurk in the brush. We know from the occasional diaries of planters that they were bedeviled by such conduct. But the correction of slave misbehavior was largely left to the master himself; in a sense, it was a "family" matter. It became a public matter only when a black was discerned as threatening in some way the security of the larger society. Then— when slave conduct aroused public suspicion—suspicion died hard if it died at all. In the early 1720s, for example, eight blacks from six different plantations in Middlesex and Gloucester were seized in the aftermath of a series of "frequent disorderly Meetings of great Numbers of Slaves." The slaves were suspected of conspiracy, but the fact could not be proved "by reason of their Secret Plotting and confederating among themselves." Nevertheless, "the dangers which might possibly happen" if the eight "should be discharged . . . and Suffered to go at large" were too many. The blacks were summarily sold off to the West Indies and their Virginia owners compensated.[31]

Suspicion, distrust, fear: Whatever their origins, these seem at the root of the violence, both personal and communal, directed at the black. Gray, Williamson, and Negro Peter beat Mulatto Jack to death. Christopher Robinson kept hauling his recalcitrant blacks into court—George, castrated "for runing away, lying out and distroying peoples Stocks"; Tom, toes severed for "lying out and doeing Severall Misdemeanors"; Charles, lashed in 1711 for hog stealing, pilloried and deprived of his ears as a recidivist in 1712, hanged in 1717 as a felon. Executed in Gloucester for "treason," Black Scipio suffered dismemberment, and one of his quarters was "put up in the most publick place" in Middlesex as a deterrent to other blacks.[32]

And always the contrasting attitudes: We followed Robert George and Constable Southern as they entered the Mactyre barn and surprised John Mactyre and his slave Dick packing away stolen tobacco in a Mactyre hogshead. Both were arrested for felony. Mactyre was sent to the capital for trial; apparently he was found guilty, pleaded his benefit of clergy, and came home again. At least that is where we find him a year after his arrest. Dick was tried by the justices in Middlesex and found guilty. "The said Negro slave not offering anything to arrest or stay judgment," the court had no recourse but to sentence him to death. But Dick had only been doing what he had been told to do. Wherein lay the guilt?—a question Hugh Mactyre, John's father, addressed to the court. The court considered Hugh's petition, accepted it, and forwarded an application for pardon to the governor.[33] It seems that when the black played his role, when he was the dependent and obedient child, the white in turn could play his role of patriarch—bountiful, caring, even at times tender. "My poor little [sick] slave Charlotte," Landon Carter would jot down in his diary later in the century: "Yesterday a little after 3 o'clock I had, in order to tempt her to eat, directed some bread and beer to be boiled and sweetned" for her.[34]

About attitudes, of course, the historian can only generalize and, in the end, leave room for variation. Benjamin Davis, for example, assumed control of land and three blacks when he married the widow Williamson in 1706. It is entirely possible that he looked upon the blacks as nothing more than so many hands to help with the work of the plantation. And rather than needing to rationalize the cruel exploitation of slavery by thinking of the blacks as "family," he could very well have simply accepted unthinkingly a system already established. We can make a general case for ambivalent feelings of family and fear, but we cannot apply the generalization to particular people.

Whatever attitude the blacks evoked in Davis, however, one thing is clear: The blacks were structuring his world. Davis had been born in the era of servant labor (1680). His father had followed a path typical of the early decades of the county. Entering as a servant and completing his term, he had worked as a hired laborer and a sharecropper, then rented a bit of land, and, finally, bought the hundred acres that would pass to Davis's brother. Although we do not know it for a fact, it is conceivable that the elder Davis managed to amass from his tobacco and cattle enough capital to buy the labor of a servant of his own. Or perhaps he rented out a part of his land to another ex-servant. These were common strategies of the Chesapeake farmers, the ways by which men settled themselves firmly upon the land. There were risks, and men probably failed as often as they succeeded. Some were inept. Others overextended their credit and lost all to pay their debts. A newly purchased servant might die before his labor could recompense the owner the cost. The master of the house himself could die before the process was very far along. In this last case, however, death would create an opportunity for another, who, marrying the widow, would gain control of land and property and hence gain a step in the game. The end product of the game, we must point out, was not great wealth. We would be deluding ourselves even in trying to measure social mobility in terms of movement from the very lowest stratum (servitude) to the highest (that of a Wormeley). At best men found niches for themselves among what we have called the "middling sort" and left enough to their freeborn sons so that they would not fall back again. Great wealth was dependent upon a start in life that very few of our Middlesex men had.

Davis's world would not have been his father's world in any event. In another context, we traced some of the changes taking place between 1680 (when Davis was born) and the turn of the century (when he entered his manhood): the decline in the number of servants entering annually from England and in the number of ex-servants entering the pool of would-be sharecroppers and renters; the inexorable pressure of demography that was at work, always producing more sons than fathers, forcing the division of lands, and even leaving some sons without any. What would have happened if the blacks had not arrived in numbers and if men like Wormeley had not begun replacing gangs of white laborers with gangs of black is an interesting conundrum. But the fact is that the blacks did arrive, and, as we have said, they fashioned Davis's world.

For one thing, the blacks introduced into Middlesex and the Chesapeake a more virulent form of malaria than had come with the English from Europe. It is a common enough phenomenon in the history of humankind. Peoples isolated from each other develop diseases and immunities particular to themselves; when they come together, they exchange diseases but not immunities, with the consequence that each suffers the other's illnesses in greater measure than does the original carrier. On occasion the results have been catastrophic. Whole peoples have been devastated and cultures wrecked. The effects of the malarial exchange were more subtle. An annual fall season of "Endemical Distempers" was introduced. The Virginians had no name for the disease, calling it simply the "Fever or Ague." Anybody could be afflicted, and while the results were not usually fatal, victims were debilitated and hence more likely to be carried off by other diseases circulating in the society. The death rate in general rose; the years the average man or woman had to live dropped. As malaria settled into the Chesapeake, however, three groups were most often struck: new arrivals from England (so prone were they that the Virginians came to speak of a bout with what we know to have been malaria as a necessary acclimatization, a "seasoning"); children between roughly five and ten years of age; and pregnant women. The susceptibility of the first affected all those processes within the society dependent upon a steady supply either of newcomers entering as servants or of former servants entering the free population, for paralleling the decline in the number of new servants was a decline in the proportion of servants surviving to become freedmen. The susceptibility of the last—of pregnant women—ultimately meant fewer births to the white women of the county and limited growth.[35]

For another thing, the coming of the blacks changed the

microeconomy within which the individual planters of Middlesex worked. The increase in the initial cost of a laborer can be expressed in straightforward terms: In the first decade of the new century, an adult black male cost roughly two-and-a-half times as much as a white servant with four or more years to serve purchased in the early 1680s.[36] But the differential masks what were in effect entirely different investment strategies. Between two to three tobacco crops produced by the white servant would cover the initial outlay and whatever costs a modern accountant might debit for the food, clothing, and shelter the planter provided, leaving between one and two crops (if the servant served four years) as profit. But it would not be until sometime in the sixth year that the slave's cost was recovered—later if the slave was female or a child—although from that point on all the product of the slave's labor (less support costs) would be profit. White servitude, in other words, involved a relatively short-term investment. If the intention was to maintain a permanent labor force, servitude posed a fundamental cash-flow problem, for somehow from the profit from one servant the planter had to find the cost of a successor. In contrast, black slavery involved a long-term investment. Barring demographic disaster, there was no replacement cost. The different strategies clearly involved different risks. The planter buying the servant's labor risked less for a shorter period of time than one buying the slave. If the servant died in his third year of service, the planter had at least the two crops produced—roughly the equivalent of the original investment—and lost only the promise of a few years' profit. If the newly bought adult male slave died during the third year, almost half the investment was lost, along with the promise of a lifetime of labor.

There was, moreover, a hidden cost associated with slavery. The cargos carried by the slavers consisted overwhelmingly of young men and women in their late teens and early twenties, with males outnumbering females by a ratio of some two to one. To the planters, these were "prime hands," capable of peak production and peak profits. Yet populations are never static. Children appeared. As early as 1701, one-quarter of Wormeley's blacks were fifteen or under, and 16 percent were under ten. Prime hands aged. Surviving to their early forties, they would appear on inventories as "old"; and to their fifties as "very old," "aged," "decrepit." Fourteen percent of Wormeley's labor force were over forty. At both ends of the age spectrum, the productivity of the blacks—and the planter's profit—trailed off, with the very young and very old being simply mouths to feed and bodies to care for, costs with no return. Even the planters realized this. Slave values assigned by estate appraisers, when plotted by age, form a bell, low in the early ages, rising to a peak, then falling again. A law of 1680 referred to children under twelve as incapable of working. An account of 1697 called them "so many useless Hands."[37]

In the long run, given luck, procreation and aging more than balanced each other, and the planter—or, more likely, his heirs—would end up with a significant, even spectacular gain. Sharlott, a girl purchased by Henry Thacker in 1720 and adjudged by the county court to be twelve years old, is a case in point. She was among the most prolific of "a prolifick people," giving birth to at least thirteen children. Forty-four years after her purchase, she, her surviving children, and her children's children—twenty-two individuals in all, ranging from Sharlott at fifty-six to her great-grandson, Isaac, age two—were still Thacker slaves. His original investment had grown by a factor of twenty-five, from an estimated 17li 6s to approximately 431li. And Sharlott's labor, together with that of her descendants, had produced annually a net profit for Thacker that summed up over the years through 1764 comes to twenty-seven times her original cost.[38]

Sharlott exemplifies the possibility of gain. But we must always keep in mind the risk. What if she had died a year or so after giving birth to her first child? Sharlott's labor to that point would have returned only a small part of Thacker's original investment; the rest (roughly 85 percent) would have been lost. And Thacker would have been left with an additional mouth to feed, Sharlott's child, who would not be capable of income-producing labor for at least ten years and would not reach peak or prime labor for almost twenty. In this instance, Thacker, who was relatively well-off, could probably have absorbed the loss. But what if he had been simply a freedman a few years past his majority and struggling to make his way, all of his capital wrapped up in his land and in this

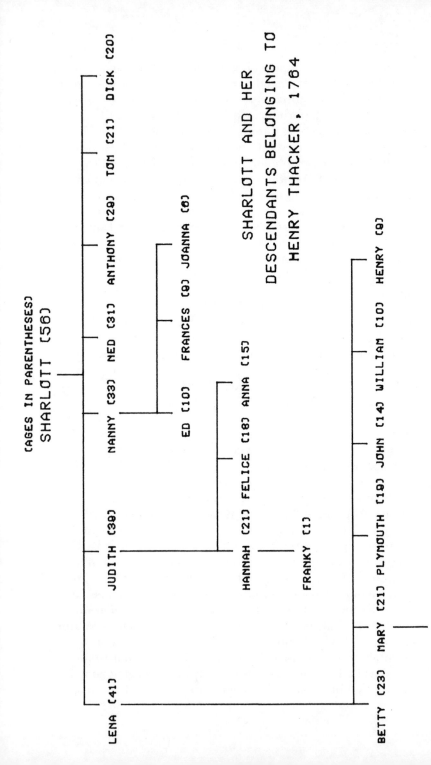

(AGES IN PARENTHESES)

SHARLOTT AND HER
DESCENDANTS BELONGING TO
HENRY THACKER, 1764

one young girl and whatever black male had fathered her child? With Sharlott dead, he would have lost half his labor force. He probably would not have the capital or credit to replace the loss. And by the time Sharlott's child was of prime laboring age, its father (if still alive) would be past prime. This was, recall, the very situation facing Benjamin Davis when his female died and he was left with but one black male adult and one child.

Inventories afford us our best overall view of the profits and losses associated with slave ownership. We assume the slaves listed constituted the planter's labor force for the year in which he died and estimate the net annual profit (or loss) for that year in relation to the capital represented by the blacks. Thus Philip Warwick, Jr.'s 1744 labor force consisted of two adult males, an adult female, one female over fifty, and two boys between ten and fifteen years of age. In his case, an adjusted capital value of ninety-three pounds was yielding a return of approximately 17.5 percent per annum. Henry Gilpin's 1728 inventory listed six blacks: one adult female, two girls between ten and fifteen, and three children under ten years of age. In Gilpin's case, capital of ninety-one pounds was yielding a net annual return of under 6 percent. John Shorter's inventory of the same year listed five blacks: a woman, three small girls, and an infant. Shorter's blacks actually cost him in maintenance four to five shillings more than their labor could have brought in.[39] The three cases illustrate a truism: The profitability of slavery was highly dependent upon the demographic characteristics of the individual planter's blacks, specifically their distribution by sex and age. Applied generally to slaves listed in Middlesex inventories, the procedure highlights (in the wide variation of annual returns on slave capital) the risks imposed by demography on small holders and (in relatively constant returns) the security accruing to large holders who could subsume demographic chance in sheer numbers. In eighteenth-century Middlesex, annual profits as a percentage of slave capital ranged among small holders from a net loss to over 27 percent, and among large holders from 4 to 13 percent.[40]

Slavery in a word was a strategy best suited to those at least reasonably well-to-do and preferably wealthy. Given the initial costs, slave labor was beyond the foreseeable reach of the poorer sort, beyond even those like William Provert who stood low among those of middling status in the society. And given its risks, it was an extraordinarily chancy venture for those who could afford only two or three hands. For those, however, who could afford to plunge heavily, who could absorb losses and even improve their odds by, in effect, letting the law of large numbers prevail—the larger the slave force the better the chance that demographic losses would be exceeded by gains—slavery meant regular capital gains and an annual return on slave capital averaging 9 and 10 percent.

This is, however, hindsight. For the men of Middlesex at the opening of the eighteenth century, an investment in slaves seemed the only way to secure or improve a position. Although we stretch the meaning the author intended, the line from Thomas Percy's late eighteenth-century embellishment of an old English ballad is pertinent: We are not far into the new century before "everye white will have its blacke." Men without slave labor sought to buy or inherit it; men with slaves distributed them among their male and female heirs or earmarked cash bequests for the purchase of blacks, as John Smith did when he bequeathed to three nieces fifteen pounds apiece to be used at their coming of age to buy each "a young Negro."[41] And by purchase, inheritance, and marriage—men without slaves marrying widows or young heiresses with them—slave labor became associated with more and more of the households of the county. Between 18 and 19 percent of the heads of household of 1704 owned at least one slave; 46 percent did so by 1724; half by 1740.[42] Yet to complete Percy's couplet: "And everye sweete its sowre." While some families found sweet success in slavery, others found only sour failure.

The records of the county are replete with indications of blasted expectations.[43] John Guttery's hopes were denied. A Middlesex-born sawyer, Guttery purchased eight-year-old Harry in 1717. It is not at all unlikely that he anticipated teaching the boy his craft and working with him in the saw pit, much as carpenter Thomas Hipkins purchased young blacks and trained them into an efficient and profitable house-building crew. Harry, however, died soon after the purchase. Guttery did not, probably could not, replace him, and when he died in 1733 he left an estate worth only fourteen pounds. His widow lived on as an object of charity until her death in 1744. Ordinarykeeper Jacob Rice was another who ventured on the Negro road and failed. In 1720 he bought a female with a one-year-old infant that had been conceived or born aboard the slave ship. Both blacks died soon after, and seven years later, following his death, Rice's estate was sold at public auction for a total of thirty-two pounds, eighteen shillings and eight pence. His son Jacob junior remained in the county and died in poverty in 1763.

John Tuggle—the son of Henry Tuggle and grandson of the Thomas whose house we visited in 1668—was another loser. In 1725, by marriage to a widow, he gained control of Lucy, a sixteen-year-old girl purchased in 1722 by Patrick Kelly and left by him to his wife Catherine (Nichols) Kelly-Tuggle. Lucy, in 1726, gave birth to a son, Ned, but two years later she died. Ned survived a year without his mother; then he too died. Lucy's labor for first Kelly and then Tuggle never produced enough profit to return her purchase price. During the year of young Ned's life following the death of Lucy, moreoever, support of the child represented a net loss to Tuggle. And the death of both represented a capital loss of thirty pounds. Tuggle's fortunes never recovered from the blow. At his death in 1759, he owned one black, another Lucy, a fifteen-year-old girl inherited from his father's estate after the death of his stepmother a decade earlier. Tuggle's profit from this second Lucy over the ten years he owned her could have been no more than four pounds, an average of eight shillings a year, barely enough to pay the county levy on himself.

John Curtis was still another loser. In 1734 he owned six blacks: Dinah, a woman in her mid-thirties; an infant named Jenny; six-year-old Nan; a fifty-five-year-old man named Pompey; Soper, a thirty-one-year-old male; and Peter, a male of unknown age, presumed for the purposes of these calculations to be in his prime working years. Dinah and Peter both died in March 1735; little Jenny followed in the fall of 1736; and Nan died in 1740. When Curtis's estate was settled in April 1741, the holdings in blacks consisted only of old Pompey, now over sixty, and Soper, thirty-eight. In the seven preceding years, the estate had a net profit from its blacks of roughly seventy pounds. But capital losses amounted to over seventy-five pounds. And, severest blow of all, the possibility for natural increase (and an increase in capital) was now zero. Pompey would soon die; Soper could only grow older, losing value every year.

By way of contrast, chance smiled on Alexander Graves. Arriving from Maryland in late 1707, Graves purchased the next year an eight-year-old black girl, Sarah. Sarah survived and, like Thacker's Sharlott, was prolific, bearing at least four daughters and five sons before her death in 1742. When Graves's estate was inventoried in 1740, his holdings in blacks amounted to some 110*li*—101*li* of the total accounted for by Sarah; her daughter Frank, age twenty-three, and Frank's infant son Dick; Sarah's son Jemmy, sixteen; her daughters Judy, nine, and Hannah, five; and Mingo, a year-old boy. Graves had purchased Sarah for approximately 12*li* in 1708. In addition to the current capital that she had produced, the income from Sarah and her descendants over the thirty-two years amounted to another 100*li*. But not every year had been profitable. There had been periods in which returns from labor had barely matched costs, even years of loss, when Sarah was young and her children only a charge on the estate rather than income-producing members of it. It had taken luck and time to bring Graves's economic position to its healthy condition.

Luck smiled on John Gibbs as well—at least for a while. We cannot trace the growth of his holdings from one purchase (as we can with Graves), but by the time of his death in 1726 he had six blacks: an adult male, two adult females, and three children under ten years of age. Four years later, following the death of Gibbs's widow Mary, the estate was once again inventoried. The intervening years had seen the county struck by epidemic. One black had been born but two (the adult male and one adult female) had died. The loss was not simply a matter of slave capital but of income as well. Before there had been three laboring adults and three children. Now there were four children and only one laborer. Gibbs's blacks had produced roughly ten pounds profit in 1726; Gibbs's widow's blacks produced less than a ten-shilling profit in 1730. In this particular case, the disaster was followed by departure from the county, Gibbs's sole surviving son, Zacharias, and his wife and child and Zacharias's two married sisters and their husbands and children all leaving to settle in the far western reaches of Spotsylvania County.

Again, however, we offer a contrast. Like John Gibbs, John Price died in 1726. Like Gibbs, too, Price's estate was inventoried twice, in 1727 and again in 1731. The same epidemic that hit Gibbs's blacks hit Price's. In the very year of Price's death, the estate lost two adult males and three children; the following year his female, Judy, died and another adult male. But severe as the blows may have been, the size of Price's black force (fourteen in 1727) was large enough to cushion their impact. In 1731 there were still thirteen blacks, five of them children, valued at roughly 235*li* and producing an annual profit of some 30*li*, a return on slave capital of 13 percent.

Winners and losers, with the coin weighted in favor of those who had already won something—such in part was the world being fashioned by slavery for Benjamin Davis as the eighteenth century opened. In 1710 Benjamin felt himself losing, took umbrage when George Wortham offered him an overseer's position, and was killed in the argument that followed. Even his umbrage is understandable in terms of the incoming blacks. Blacks as well as whites served as overseers. Ralph Wormeley's "Captain" seems to have held some sort of supervisory position at Rosegill; while Henry Thacker, in his 1704 will, recommended that his "Doctor Jack" be "Imployed to Look after the rest of the . . . Negroes" with "provisions Equall to an overseer."[44] If the black slave could be an overseer, the status of a freeman accepting the position would be clearly diminished.

But as widespread slavery settled on the county, an evident prosperity and the anomalies embedded in that prosperity fascinate us. Prices for the county's sweetscented tobacco rose in the first decade of the new century. These were, moreover, years in which, in the aggregate, the best of all possible ratios of prime blacks to unproductive children and elderly blacks prevailed. New blacks—overwhelmingly prime—were entering in considerable numbers; the demographic dynamics had not yet had time to erode the favorable ratio. Our best estimate is that around 1710 roughly 70 percent of the black labor force was prime, a percentage that would drop into the forties in the 1720s.[45]

In this surge of prosperity, however, the economic levels of society were diverging. In the first decade of the eighteenth century, those whose personal estates were such as to place them in the bottom levels of society—roughly two-thirds of the male heads-of-household—owned on average goods valued at no more than the average goods of their compeers of the seventeenth century. In contrast, the rest owned more, with the highest levels on average doubling the personal property of their earlier counterparts.[46] To put the point another way: In the earlier century, to judge from inventories of personal property made as part of probate proceedings, what we have called the cosmopolitan families of the county were roughly forty-six times as wealthy as the poorest families, and the leading county-oriented families—Worthams, Joneses, Seagers—eleven times. In the first decades of the eighteenth century, the distance between the poorest sort and the uppermost economic levels almost doubled. By mid-century, the county-oriented families were on average thirty times as wealthy as the poorest, and the great cosmopolitan families well over a hundred times.

We sense the overall prosperity most directly in the changing life-styles of the county's men and women. William Brocas, for example, was among the premier men of the early county. To judge from the 1655 inventory of his personal property, however, he surrounded himself with few amenities. True, he had a curtained feather bed, an "old lookinge glass and a broken frame for a bason," a silver seal, and "a parcell of old torne books most of them Spanish, Italyan, and Latin." But the image reflected is of semi-Spartan and certainly seedy surroundings. What there is is invariably described as "old," "worne," and "knockt up." Richard Allen, in terms of relative wealth and standing, was certainly not Brocas's equal; Allen's personal property of 137*li* places him among the middling sort in 1715. Yet he, too, slept in a feather bed; warmed before entering with a brass warming pan; had a new set of pewter plates, dishes, and "basons"; and owned a handsome case to hold his knives and forks. An hourglass graced his mantel, and three "Looking Glasses" his walls. John Vivion was closer to (but still not the equal of) Brocas in relative rank and wealth. Yet he had "New fashon Rushin Leather Chaires" in his chamber and "New fashon Caine Chaires and Cushions" (two with arms) and a cane couch in his hall. Robert

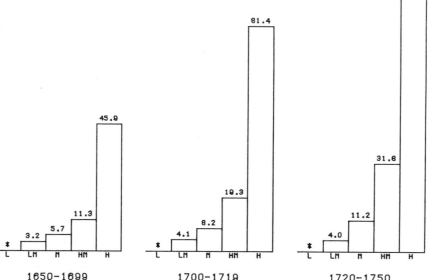

THE CHANGING DISTANCE BETWEEN THE POOREST IN MIDDLESEX AND THOSE ABOVE THEM

1650-1699

1700-1719

1720-1750

KEY TO WEALTH GROUPS:
L = LOW;
LM = LOW MIDDLE;
M = MIDDLE;
HM = HIGH MIDDLE
H = HIGH.

THE TOWERS REPRESENT THE MEDIAN ESTATE EVALUATION OF EACH GROUP DIVIDED BY THE MEDIAN OF THE LOWEST. THUS, IN THE FIRST PERIOD, THE MEDIAN OF THE HIGHEST WEALTH GROUP WAS 46 TIMES THAT OF THE LOWEST. SEE EXPLICATUS, "WEALTH," FOR A DESCRIPTION OF THE SAMPLE AND WEALTH GROUPS.

Dudley was on a par with Vivion in terms of wealth. He covered his table with a "large holland" cloth, sat on cane chairs, used bone-handled knives and forks, and hung calico about his bed. Emulating Madam Wormeley, Madam Dudley kept her closet in a similar style, complete with a cane couch, a "Linsey Woolsey quilt" and pillow, a brass chafing dish, a bellows, and a candle box.[47]

Clearly the personal space about the middling and upper sort of the county was becoming more lavish at the end of the seventeenth and beginning of the eighteenth centuries. At the same time, the volume of that space seems to have been increasing, for, in the 1690s and early 1700s, we sense a dramatic building surge underway. A new and larger glebe house, recall, was built in the late 1690s, and still another—complete with separate kitchen and dairy—at the end of the first decade of the new century. Rosegill seems to have been expanded in the 1690s, its several structures merged into one and new outbuildings erected. George Wortham's new house, built also in the 1690s, boasted six rooms and a separate kitchen; his father's house, fitted out for a courthouse about the same time, had but two rooms on the ground floor and a loft. Just before his death in 1700, Richard Willis, almost a peer of the Wormeleys in wealth but not in status, abandoned his old house of four rooms for one of six that also had a separate kitchen and dairy. Tobias Mickleburrough, a man of means, although far less so than Willis, and something of a dandy to judge from his silver-handled cane and the three gold rings he wore, requested in his 1702 will that his executors insure that his "new house" be "finished with all the reasonable Expedition that may be . . . and that It may be laid with oyl and Colours which I have ready for the same purpose." William Needles, too, moved into a new house just before his death in 1701, housing cows, calves, and heifers in the old. Needles's inventory places him among the lower middle householders of the county.[48]

The changing life-style reached even into the lower economic levels of the society. Again examples: Paul Brewer, who died in 1655, had in the way of luxuries but a "small brass kettle" and two books. He slept on a rush bed and ate from an "Indian Bowle." His only furniture other than the bed was a single chest. His fireplace utensils consisted of a pot, frying pan, and rack. Most of his estate (60 percent) consisted of his animals and a crop of tobacco. John Somers, who died in 1702, was no better placed than Brewer, either relative to the county society (he, too, was among the poorer sort) or in terms of the total worth of his personal belongings. Sixty-one percent of his estate consisted of animals and tobacco. His bed was no better than Brewer's, and his only other furniture was four "old Chests." Yet somewhere along the line he had managed to acquire pothooks and fire tongs for his fireplace and pewter plates, earthenware, two brass skillets, and a butter pot. John Hickey, who died in 1710, was of the same sort. Again, 60 percent of his belongings consisted of his animals. But the remainder included "two lookeing glasses," "eighteen pounds of best pewter," "one tin Candlestick," and "two butter pots." One final example: Thomas Tuke, who died in 1728, like the others can only be categorized as poor. Like their houses, his boasted crude beds and old chests. But in addition there were chairs (seven in all), an "old Japan Table," and an "oval Table." Like Somers's, his fireplace boasted pothooks and other utensils. He had pewter, as Hickey had—four dishes, eleven plates, and two "basons." But he also had a porringer and six spoons, two candlesticks to Hickey's one, and a chamberpot.[49] In no way can we think of Tuke's surroundings as lavish. The space about him was still the one room and loft so common in the seventeenth century. And its furnishings pale when contrasted to those in the house of a Vivion or Dudley, or even an Allen. Indeed, as we said of Tuke's kind in general, in total valuation he had no more than his sort had three-quarters of a century before, while Vivions, Dudleys, and, to a lesser degree, Allens had far more than their earlier counterparts. Having said that, however, we must stress the linear progression in things owned extending from Brewer in 1655 to Tuke in 1728. The crude sparseness of Brewer's surroundings looks even cruder before Tuke's, even though two men's total estates were roughly the same.

A number of phenomena account for this spread of amenities through the society. Slavery and its profits surely comprise one. But it is by no means the whole story. It does not directly account for the spread of amenities among those who held no slaves. The simple maturation of the county is another. There is, after all, only so much productive capacity in a single piece of land. Once the farmer had brought his land close to that capacity—in the process expending the surplus his farm produced on acquiring the tools, animals, and, in the case of the Chesapeake, the labor necessary—he and his wife could turn the surplus toward acquiring amenities that, while building the farm, he could not afford. Developments in England (the growing production of cheap earthenware, for example) and improvements in the distribution of English goods in the Chesapeake (about which more in the next chapter) played a part, too. As time passed, goods were simply more readily available to the men and women of Middlesex. And we must take into account the fact that ours was not a society much inclined to throw things away. What was amassed in one lifetime was distributed at death to form the basis of a new and somewhat more lavish collection. We already have one clear example of this: John Hickey had married John Somers's widow; Somers's one butter pot was one of Hickey's two.[50]

None of this, however, really accounts for the anomaly represented by Brewer, Somers, Hickey, and Tuke—that, over time, the poorer sort had no more in gross terms and yet more in the way of life's comforts. The same anomaly applies to an extent to the men of the middling sort. In gross terms they had more; relative to the poorest they had more; but in terms of amenities they gained more than their overall gains would seem to warrant. What we seem to be glimpsing here is another facet of the fundamental difference between Benjamin Davis's world and the earlier world of his father, another and an ironic aspect of Davis's frustration. Blocked by the costs and risks associated with slavery, men like Davis could not afford to develop their land to the fullest. Turning onto the Negro road, the society, in brief, forced such men away from those productive investments that would have allowed them to get on in the world. Perhaps in recompense they turned to what for want of a better phrase we can call investments in consumption—amenities that made merely getting by more comfortable.

A statistical aggregation is suggestive. By dividing the personal property listed in almost three hundred inventories into

productive goods (laborers, animals, tools, cash and its equivalent) and other goods (household goods, clothing, amenities
per se), we see that those at the lowest economic level devoted—
as inevitably they do—a larger part of their worldly goods to
living poorly while those at the upper level devoted a smaller
part to living well. (Note the upper bar graph in the accompanying illustration.) When we look at the percentage of total
value in household goods and amenities in discrete periods,
the fact that over time the poor devoted a greater percentage
to simply living and the rich a smaller percentage stands out
(the bottom graph).

The point comes home even more directly when we consider individuals. Paul Brewer's goods in 1655, for example,
clearly reflect the economic strategy current in the seventeenth century: 175 acres of land, two cows, a heifer, four
calves, a bull, some pigs, his tools. Brewer, an ex-servant, could
anticipate that his cows would steadily increase his capital by
virtue of their natural increase, all the while providing milk
and occasionally meat for his family and even expendable
capital—a surplus—should he choose to sell an extra calf or
two. The care of the animals, moreover, took minimal labor
away from the corn and tobacco fields; indeed, the care of the
animals was undoubtedly in the hands of Brewer's wife. He
could anticipate, too, that cattle, crops, and even the land itself
(by renting or selling a part) might ultimately furnish the
wherewithal to buy servant labor, thereby expanding his economic base, perhaps allowing him to open another field or
two. Getting on in this fashion was implicit in a virgin land
where farms had to be eked out of a wilderness and where
labor—a relatively inexpensive and short-term investment in
a servant or two—was so obviously the key to advancement.
If we imagine the Brewers (husband and wife) faced with a
choice between purchasing a butter pot or something more
useful to the work of building the farm, then we must also
imagine them opting for the latter.

John Hickey's holdings, however, reflect Benjamin Davis's
changing world. Hickey, too, was an ex-servant, freed in 1691.
In 1700 he was still a renter. Land was scarcer in the county
and more expensive than it had been before, and he had not
been able to amass enough money to buy. Marrying John

WHERE THEY PUT THEIR MONEY

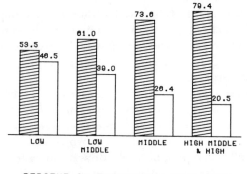

PERCENT IN PRODUCTIVE GOODS AND
AMENITIES BY WEALTH GROUP

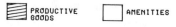

PRODUCTIVE GOODS   AMENITIES

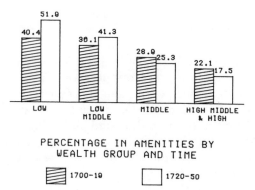

PERCENTAGE IN AMENITIES BY
WEALTH GROUP AND TIME

1700-19   1720-50

Somers's widow, Hickey occupied the Somers's 110 acres for a while, then had to give them up when Somers's son came of age, shifting his cattle back onto rented land, where they were when he died in 1710. During his last ten years, Hickey could have little expectation of getting on in the world in the sense of making a farm. His cattle might increase; they would produce milk and meat for his family, even expendable capital, as Brewer's had. But land and labor—slave labor now, expensive and risky, involving a long-term investment—were beyond his means. In this situation, he understandably would settle for getting by rather than getting on. Faced in our imagination with the same choice Brewer faced—a butter pot or something useful to build a farm—Hickey and his wife would probably choose the former and make their lives a bit more comfortable.

Finally, Thomas Tuke exemplifies the extreme of our progression. Appearing in the county in 1721, he did not even try for land, let alone labor. He was a tailor and needed only the tools of his trade and a houselot for his family, his cow, her calf, and a heifer. In brief, he had no farm to build, hence no need to scrimp in order to get ahead with one. Should the Tukes choose to sell the heifer (saving the cow for milk and the calf for meat), they would without doubt use the proceeds to buy amenities. What else was there to spend them on?

Let us return to a point made earlier—the divergence of the economic levels of the county and the greater and greater distance between poor and rich. One clear aspect of this divergence was the increasing burden of welfare in the county.

That the "lame, impotent, old, blinde, and other poore not able to worke" were the responsibility of the community at large was explicit in the English tradition carried into Middlesex. The quotation itself is from Michael Dalton's *The Countrey Justice* of 1622, a book required by a Virginia law of 1666 to be part of every county court's "library" and known to be part of Middlesex's from 1688, when Christopher Robinson was reimbursed 216 pounds of tobacco for its purchase.[51] And from the very beginning of settlement, both county court and vestry played a role in administering welfare. When, for example, widower William Baldwin died in

1664, before the formation of Middlesex, a neighbor seems to have taken in his children. The Lancaster court subsequently assumed responsibility for their care, ordering that the children remain "where they are" until arrangements could be made to bind them out as servants. One of the children, however, had a "scald head." Henry Corbin's Lancaster Parish vestry paid Henry Pickett for curing him, then bound the child to Pickett.[52]

Poor relief took many forms, from child care and the underwriting of medical bills, through direct assistance to the victims of particular calamities (fire, for example) and annual stipends, to exemption from levies and the payment of burial expenses. The sextonship of the churches was a form of poor relief. Thus John Blake, "a poore Decriped man" assisted by Lancaster Parish in 1666 and 1667, was paid two hundred pounds of tobacco for cleaning the Middle Church and its churchyard in 1677 and in 1678 four hundred pounds "for cleaneing the Great Church yard as sexton" and two hundred pounds for keeping clean the Lower Chapel.[53] Ultimately the sextonship became largely a sinecure for poor widows. Payment for the boarding, lodging, and tending of other recipients was itself sometimes a form of charity for the housekeeper, Blake, for example, being paid five hundred pounds of tobacco in 1677 for keeping a bastard child of one of Ralph Wormeley's maids, an additional twelve hundred pounds in 1678, and one thousand in 1679.[54]

In the early years, recipients of charity were largely single individuals, kinless, without family to assist them. Indeed, law and custom stipulated that families extending in a vertical line from grandparents through parents to children and grandchildren were responsible for supporting indigent members within the line.[55] Or recipients were infants, more often than not the illegitimate children of servant girls. In the 1680s, a third of those known to have been cared for by the county or parish were children. The overall burden of welfare—estimated, of course—can be stated in terms of rates. From the mid-1670s to the end of the century, the number of adult recipients of welfare in the county fluctuated around 10 per 1,000 free, white adults, rising to a high of 12.2 per 1,000 in the years from 1685 to 1689 and dropping to a low of 8.9

from 1690 to 1695. The overall cost of all welfare payments fluctuated around fifteen pounds of tobacco per Middlesex household, between 2 and 5 percent of all money raised for public purposes in the county.[56]

Both the numbers of recipients of welfare and welfare's total cost rose dramatically in the new century, the latter doubling between 1687 and 1704, rising from fifteen pounds of tobacco per household to thirty-one, tripling if we take into account the changing price of tobacco, and accounting for 14 percent of all county and vestry expenditures in the latter year. Relatively fewer children were supported, however. Where a third of all welfare expenditures were for what we would call child support in the 1680s, the percentage dropped to 7 in the first decade of the eighteenth century and to between 1 and 2 in the 1720s and 1730s. Adults, largely women, came to dominate the rolls. And welfare tended to settle into particular families, a phenomenon commensurate with other indications that the lines between strata in our society were hardening in these years—sons of the lower sort, for example, being locked into the positions of their fathers and therefore unable to improve their lots, and even middling-level sons in greater and greater numbers dropping from the level of their fathers.[57]

Lettice Shippey and her family exemplify the phenomenon. Lettice married Thomas Bateman in 1704, was widowed in 1714, and did not remarry. When Lettice's mother, by then Mary Purvis, found herself in dire circumstances in 1716, Lettice did not have the wherewithal to provide help. Neither could Mary's son, John Purvis, who had married in 1711, fathered six children in quick order—two of his wife's births were twins—and who found himself so pressed that by 1718 he would have to ask the vestry to take over their care. Mary Purvis perforce was supported by the public from 1716 to her death in 1720. And by 1728 Lettice herself would become an object of charity.

So, too, is the Ball family a good example. Edward Ball, father of eleven children, was named sexton of the Middle Church in 1714 and served until his death in 1726, when the sextonship was awarded to his widow, Keziah, who held it until she in turn died ten years later. In that year, two sextonships

PUBLIC EXPENDITURES
IN MIDDLESEX
1668, 1687, 1704, 1724

[PERCENTAGES IN PARENTHESES]

NOTE: The size of each circle is proportionate to the total levy collected from the county for all purposes in 1668; the segments of each are in proportion to the amount expended from the monies collected for various purposes. "Colony" designates sums raised in the county for the colony government in Jamestown (later Williamsburg); "Burgesses," the compensation and expenses of the county's representatives to the legislature. By the 1720s these expenditures were paid by the colony government from tobacco duties rather than from levies. "Collection" represents the cost of collecting the levies.

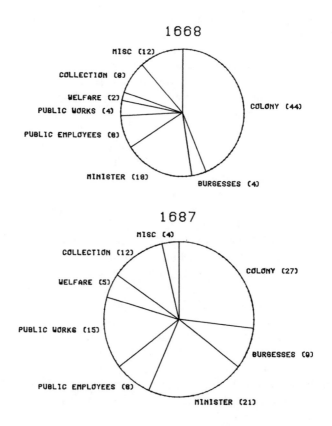

1668

MISC [12]
COLLECTION [8]
WELFARE [2]
PUBLIC WORKS [4]
PUBLIC EMPLOYEES [8]
MINISTER [18]
BURGESSES [4]
COLONY [44]

1687

MISC [4]
COLLECTION [12]
WELFARE [5]
PUBLIC WORKS [15]
PUBLIC EMPLOYEES [8]
MINISTER [21]
BURGESSES [9]
COLONY [27]

were open, one at the Middle Church (Keziah's position) and the other at the Lower Church. Widow Elizabeth Long was awarded the vacancy at the Middle Church; the Lower Church position went to Keziah's son-in-law Joseph Smith. And when Smith died in 1740, Keziah's daughter Elizabeth was named to replace him. Elizabeth had one grown son, Edward, but he could give little help to his mother, for what he had was expended on the family of his indigent father-in-law, Philip Brooks, five of whose orphans were in Edward's care at vestry expense in 1745.

One last example—the Humphreys, a four-generation welfare family. John Humphrey arrived in the county in its earliest years and himself was never a recipient of welfare.

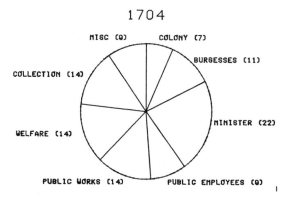

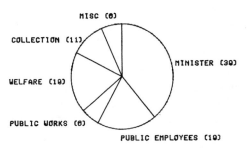

But he fathered five children, of whom four were helped in some manner by the public after his death: John's daughter Elizabeth was supported by the public from 1721 until her death and burial in 1759; his son Robert received help in 1712; and another son, Joseph, in 1748. The bastard child of his daughter Catherine was a parish child. His legitimate grandchildren, too, ultimately became objects of charity: Joseph's son John and John's widow; and Robert's daughter Mary Deagle. Harry, the stepson of John Humphrey's granddaughter Mary Anderson, and Harry's children all in turn received parish largesse. But even with these, the link between the Humphrey clan and the "parish chest" is not complete. After John Humphrey's death, his widow married John Ross, who remarried when she in turn died. Daniel Ross, Ross's son by his second wife, needed public support. In 1715 the vestry paid his stepbrother, John Humphrey's son Robert, for keeping the boy and Dr. Lewis Tomkins 1,000 pounds of tobacco for "salivating" him. In all, the county over a span of seventy-eight years contributed a total of 26,767 pounds of tobacco and something over two pounds current money to the care of this one family, the equivalent of the entire parish budget for the year 1700.

What of the gentlemen of the county, not so much the cosmopolitan Wormeleys, whose domain and concern was the colony, but the Worthams, Prices, and Seagers, the county-oriented gentlemen who did the county's business? As members of the court and vestry, they set the levies and paid out the public's money—a larger and larger percentage for charitable purposes as time went on, fully 14 percent in 1704, 20 percent two decades later. The gentlemen could not help but notice what was happening. In 1712 they petitioned the colony's legislature "That better Methods be taken for providing for poor and Impotent people," while in 1715 they cut welfare payments by 20 percent, ordering that "every Pensioner be allowed but 800 lb of Tobaco for every 1,000 . . . and Soe in proportion."[58] Yet, prospering themselves in the first decades of slavery, busily improving their own homes and furnishing them with "Rushin Leather Chaires," they set about refurbishing the county itself.

As early as the 1680s, the court had begun planning the

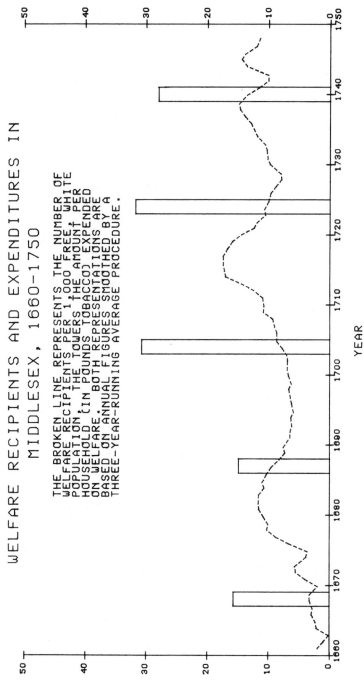

WELFARE RECIPIENTS AND EXPENDITURES IN
MIDDLESEX, 1660-1750

THE BROKEN LINE REPRESENTS THE NUMBER OF
WELFARE RECIPIENTS PER 1,000 FREE WHITE
POPULATION; THE TOWERS THE AMOUNT PER
HOUSEHOLD (IN POUNDS TOBACCO) EXPENDED
ON WELFARE. BOTH REPRESENTATIONS ARE
BASED ON ANNUAL FIGURES SMOOTHED BY A
THREE-YEAR-RUNNING AVERAGE PROCEDURE.

YEAR

building of a courthouse, and in 1692 it allocated twenty-three thousand pounds of tobacco for the work, although, as we shall see, the project fell afoul of Ralph Wormeley's pretensions. In 1695 the court leased from George Wortham the "good strong house"—his father's—that Wortham had remodeled to meet the court's purpose. By 1700, however, the justices were complaining that their quarters were "very leakey," and in 1704 they contracted with John Hipkins to build a new courthouse "with all the Expedition Immaginable" for twenty-five thousand pounds of tobacco.[59] Despite a bitter controversy as to where to locate the new building, it was completed by January 1706.

In the meantime, the vestry had been busy. The repair and refurbishing of the glebe was a constant concern during these years. In 1690 a complete remodeling of the Upper Church was undertaken (9,000 pounds of tobacco), of the Middle Church in 1696 (14,815), and of the Lower Church in 1697 (11,650). By 1710 the Upper Church was again "gone to ruin," and the vestry determined to build anew, taking the opportunity to relocate the building on the main road, nearer the center of population of the upper precinct. Then the vestrymen decided to embark on a program of rebuilding anew all three churches, the Upper Church in wood, the Middle and Lower churches in brick. By 1717 the work was completed at a cost of 312,000 pounds of tobacco, roughly eighteen hundred pounds sterling, an enormous sum equivalent to almost half of the total budgeted expenses of both county court and vestry during the whole of the previous decade (680,000).[60]

There was a self-conscious lavishness about this building spree, something akin to modern boosterism. The first courthouse planned was to have been done in brick and to have been "at least of equall goodness and Dimentions with the Brick Courte howse lately Built in Gloucester County." "Sash windows" were carefully stipulated for the courthouse and for all three new churches, a style of window that replaced the old casement window and that first entered Virginia during the building of Williamsburg as a new capital to replace Jamestown.[61] When all was completed, the gentlemen of the county could glance around from the "high framed pews" so carefully included in the building directions for the churches or from the raised "justices seat" in the courthouse and know they had the best that could be had: arched and painted ceilings, whitewashed plaster walls, the great windows—in the Lower Church ten feet high, five across, "Arched A top," their frames, together with the doors and cornices, "all laid in Oyle and Colours"—and "commendable" screens dividing church from chancel.[62]

The visitors, too, standing in the one church that survives in a form approximating these Middlesex churches must murmur quiet appreciation.[63] But we must also remember the cost. The levies paid by the county's inhabitants to offset the expenditures of court and church—so much for every male sixteen or over and every slave, both male and female, of the same age—rose from an average of 77 pounds of tobacco during the first five years of the century to 110 pounds for the years 1711 to 1717, peaking at 152 pounds in 1712, but remaining above 100 for five of the seven years. For the prospering gentlemen who voted the sums, the personal burden undoubtedly seemed worthwhile. The welfare rolls offer mute testimony to the burden on those at the other end of the economic spectrum, the average number of recipients in a year doubling between the two periods.

7. Urbanna

God made the country, and man made the town.
What wonder then, that health and virtue, gifts
That can alone make sweet the bitter draught
That life holds out to all, should most abound
And least be threatened in the fields and groves?
— William Cowper, *The Task*

IN BOTH fact and imagination, the visitors have often stood on the point of land formed where Rosegill Creek joins the Rappahannock. Ahead and to the right the majestic river dominates—even overpowers—the scene, flowing toward the observer from the northwest, then angling slightly as if consciously sparing this particular land and the Wormeleys' "great house," which stands upon it. North and east the Lancaster shore is a dim brown line, so far away that details are invisible. The view to the left is gentler, more on a human scale. The level land of the point drops abruptly, falling about twenty feet to the creek itself, although "creek" is something of a misnomer. Here the Rosegill forms a small harbor some thirty yards across, perhaps a thousand long. Today there is a pleasant town across the water—Urbanna— and the creek is called Urbanna Creek. Small boats of various kinds ride at moorings or nestle against the docks extending from the far bank. The wood and brick of the town itself peeps at us through trees.

Urbanna, too, was a product of the building boom of the turn of the century. But to understand the genesis of the town and the profound effect that it had upon the county, we must first understand the way in which Middlesex was linked to a larger world of trade and commerce, a merchant community that sprinkled the Atlantic with a myriad of sailing ships and imparted value to the tobacco our people tended.

We can start with Tobias Mickleburrough. We have already mentioned him in passing. His silver-handled cane and three gold rings caught our eye when referring to the new house he was building at the time of his death early in 1703. We bring him to mind again because Mickleburrough, from the early 1680s on, kept store at his house on the south branch of Sunderland Creek in the lower part of the county's upper precinct.

Mickleburrough's was by no means a "store" in the modern sense. His business was conducted anywhere and everywhere—in the hall of his house, while standing in the entry, at church during the time before and after service devoted to "strolling round" and "consulting," and at court day. It was an almost casual matter of a neighbor mentioning needs, Mickleburrough answering in terms of items on hand or to be had through his "connections," a bargain struck—so much in goods in return for so much in tobacco when the crop was made—and its careful recording in "a book of Sales."[1] Most of the goods he had on hand Mickleburrough kept in a storeroom, probably a separate building, but others were tucked here and there about his house. In all, "store goods" amounted to roughly twenty pounds current or 5 percent of Mickleburrough's personal belongings as inventoried after his death.[2] For, notably, he was a planter as well as storekeeper, owning twenty blacks in 1703, a home plantation of just over two hundred acres, another, largely undeveloped, of six hundred acres some two miles away, and he was operating still a third as guardian of a Seager orphan.

It is the store goods that interest us, however, for they allow a glimpse of what he and his neighbors needed in the way of imports: nails in a variety of sizes from threepenny to twenty; cloth and thread; buttons; bone combs; mirrors; pewter; gunpowder; a variety of locks and hinges; window glass; linseed oil; and the white and red lead that, when mixed, made colored paint. But the last was probably not for sale; in all likelihood it was the "oyle and Colours" that Mickleburrough had laid aside for his own new house. The inventory of another storekeeper with a somewhat larger stock adds to the list: again, nails and cloth, but also "5 women's Gownes" and "a Girls petticoate," "a parcell shoe buckles," hat bands, pots and pans, hoes and axes, two hammers, a saw, and "3 horne books."[3]

A list of thirty debtors compiled by the executors of Mickleburrough's estate, moreover, allows us a glimpse of his customers. When plotted on a map, they form a tight circle extending three miles in every direction about his house. Twelve were renters; seventeen were small planters with holdings ranging from 50 to 272 acres and averaging 124; only one was another major holder, Mickleburrough's brother-in-law, Henry Thacker (1,375 acres). Their debts to Mickleburrough, too, were small, ranging from 16 pounds of tobacco to 850 and averaging just over 300. Were all the tobacco owed him in February 1703 collected and packed in hogsheads for shipment, it would amount to roughly seventeen hogsheads, by no means the equivalent of the fifty-three hogsheads shipped from Ralph Wormeley's Rosegill in 1701, but a significant quantity nevertheless, particularly when we add the hogsheads from Mickleburrough's own land. If Wormeley's tobacco made up roughly a quarter of a ship's cargo, Mickleburrough's would have made up a tenth.[4]

In our mind's eye we must envision small retail operations such as Mickleburrough's sprinkled all across Middlesex—the "merchants . . . seated with their Stores in their Country Plantations, and having their Customers all round about them," as commented upon in a contemporary pamphlet, the "Men in Number from ten to thirty" on every Chesapeake river who "take care to supply the poorer sort with Goods and Necessaries."[5] Seldom do we see such operations in any detail. Most often our information comes in the form of sparse hints entered in the records for one purpose or another: a judgment against Edward Spark "to be paid in a Store" (1691), another judgment using the same language (1693), the trial of two slaves (1696) accused of theft "out of the Stoore" of a planter whose court actions and inventory imply retail trading.[6] They were, however, the top opening of a funnel through which the produce of the small and middling planters of Middlesex flowed out to the Atlantic. Still, store-keeping planters like Mickleburrough were only part of a larger structure. For just as earlier we made a distinction between county and cosmopolitan gentlemen, we must here make a distinction between county and cosmopolitan merchants.

Mickleburrough himself was but one of several customers of another Middlesex man, William Churchill, who had what Mickleburrough did not have, that is, those close relationships with merchants in England that, by virtue of mutual trust, allowed the conduct of business across three thousand miles of water. A Virginian of a later date put the matter neatly. Asked by a friend to send tobacco to a particular merchant in England (who in turn would sell it, deduct costs, and use the proceeds to establish an account against which the Virginian could draw to pay debts or buy goods for import into Virginia), John Custis at first refused on the grounds that "Mr Hanberry"—the merchant in question—"is an utter stranger to me." Subsequently Custis agreed, but cautiously, giving to "Mr Hanberry . . . (who I understand is your particular friend) the trouble of a small consignmnt." "The gentleman is an utter stranger to me," he repeated, "but I depend he is a man of honor and probity otherwise you that understand mankind so well would never have listed him in your friendship. . . . If Mr. Handberrys uses me well [and] if I live we may have greater dealings."[7]

Churchill, entering Middlesex from England in 1675 as a young man of twenty-five and buying land along the lower Rappahannock, had such relationships from the start, specifically with his "kinsmen," merchants Nicholas and John Goodwin of London. To these he added others over time and, importantly, he acquired Middlesex connections—Christopher Robinson, for one, who also had extensive English ties. In partnership or alone, Churchill bought, sold, rented, mortgaged, and foreclosed land throughout the county, but primarily in the lower precinct where he lived. He traded with a variety of English mariner-merchants—men whose ships plied the rivers on an itinerant basis, putting off English goods and taking on tobacco. He entered into a variety of engagements with his English connections, acting for them as agent or factor, gathering cargoes for them and selling their goods. But he also traded on his own account, sending tobacco on consignment to one or another English merchant to create a balance upon which he could draw. Like Mickleburrough, he operated a store; in 1688 he had a servant working there exclusively. But he also wholesaled goods to others, including Mickleburrough, advancing him English goods on the promise of a return in tobacco. In 1703 Mickleburrough owed Churchill just under four hundred pounds. So extensive were Churchill's operations in the county that at one time he engaged William Killbee of the lower precinct to serve as *his* factor and to collect debts owed him. By 1698 Churchill was styling himself "William Churchill and Co."[8]

Mickleburrough served the small and middling planters in effecting the vital exchange of tobacco for English goods; so, too, did Churchill to an extent. But Churchill also served Mickleburrough, giving a structured appearance to trade within the county. In sum, Churchill was Mickleburrough's "connection," while Churchill's own connections led outward to the mariner-merchants and London houses. The arrangement was by no means unique. Indeed, when we track the various credit arrangements in the county through lawsuits and the like, territorial hegemonies begin to suggest themselves.

In his early years, Churchill's network of debtors within the county was confined to the lower precinct between the Rappahannock and the road. South of the road, Matthew Kemp held sway, operating in both Middlesex and Gloucester from holdings on the lower Piankatank, with Richard Stevens and Robert Dudley having to him the same relationship as Mickleburrough had to Churchill. Robert Beverley, Christopher Robinson, and Richard Willis divided the rest of the county. (The Wormeleys of Rosegill had little part in these intracounty credit relationships after roughly 1680; with their own connections in England, they exported and imported largely for themselves.) Notably, the connections abroad and within the county that allowed these hegemonies did not automatically pass from father to son as land and personalty did, but shifted from one planter-merchant to another. We will return to the point. Suffice it here to note that Beverley had fallen heir to the connections of John Burnham, a major planter-merchant of the 1670s who died in 1681. When Beverley died in 1687, Robinson's area of influence grew. When Robinson died in 1693, Churchill's influence spread from the

lower precinct into the middle, while Gawin Corbin—Henry
Corbin's son, now grown to manhood, with extensive relations both in Middlesex and England—entered the scene to
take Robinson's place on the Rappahannock side of the county
from the Essex boundary to just below Sunderland Creek.
And when Willis died in 1701, Corbin's and Churchill's influence swelled to fill the vacuum. Willis was much married but
childless; his lands went to a nephew, John Alden, but Alden
never assumed the merchant role of his uncle.

If credit relationships suggest an element of rationality in
the economic structure of our county, we must nevertheless
confess that the point escaped observers at the time. Each year
toward the end of the century, some 150 ships arrived in the
Chesapeake in the late fall carrying goods consigned to planter-
merchants at their various locations or sent on speculation to
be bartered for tobacco on the spot. For three to four months
the ships sailed the waters of the bay and its rivers, each taking it own course until, their English goods gone and their
holds filled with tobacco, they set canvas for England.[9]

Viewing the comings and goings from his vantage point
in Gloucester County, the Reverend John Clayton was led to
comment that "the great number of Rivers and the thinness
of the Inhabitants distract and disperse a trade. So that all
Ships in general gather each their Loading up and down an
hundred Miles distant; and the best of Trade that can be driven
is only a sort of *Scotch* Pedling." To others, merchants such as
Churchill and Mickleburrough lived "the best of any" but still
were "subject to great Inconveniencies in the way of their
Trade." "They are obliged to sell upon Trust all the Year long,
except just a little while when Tobacco is ready," "drive a pity-
ful retail Trade to serve every Man's little Occasions, being
. . . in Effect but Country Chapmen," and all the while pay
damaged tobacco and high freight rates for the "scrambling
Manner" in which the ships offloaded and loaded their cargoes.[10] The apparent disorder suggested towns as a cure, for
with towns business could be centralized and the crop assembled in but a few spots, allowing the ships a quick unloading
and loading. The thought linked to a concern (at least among
some) for the scattering of the population across the landscape—"our wild and Rambling way," one Virginian called

it—and the lack of "cohabitation," and hence a lack of the
"Christian Neighbourhood" and "brotherly admonition"
associated with towns. And both thoughts linked to a more
general concern over Virginia's single-minded attachment to
tobacco and the failure of every attempt to encourage diversification. Towns, some felt, would attract craftsmen and artisans, even manufacturers, and these in turn would lessen the
dependence on English imports and the tobacco that paid for
them.[11]

Over the years such concerns had provoked occasional
action from Virginia's government. In the 1650s the legislature of the colony ordered that in every county there be established "one or two places and no more" where "the marketts
and trade of the county shall be and not else where." Con-
forming, the Lancaster court voted to establish two places "for
Stoars and Markets" in what would become Middlesex, one
on the Rappahannock several miles above Rosegill Creek, the
other on the Piankatank. But "markets" on paper were not
markets in fact. The ineffective act was soon replaced by
another that simply provided that if any county or particular
person set up a place "whether the merchants shall willingly
come for the sale or bringing of goods such men shall bee
lookt uppon as benefactors to the publique." Berkeley, as governor, attempted to force the development of Jamestown and,
by ordering the tobacco ships to anchor only where they could
be protected by forts, other towns as well. "If the shipps had
soe ridd," wrote a commentator later, "and the tobacco of every
County had beene brought to p'ticular places," it would be
very advantageous in "causeing Warehouses to be built, and
soe in p'cess of times Townes."[12]

In 1680, under the leadership of Middlesex's own Robert
Beverley, acting as clerk of the House of Burgesses, the Virginia legislature passed a comprehensive bill "for Cohabitation and encouragement of Trade and Manufacture" under
which the colony's trade would be funneled through twenty
towns to be established in the various counties, including one
in Middlesex. The authorities in England suspended the bill
late in 1682, objecting largely to the provisions that might have
encouraged diversification and taken Virginians away from
tobacco. Beverley tried again in 1685 only to have the effort

swamped in the wake of, first, an Anglo-American constitutional squabble, and then England's Glorious Revolution, which saw the replacement of James II by William of Orange and Mary, his Stuart wife. Finally, in 1691, another port bill, only slightly different from that of 1680, was passed. This, too, was rejected by English authorities, as was another drafted by Beverley's son, another Robert, and passed in 1705.[13] But the whole sequence of acts created enough of a legal framework to allow prominent Virginians here and there to proceed with the business of erecting towns. In Middlesex the effort first pitted the county's cosmopolitan merchants against Ralph Wormeley of Rosegill, and then a group of young men aspiring to be cosmopolitan merchants against those whose aspirations had already been fulfilled.

At this point, we must make something of a digression to consider Ralph Wormeley, the master of Rosegill during the last decades of the seventeenth century.

We know a great deal about this man: his birth in 1650 to a prominent father; his education in England; his return to assume the management of Rosegill and of lands elsewhere in Virginia from his stepfather Sir Henry Chicheley; his political offices. We know his wives—first his second cousin, the Lady Katherine Lunsford, daughter of Sir Thomas Lunsford and of Ralph's cousin Elizabeth; then, after her death in 1685, Elizabeth Armistead of Gloucester. We know his children: Elizabeth and Katherine by the Lady Katherine; young Ralph, John, and Judith by Elizabeth. The provisions of his will tell us a little of his concern for his children and for precedence. John, the second son, was to have the Wormeley lands on the York River and one-third of the personal property; Ralph, the elder, all the rest of the land, including Rosegill, and two-thirds of the personalty. (As it turned out, Ralph died young and unmarried in 1713 and everything went to John.) Daughter Katherine was to have 50li sterling inasmuch as Ralph had already "paid her portion," presumably at her marriage to her cousin, Gawin Corbin. Judith, the youngest daughter, was to have 250li at the time of her marriage and fifteen hundred acres laid out from the York River lands by her brother John. The provisions for Elizabeth were the most particular: 300li

sterling when she married, plus the choice of either a male or female black, the mulatto boy Daniel, a feather bed, its linens and curtains, a table, a chest of drawers, and assorted silver pieces—a lavish dower, indeed. Until she needed it, moreover, she was to be supplied with a room at Rosegill, furniture (including "one of the new best Standing beds"), two riding horses, and an allowance of 20*li* a year "to buy her Cloaths with till she be marryed."[14]

Still, there is much we do not know about this Wormeley. Did he—as visitors to Rosegill's great house so automatically do even today—walk out to the point, drawn to it by the awesome majesty of the river and pure beauty of the creek side? His sons and grandsons might well have. William Byrd visited John Wormeley at Rosegill in 1720, noting in the laconic style of his diary: "We walked about the plantation which is very pretty." Sometime later an occupant of the house (probably John Wormeley) built an eighty-foot gallery across its back, the windows framing a view of the river. Indeed, nature was in general romanticized in the course of the eighteenth century. To an English poet at its end, towns were made by men, the country by God. And a visitor to a prominent Virginian's home (not Rosegill) wrote of walking and chatting with the mistress of the house: "She observed with great truth, that to live in the Country, and take no pleasure at all in Groves, Fields, or Meadows . . . would be a manner of life too tedious to endure."[15] But perhaps our Wormeley accepted nature only pragmatically. The river was simply transportation, and the creek a secure landing. We do not know. His character intrigues us; yet we have only snippets of information and our imagination to guide us into it.

At our first glimpse of Wormeley—when, at eighteen, he carried a petition to the Lancaster court asking that it meet alternately on both sides of the Rappahannock and stalked out when the justices spurned the petition—he seems every bit the archetypical young aristocrat. We imagine him flushed by the rebuff, gripping his sword hilt as he stomped from the court, perhaps of necessity calmed by John Curtis, his fellow (and older) delegate from the Southside. A dozen-odd years later, in his early thirties, Wormeley seems more subtle in the complicated politics surrounding the petition for a tobacco stint, the subsequent riots, and Robert Beverley's incarceration. The very silence of the records as to his activities in an affair in which, simply on the basis of his proximity to events, we conceive he must have been involved, argues for a Richelieuian role. And clearly during the last decade of his life, when, as secretary of the colony—"Mr. Secretary" was how he liked to be addressed—he took control of the appointment of county clerks throughout Virginia and in effect professionalized that office, he proved himself the consummate bureaucrat. He was "the greatest Man in the Government, next the Governor," according to contemporaries, and his power emanated from his command of the flow of official paper.[16]

At home in Middlesex, Wormeley could be convivial among those of his own sort. In a different context, we glimpsed him "in company" with another gentleman teasing a snake along the road, then dropping into a nearby house for refreshments. As a host he could be bluff and cheerful. A traveler sojourning at Rosegill wrote of Wormeley's laughing when his guest diluted wine with water, playing the night away at cards, and offering to arrange a marriage with a "good-looking" and wealthy widow over whom he had some influence.[17] He could, too, be the bountiful patron. In the 1690s he seems to have taken Robert Beverley's orphaned sons under his wing. One son (Harry) married Wormeley's ward (Elizabeth Smith, also his niece and second cousin); their first child was baptized at Rosegill the next year. Another son (Robert) was named clerk of King and Queen County in 1699, presumably through Wormeley's influence. Yet from his mid-twenties on, Wormeley seems aloof from the county in general, reserved, approached cautiously even by its gentlemen justices and only when necessity required, and seldom making approaches to them. And in his constant efforts to expand Rosegill, he was ruthless toward his neighbors, trimming in a series of complicated maneuvers George Wortham's patrimony, moving as an officer of the crown to force lands to escheat, then taking title to them. When we plot the additions he made to Rosegill over the years, his intentions seem clear enough: He would have the property extend clear across the county from the Rappahannock to the Piankatank, dividing Middlesex in half. Indeed, Wormeley's attachment to Rosegill seems central to an understanding of the man. Rosegill was Wormeley's manor and he, quite self-consciously, was its lord. The Mother Church, located in the middle of Rosegill and embellished with his silver and linens, was his manor church. And if a town was to be built in Middlesex, it seems he would have it his manor town.

The act of 1680 first specified where any town in Middlesex would be located: on a fifty-acre tract on the upriver side of Rosegill Creek—Wormeley land. It was to Wormeley, therefore, that the leading planter-merchants of Middlesex applied when, each presumably acting because he saw his own profit in the venture, they sought through the county court to make the town a reality. A bare six weeks after the passage of the act, the Middlesex court designated Robert Beverley and John Burnham its agents or "feoffees" to arrange the purchase of the land for ten thousand pounds of tobacco and receive it on behalf of the public. The same order charged the feoffees with laying out streets and half-acre town lots—Beverley to do the actual surveying—and empowered them to "make Sale and [pass] good and Sufficient Deeds and Conveyances to all [and] every Person . . . that shall Desire [to] Purchase." Beverley's survey seems to have been completed in October 1681. In November the court anticipated moving itself to the town, ordering Beverley and Christopher Robinson to contract with "workmen" for a courthouse to be built there "of Such Dimentions and with Such Conveniency as in their discretions they Shall thinke Convenient." For all the activity, however, nothing happened. Certainly nobody moved into the town. More importantly, later events indicate that while Wormeley accepted the ten thousand pounds of tobacco for the town site, he withheld passing formal title.[18]

Still, the matter of a town of their own remained in the minds of the gentlemen. In late 1684—before the abortive town act of 1685, hence not an action taken in response to that act—the justices approached Wormeley about the possibility of building a courthouse on the town land. This was to be the "good Strong Bricke Howse . . . of equall goodness and Dimentions with the Bricke Courte Howse lately built in Gloucester" referred to in the last chapter. Wormeley seemed amenable, promising at the January 1685 court to give answer in February. At that court, he and Beverley undertook to build the courthouse. But before the actual work was to begin, three of the court's members were to negotiate with Wormeley and sign on behalf of "this Court and all the Inhabitants of this county" what were referred to as simply "Articles of Agreement or other Wrightings." There is no hint at this time of what Wormeley was requiring. But in the end nothing happened. Except for a Wormeley warehouse, the town land remained vacant.[19]

In June 1690—well before the passage of the 1691 port bill, hence, again, not specifically a response to it—the matter rose anew in the Middlesex court. Matthew Kemp, William Churchill, and Robert Dudley were delegated "to Waite upon" Wormeley at Rosegill and "discourse his honor about the Land . . . for to build a Town upon" and particularly about building a courthouse there. The records are mute as to the outcome, but a year later, with a new town act on the statute books (at least temporarily), the court bestirred itself again. In an unusual step, the justices first announced where and when they would meet to consider the matter of "the Towne Land," then charged the sheriff to "give Notice to the Severall Gentlemen." On the appointed day, they designated new feoffees—Matthew Kemp, Christopher Robinson, and William Churchill—but also charged their clerk with drawing up a deed of sale. Their language was unequivocal: The deed so drawn was to "be presented to the said Ralph Wormeley Esqr." by the whole court meeting on the town land at seven o'clock on the morning of July 27. And inasmuch as Wormeley had "allready received the Consideracion of the aforesaid fifty Acres of Land," they would require him to sign.[20] Clearly a dispute was in progress and a denouement imminent.

Wormeley did not appear at the town land to meet the justices on the appointed morning. Perhaps he let them know in advance that he would ignore their summons, saving them the trip. There is, however, a hint in the sterile language of subsequent court depositions that he simply ignored the matter, in which case the justices waited for him in vain, shuffling about in the damp grass. In any event, the feoffees and some others did go to Rosegill's great house later in the day. Admitted, they demanded of Wormeley "an Assurance and Conveyance of a good and absolute" title to the land. The deed prepared by the clerk was laid before him. Wormeley curtly refused to sign. The document, he said, did not contain certain reservations that "hee had agreed formerly."

What reservations?

"One Eare of Indian Corne or a pepper Corne yearly" as an "acknowledgement" or quitrent for the land, "with other limitattions that None liveing in the Towne should keepe a Dove Howse nor keepe any hoggs but in a Sty nor any horse but in the howse."

The feoffees refused reservations that to all intents and purposes summed up to lordship. The law was on their side, they said, citing the provisions of the 1691 statute to the effect that if the owner of lands designated for a town refused to pass title "such denial shall ipso facto be taken for a forfeiture to the feoffees." By simply noting his refusal, the feoffees told Wormeley, they would have the land for the town.

"Soe doe if you will," the master of Rosegill is recorded as replying.[21]

With that the deputation left. Later they recorded their account of the visit in the county's order book, together with those of the clerk and two witnesses—"ipso facto" evidence of Wormeley's intransigence, hence of his forfeiture. It did them no good. The town land was laid out in streets once again, and particular locations were designated for "Church-yard markitt place and fortification"; fourteen lots were actually sold.[22] But when the court contracted with James Curtis and John Hipkins for "a good Strong, Substantiall . . . Built house, for a Court House" in the town in April 1692 and the builders started work, Wormeley sent his servants across the creek to stop them. The court could only dispatch another deputation "to Know his Reasons for hindering" Curtis and Hipkins. The answer is unrecorded, but, in early 1693, the court relieved the builders of their obligation to continue and took possession of what materials remained. Subsequently they sent another deputation to Wormeley, not to protest—that apparently was futile—but to attempt to "agree" with him "for the Building and Erecting of a Court house" on the land. No agreement was possible, and the court proceeded to make other arrangements for quarters. In October 1693 Christopher Robinson had a "house frame" on the town land—the only private construction recorded. Presumably Wormeley had stopped Robinson's builders as he had stopped the county's.[23]

In the early years of the new century, the town again became a matter of contention. The situation, however, was altogether different. Old economic networks once paramount in the county—what we have referred to as hegemonies—had waned while new ones waxed. Robert Beverley's death in the mid-1680s, as we noted, saw the rise of Christopher Robinson, who married his widow, assumed the administration of the estate (almost 1,600*li* in personal property, 2,300*li* in debts due, plus land in four counties), and added Beverley's English connections to his own. Beverley's eldest sons, Peter and Robert, left Middlesex in the 1690s to take up lands and careers elsewhere; a younger son, Harry, bequeathed lands upriver in Rappahannock County, remained in Middlesex on land he controlled by virtue of his marriage to Elizabeth Smith, Wormeley's ward.[24] Then Christopher Robinson died. His 1693 will left his "true Friend Mr. William Churchhill" only his "best horse" and equipage. But the death left Churchill the principal executor of the estate and, for a brief time, of the Beverley estate as well. When Beverley's sons won control from him in 1694, there were only 528*li* in personalty and accounts receivable remaining.[25] Robinson's death also left Churchill heir to Robinson's English connections, most notably the Jeffreys of London, for whom Robinson had served as principal factor and who now looked to Churchill. Churchill seems also to have taken charge of Robinson's two minor sons, Christopher and John, and until they came of age in 1701 and 1703 respectively, of the lands devised to them by their father. Ralph Wormeley died in 1701 and two years later Churchill married his widow. Wormeley's sons, like the Robinson brothers, were minors—and in England at the time; hence Churchill moved onto Rosegill, adding its resources to his own, much to the dismay of at least one leading planter, who wrote complaining that "Churchills living upon the place together with his relations [connections] have given him the Opportunity to fix himself absolutely in [its] Government."[26]

Churchill's rise to preeminence on the one hand and, on the other, the presence in the county of three young sons of once preeminent fathers—Christopher and John Robinson, and Harry Beverley—set the stage for what followed. Churchill, together with Gawin Corbin from his plantation on the Rappahannock side of the upper precinct and Matthew Kemp on the Piankatank, dominated the trade of the county by virtue of their near-monopoly on the vital connections with English merchants. The young men seem to have seized upon the notion of a town as a vehicle by which to make such vital connections for themselves.

The issue was joined in June 1704 when Beverley and the Robinson brothers presented a petition to the county court asking that feoffees for the town be revived and themselves appointed.[27] Corbin, as one of the executors of Wormeley's will, and Churchill, "as marrying the Widdow," both members of the court, left the bench—an act carefully noted later as testimony to their "impartiallity" in a matter involving their own interest—and from the bar "offered such reasons against [the petition] as then occurred to them." Beverley and John Robinson, also justices, apparently kept their places, voted for their own petition, and saw it carry.[28] Exactly what Churchill and Corbin offered by way of argument is not stated. It is possible, but unlikely, that they propounded old Ralph's lordly "reservations," although certainly they cited those reservations and the forfeiture proceedings as putting at least a question mark on the county's title to the land. And we can only guess at what lay behind their opposition. Churchill's change of mind seems the key. He had been an advocate of the town and a feoffee himself in the 1690s when he was building his English connections. Now he, with Corbin and Kemp, had those connections secure and conceivably saw no need for a town.[29] Still, at this stage, the difference that had surfaced seems relatively minor.

Within two months, however, the affair became a major contretemps. The nagging question of a county courthouse had arisen again the year before when the justices realized that their lease of Wortham's building would soon expire and began considering "the best ways and meanes for the Speedy building and Erecting" of a new courthouse, referring the matter from one court to another. Finally, at an evening meeting on March 15, 1704, after earlier ordering the sheriff to "make Proclamacion" of their intent "to the end all work-men may have notice," they read aloud the specifications of the building they had in mind—the century's way of inviting bids on public works. They also designated justices John Smith, Harry Beverley, and John Robinson to survey a two-acre site for a courthouse in Smith's old field, a location on the main road a mile or so below the then-location at Wortham's. Pre-sumably, too, the three were to accept securities from which-ever workmen took up the contract and oversee the work.[30]

But Beverley and the Robinson brothers had a different idea—the town. Winning the feoffeeship in June and out-weighing John Smith on the committee, they ignored a July order of the court to get on with the business of the court-house as planned, suggested informally that a Robinson building near or on the town land could be fitted out for the court at a lower cost than building anew, and then, in August, petitioned "for the Courthouse to be built upon the Town land." At the same time, they asked that a public landing be established on the opposite side of Rosegill Creek from the town and for "maine roads" to be built "up and down the County," connecting the town to the network of existing roads. The landing entirely and the roads for the most part would perforce be built on Rosegill. In a heated session, the court rejected their petitions, agreed summarily with John Hipkins to build the courthouse for twenty-five thousand pounds of tobacco, and named Churchill, Smith, and John Grymes to lay out a site at Wortham's.[31]

In the aftermath of the court's action, something new in the ever-changing situation in the county shows itself. All of the principals in these affairs were men we earlier termed the cosmopolitan few, marked as such by status and wealth but more importantly by outlook—a comprehension, if you will, of a society and economy larger than the single county as a stage for their actions. But where, earlier, there had been among such men no great disjunction between economic and political influence, one now appeared. Churchill, Corbin, and Kemp controlled the economic ties that led outward from the county; the young men were virtually without such ties. Yet strands of kinship led outward from Robinsons and Beverleys to prominent families elsewhere in Virginia—to Peter Bever-

to the Main Road
and New Dragon Bridge

URBANNA

Rappahannock R.

Rosegill Creek

THE GREAT
HOUSE

PUBLIC
LANDING

WORMELEY'S
MILL

Road to the
Landing

the
Glebe

R O S E G I L L

to the
Middle Church

to Dragon
Bridge

the Road

to the
Ferry

COURTHOUSE

CHAZAUD

Urbanna and Vicinity

ley, for example, clerk of Gloucester County and at the time speaker of the House of Burgesses in Williamsburg; to William Byrd of Charles City County, whose sister Ursula had been wife to Robert Beverley the younger. Time and an inexorable demographic dynamic—fathers begetting sons who married wives from families of equivalent status anywhere in Virginia—were weaving an elaborate spiderweb of relationships at the highest level of Virginia's society. One consequence was that the young men had a political awareness and influence quite apart from the economic networks that tied Virginia to the commerce of the Atlantic. They lost no time utilizing their influence.

By September 1704 the young men had a petition before the governor and council in Williamsburg "complaining of diverse irregular Proceedings of the Court" in Middlesex. By October there was another, "praying the building of the courthouse may be stopped until the petitioners be heard." To the second was attached "a Paper signed by the Major part of the Freeholders" of the county, complaining that "the building of the . . . Court house in the Place appointed by the Court is a Grievance." The governor and council concurred with the second petition to the extent of ordering construction stopped until the whole matter could be disposed of by the general assembly. In February 1705 there was still a third petition from the three before the council, "praying" for authority to take "Depositions of witnesses for proving their Complaint against the Court." Either the council had had enough or, more likely, the counterinfluence of Churchill, Kemp, and Corbin finally proved effective. The council determined not "to meddle further" in the business and refused the last petition.[32]

We need not follow in all of its complexities the course of this dispute. As visitors dispassionately observing, we cannot help but be struck by the passions it evoked—that, for example, of John Robinson when he accused Matthew Kemp of drunkenness while sitting on the bench and Kemp's impassioned reply: He had, he said, always given "his due Attendance at all Courts . . . not being Misled nor Joyned in faction with any troublesome person to the hindrance or perplexing of the Court but doing Justice and Right to every person to the best of his Judgment always having regard to that Golden Rule do as he would be done to." At one juncture, four of the justices formally complained to the governor about a fifth as "a person most notorious by abusive, prophane, and Imoral Qualities, so misbecoming the seat of Justice, that we humbly desire to be excused Sitting with him." At another, Harry Beverley approached justice John Grymes as the latter sat under the mulberry trees outside the courthouse. Beverley complained that Grymes "had tax[ed] him with Something that he did not know nor had never read."

"You did," retorted Grymes from his seat.

"You lye!"

"Nay, you lye!"

With the last, Beverley raised his cane and struck. Grymes rose, his own cane in the air.

"Strike," shouted Beverley.

"No, I will not!"

"Hypocrite!" And Beverley struck again.[33]

Passions, however, should not detour us from essential elements of the matter. It was, as we have said, a quarrel among the cosmopolitan few, those who occupied the very highest niche in Virginia (not just Middlesex) society. But the county was inevitably drawn into the battling among its preeminent few and changed by the outcome.

The court was the arena of the internecine battling inasmuch as by law and tradition it had charge of the administration of county affairs such as courthouses, roads, and towns; when preeminent gentlemen argued about such things, they of necessity came to court to do it. Churchill and Christopher Robinson are clear examples. Each for his own reasons had formally withdrawn from the court earlier; each returned— Churchill to attend regularly during the period of the dispute until appointed to the council of the colony in 1705; Robinson only twice at crucial sessions, although he could always rely on the attendance of Beverley and his brother.[34] Their court an arena, the more county-oriented gentlemen-justices perforce took sides according to the ties that linked them to one group or the other. Thus John Hay stood with his brothers-in-law, the Robinsons, Roger Jones with Churchill, the godfather and namesake of his children (Churchill and Susannah Churchill Jones), and George Wortham with Churchill, his major creditor.

County men of lesser status—the plain freeholders and inhabitants—were caught up in the fray as well. The feoffees sent their friends "about the County to all meetings, horse-races and feasts and to Peoples houses" to solicit signatures to the "paper" they dispatched to the council in Williamsburg. As they had twenty years before with the petition for a tobacco stint, the few (in this case the feoffees) were appealing to an authority that they perceived as residing in the many to support their cause. The similarity did not escape their opponents. "We humbly Conceive that the nature of getting that Paper signed is illegal and looks with a face more like the beginning of the plant cutting year then a just grievance," the Churchillian majority on the court complained. "This County has Ever bin Esteemed to be the most United of any County in Virginia and never had any differences in it Self but in [that] year." But the majority, too, grounded its position in part on at least a presumption of general support. The courthouse location it preferred was "within a Small mile upon the Same Lyne the Courts has been kept ever since the division of the County without the least regrett or murmering and Generally thought by the people . . . to be the most Convenient place." "The people are well Satisfyed and Sees into the depth of the Selfe Interest Intrigues" of Beverley and the Robinsons.[35]

In still another way, the county as a whole seems to have been drawn into the dispute. When the affair began in 1704, Churchill and Corbin represented the county in Virginia's House of Burgesses, the lower house of the legislature. As chance would have it, new general elections were called for the fall of 1705, when the dispute was at its height. We have no knowledge of candidates or electioneering (except that Churchill, named to the governor's council that year, could not himself have stood for reelection), only the indirect evidence of results that the feoffees carried their case to the hustings. When the balloting was over, Christopher Robinson and Harry Beverley were the county's new burgesses, and

Gawin Corbin and Matthew Kemp, "in Behalf of Themselves and others the Freeholders," were unsuccessfully protesting the outcome.[36]

Whatever the appeals to the populace, however, it was the larger community of cosmopolitan gentlemen that resolved the affair, not the county. No less a personage than the attorney general of the colony came up to Middlesex in June and July of 1705 to gather depositions and prosecute Beverley for his breach of the peace in assaulting Grymes.[37] Earlier (in May) the feoffees' petitions had been considered in the House of Burgesses and debated at length, the house in the end attempting a compromise by ordering that the courthouse be built at Wortham's and that a road be laid out from the lower part of the county, across Rosegill, to a "Convenient Landing upon The Creek Side" opposite the site of the town.[38] The building of the courthouse proceeded rapidly, and by January 1706 the court was meeting in its new quarters. But the dispute continued as Churchill in particular fought the road and landing. Partisans of one side or the other refused to sit with their opponents, forcing adjournments for lack of a quorum. "The County begins to lye in confuestion for want of a Court," the sheriff (Kemp) complained in August; "Some actions has layn above a year, and cant be brought to tryall"; without a court soon, he went on, neither colony nor county levies could be assessed and collected.[39]

Again, the wider community acted. The governor and council first added new names to the court and, when that did not work, named a new court altogether. The quarreling continued. The road and landing were built, but the former was "stopt," presumably by Churchill. Petitions and cross-petitions were considered by the court. At one session in 1707, partisans of one side or the other challenged so many justices as parties interested in the outcome that a quorum was lost. Ultimately the whole matter was again referred to Williamsburg by way of a judicial appeal from a decision of the court—in this instance one adverse to Churchill, Corbin, and young Ralph Wormeley, who had come of age and was assuming control of his patrimony. The appeal was summarily denied. In 1708 young Ralph sought to carry still another appeal to

Williamsburg but without success.[40] The long affair was at an end, perhaps in part because by then Urbanna was a fact.

Through all the long controversy, the young men—Beverley and the Robinson brothers—never seem to have lost sight of what they were about. Between June 1704, when they were designated feoffees, and March 1708, twenty-three lots in the town were sold.[41] The long-empty town site throbbed with the sounds of hammers and saws as houses and outbuildings were erected. Indeed, with building going on so generally in the county, Middlesex's own force of carpenters and craftsmen seems to have been inadequate. Between 1706 and 1710, the number of tithables (laboring adults) in the county surged upward, then fell, forming a bulge in an otherwise roughly linear increase in the population, which can only be accounted for in terms of the temporary sojourn of itinerant laborers drawn or brought into the county to serve the building boom.[42]

As the feoffees had hoped, merchants were attracted to the town, minor merchants at the moment, but some would build rapidly from an Urbanna base. (The town finally received its name in 1706.) Among them were the Walker brothers, James and Richard. James, we know, had been involved in minor trading along the Rappahannock in Middlesex and Essex since 1698. In 1704 he was one of those circulating the feoffees' popular petition, and in November of that year he and his brother each bought lots in the town. Edmund Hamerton was another circulating the petition who bought a lot. A minor trader along the coast, he was a friend of the Walkers and at the same time something of an antagonist of Churchill, Kemp, and Corbin, against whom he had suits pending. Samuel Brown and his cousin William Gordon were attracted in from Maryland. Gordon, to judge from the inventory of his books following his death, might well have been a Catholic. Perhaps it was his presence that prompted the opponents of the town in the heat of 1704 to write of Urbanna's being intended as a "harbour for disaffected people."[43] Men from the county moved into the town as well. Christopher Robinson built a house there. So, too, did James Curtis, his cousin, whose farm abutted the town land on the south. In February 1707 Curtis was licensed "to keep an Ordinary at his dwelling house in the Burgh of Urbanna," giving bond to provide "good wholesome and Cleanly lodging and dyet for travelers and Stableage . . . for their Horses" and promising that he "Shall not Suffer or permitt any unlawful gameing in his house Nor on the Sabboth day to Suffer any person to Tipple or drink more than is Necessary." By August of that year, there was a second ordinary licensed, and Curtis was appointed "Constable for the City of Urbanna."[44]

"City," of course, was simply a grandiloquent embellishment. At the time, Urbanna straggled along the creekside, not half its lots built upon; at its zenith later in the century, it would be no more than what a traveler called Yorktown, "a delicat Village" encompassing at the most no more than thirty houses, a hundred-odd buildings if all its kitchens, warehouses, stores, and sundry outbuildings were counted. But even then it would appear to a visitor as simply an extension of the countryside. Chickens scratched in its dusty streets, scurrying away from the hoofs of passing horses. Cows grazed its backyards. We have already met Thomas Tuke; his home and tailor shop of the 1720s were in the town, as were his cow, calf, and heifer. In the 1730s, the physician John Mitchell's two-acre lot would boast a barn for his horse, vegetable and herb gardens, fruit trees, and a "physic garden," where he grew the medicinal plants that he processed into the emetics, purges, lenitives, and alexipharmics he prescribed to his patients and sold in his apothecary shop.[45]

To some extent, the growth of Urbanna—and of the other small trading towns appearing in Virginia at about the same time—is to be associated with colonywide efforts to improve the quality of Virginia's export. In 1713 and again in 1730, these efforts took the form of warehouse acts. The first, pried from Virginia's legislature by the then-governor, Alexander Spotswood, required that public warehouses be constructed throughout Virginia and that all tobacco used in payment of taxes or debts be delivered to a warehouse for inspection by tobacco agents who, if they found it acceptable, would hold the tobacco, issuing receipts or notes that could pass as money until ultimately used to redeem the tobacco for export.[46] Virginians of all sorts objected to the act, lesser planters complaining of the fees that the agents were to collect, major planters of both the fees and the fact that tobacco—even theirs—would pass through public facilities on its way to market rather than through their own warehouses and docks. Once again, in what was becoming the timeworn way of Virginia, the major planters appealed to the populace, and, in assembly elections in 1715, most of those who had supported the act in the legislature were ousted. The appeal fired the populace, inspiring agitated meetings that here and there gave over to riot, the sheriff of Essex County, Middlesex's sister to the north, writing of "the peoples' inclinations . . . so great against The Tobacco law that they have not meet me to pay their Dues [levies]" and signifying "Their Dissatisfaction" further "by burning one of Mr. Buckners' Storehouses, with some Tobacco and his Scales in it." Yet, inevitably, resolution came apart from the populace. The major planters complained to their English merchant friends, who pressured the government overseas into disallowing the act in 1717.[47] Within thirteen years, however, the major planters of the colony and the English tobacco merchants had undergone a change of mind. With their support, the second warehouse act was passed (in 1730), a near duplicate of the first but with even stronger provisions for inspection, including the burning of inferior tobacco by the agents.[48] The act survived English scrutiny and became a permanent part of the Virginia scene.

All of this history was echoed in Middlesex. The Robinson brothers represented the county in the legislature that passed the 1713 act, Christopher having served from 1705, John from 1710. The brothers supported the governor and were rewarded for it, Christopher contracting to build Middlesex's warehouse and a dock in Urbanna for an annual rental of three thousand pounds of tobacco or fifteen pounds current money, John moving into Urbanna in 1713 and assuming the position and fees of agent when the act went into force in November 1714.[49] Cleavages among the gentlemen show themselves in petitions submitted from Middlesex to the legislature. In 1714 some of the county's gentlemen asked that tobacco agents be prohibited from trading on their own account or serving as a factor for others, a provision that would have reduced John's agency to little more than a clerk's role. The next year the

gentlemen asked that a second warehouse be designated for
Middlesex, to be erected outside Urbanna, presumably in the
lower precinct where so many of the major holdings in the
county were located.[50] There is no evidence of rioting in the
county, but in the elections of 1715 the brothers were both
ousted from the legislature. Edmund Hamerton, who had
failed in Urbanna and had settled for marriage to an upper
precinct widow, and William Blackburn, a middling planter
from the lower precinct, were returned to a short session of
the legislature in 1715, while major planters Gawin Corbin
and John Grymes replaced Hamerton and Blackburn for the
next session in 1718. The 1730 act, establishing public warehouses in Middlesex at both Urbanna and on Kemp property
in the lower end—the major planters had their way in this
respect—provoked no ripple of controversy in the county.

The benefits accruing to Urbanna by virtue of the warehouse acts were conceivably many. From late 1714 through
1717 and again after 1730, tobacco flowed into the town as a
matter of law, its presence there in quantity, together with
facilities for ready loading and unloading, attracting ships to
the town. The boon to any stores that might be established in
the town was twofold. The ships attracted to the town carried
in English goods, while the county men carrying their tobacco
to the warehouses were ready customers for them. The tobacco
notes, moreover, constituted a handy medium of exchange;
the county man had only to pass over notes in payment of
goods or old store debts, while storekeepers need only keep
the notes, leaving the tobacco in the warehouse until the ships
arrived, then redeeming inspected and approved hogsheads
to make an outward-bound cargo.

Nevertheless, we ought not overestimate the effect of the
acts in forwarding the town. Urbanna was devoted to stores
and storekeepers from the very beginning, that is, from before
the act of 1713, and was already dominant in the trade of the
county by 1730 and the second warehouse act. Indeed, the
ready acceptance of the second act can be accounted for in
part by the fact that, in effect, it was legislation attuned to an
existing situation.

The earliest merchants attracted to the town—the Walkers, Hamerton, Brown, Gordon—used it initially as a base from

which to conduct the itinerant trading to which they were accustomed, all running sloops along the Rappahannock and across the bay to the eastern shore. Brown died soon after arriving. Hamerton, as we noted, failed; undercapitalized and overindebted, he seems to have stopped trading by 1710. But Gordon and the Walker brothers succeeded. And more and more they came to rely less on their itinerant trading than on the settled trade of the county, sinking their capital into goods and maintaining stocks of tools and cloth and luxuries the like of which had not been matched in the county before. Gordon's—"William Gordon and Company" as early as 1707—had not only the usual assortment of nails and such in stock when Gordon died in 1720, but pewter plates and spoons, shoemakers' tools in abundance, earthenware, eyeglasses, forty-four dozen coat buttons, calico curtains and valances, "one pound and a gram of Indigo," Madeira wine and French brandy, "eighteen paper pictures," and even six "flower potts"—an inventory of almost five hundred separate items "In the store" alone.[51] The Walkers' store inventory was too diverse even to be listed in detail by the appraisers following James's death in 1721; they simply entered a single item of 406*li* value. Richard's inventory (1727) and the careful instructions that he inserted in his will to guide his executors in finishing the year's business afford a glimpse of the operations of a store. On the one hand, Richard bought goods in England, added a 25 percent markup, and put them on sale in Urbanna; on the other, he bought tobacco for shipment on account to a number of separate English merchants, paying 12*s* 6*d* per hundred pounds tobacco if cash was what the seller wanted, but preferring to pay in store goods or credit, for which he offered a premium 16*s* 6*d*. The latter allowed him a double profit, first on the tobacco, and secondly on the marked-up goods.[52]

Energetic and astute men, Gordon and the Walker brothers were committed to trade, specialists if you will, devoting their lives to their craft. With their profits, they obtained land and laborers, Gordon in 1710 purchasing 400 acres in the middle precinct, adding an adjoining 350 acres in 1712. When he died, he owned thirty-one black slaves and seven white servants. James Walker, at his death, had land and blacks in Middlesex and Essex counties; Richard, 1,400 acres in Spotsylvania.

The merchants linked themselves to the county by marriage. James Walker, for example, married Clara Robinson, sister of Christopher and John, in 1707. Ultimately they took seats on the court and vestry (Gordon excepted, another hint of his Catholicism). But they lived in Urbanna; trade and the operation of their stores were always their paramount concerns. In this they differed from, and gained an immediate advantage over, planter-merchants like Churchill who had dominated the county's trade earlier but for whom merchandizing had been simply one of many ways to profit. It was not, however, their only advantage.

Their stores offered variety to the men and women of Middlesex and a more stable source of goods than had the planter-merchants. A Middlesex man (or his wife) in need of a particular item could count more readily on its immediate availability and judge its quality on the spot. Indeed, Say's Law seems applicable in the sense that the rich supply of goods offered in Urbanna's stores provoked demands that planter-merchants, operating their own stores more casually, could not meet. The stores offered ready credit as well, actually pursuing store accounts; recall that by virtue of Walker's pricing policy our Middlesex man and his wife could buy a third more in goods by promising tobacco in payment than they could paying cash. Six volumes of Gordon's store accounts dating from 1708 to 1720 testify to the extent of the network of credit emanating so quickly from Urbanna.[53] The very size of the operations of the stores, moreover, and the limited number of middlemen involved tended to free their debtors from harassment. Accepting credit from a Mickleburrough in the 1690s, for example, tied one to a complex network of transactions inasmuch as Mickleburrough was simply one of many indebted to Churchill, who in turn was a creditor to many and himself indebted to English merchants; should Churchill fall behind for some reason—perhaps because the death of a major debtor, by throwing the estate into probate, delayed payment to him—he would be pressed by his English connections and would in turn press Mickleburrough, who would press his debtors. Notably the Urbanna merchants were involved in few suits for debt before the county court, while Churchill and Mickleburrough had been regularly before the court as both defendants and plaintiffs.

Given such advantages, Urbanna and its stores brought about a reorientation of the internal trade of the county, one strengthened, not inspired by the Warehouse Act of 1730. Major planters retained their own connections to English merchants, sending tobacco on consignment and buying English goods for themselves directly. But as Urbanna rose, the evidence of their retailing to their Middlesex neighbors declined. Small stores still sprinkled the countryside, although even they changed character, being more reflections of Urbanna's establishments in the variety of their stock and the single-minded attachment to trade of their owners than continuations of Mickleburrough's casual trading. Even peddlers made their appearance, stocking pack animals in Urbanna, then crying up a trade in small goods along the more remote roads and paths of the county and beyond.[54] But a new sequence of hegemonies appeared to serve the small and middle planters, successors to but different from the hegemonies of Burnham, Beverley, the first Robinson, and Churchill in being town-based rather than plantation-based: Gordon and the Walker brothers until 1720, Christopher Robinson II as Gordon's principal executor and Richard Walker until both died in 1727, James Reid and Patrick Cheap thereafter. The last—Reid and Cheap—were even more single-minded in their devotion to trade than their immediate predecessors. Entering the county from Scotland in the mid-1720s and remaining unmarried until their deaths (Cheap in the 1740s, Reid in the 1760s), they never owned more in the way of land than their Urbanna lots.

Let us return for a moment to William Churchill. While in Williamsburg in 1709, he was the butt of what passed for a practical joke among the young men of the capital. William Byrd jotted the incident down in his diary: "We drank some of Will Robinson's cider till we were very merry and then went to the coffeehouse and pulled poor Colonel Churchill out of bed." It was apparently so much fun that a few nights later "We Were very merry and in that condition went to the coffeehouse and again disturbed Colonel Churchill." Perhaps such rowdiness was on the old man's mind when, a year later, he wrote his will. Or perhaps he was thinking of the rowdiness that the Robinson brothers and Harry Beverley had injected into Middlesex as they fought for Urbanna; for Churchill stipulated that he be buried "without any great doeings, Saveing a funerall Sermon to Admonish the Liveing upon these words, 'Set thine house in Order for thou shalt dye and not Live.'" And he bestowed one hundred pounds sterling on Christ Church parish to pay for quarterly sermons against "the four reigning Vices vizt Aetheism and Irreligion, Swearing and Curseing, fornication and Adultry, and Drunckeness."[55]

Obviously we cannot read too much into the scene of an old man plagued by tipsy carousers. One thing seems clear, however; Churchill was of a type opposite enough from that of his bedevilers to make rousing him from his bed a merry prank. And it is the hint of two types among the cosmopolitan gentlemen that is of interest.

Churchill was a planter-merchant, one of a breed of men who spent their lives, in Wordsworth's phrase, "getting and spending," entrepreneurs who dealt diffusively from a plantation base in lands, laborers, and goods, always ready to chance sixpence here to make a shilling there. But in Middlesex we see the hyphenated "planter-merchant" rapidly dissolving into its component parts during the first decades of the eighteenth century, into merchants like Reid and Cheap on the one hand and planters like Armistead Churchill, old William's son, on the other. Armistead did not trade as his father had. He was content to direct the operation of his plantations and live off the produce eked from the land by his blacks, hedging against the future by investing in more land in the western counties, but leaving retailing to the storekeepers.

The trend coincided with another. Young men born in the Chesapeake to wealthy fathers—Armistead, for example—were coming of age. Born into an ever more extended lineage as demographic forces expanded their numbers and inheritance spread them throughout the Virginia landscape, to masterdom in a world of slaves, to wealth in a society in which the extremes of wealth were growing apart, and to the relatively certain economy of planting as specialized merchants assumed the risks of trade, the very character of the sons seemed to be emerging as something other than that which we sense in their fathers. A commentator later in the century wrote to the point: "The son being made a Gentleman by the Negroes and Land given him by his father . . . This son, full of his own merit, and elevated with the figure he cuts in the world, and with his own importance, immediately assumes the swaggering air and looks big." The fault, the writer continued, was "the notion early imbibed of their being born rich." For "riches are of deadly mischief." They "render a man proud; inspire him with contempt for labour, and make him haughty."[56] The elements of this character have been presaged here and there in passing: in Wormeley's aloof baronialism, in the haughty violence displayed by Beverley in the course of his assault on Grymes, and, indeed, in the whole of the young men's audacious insistence on having their town. But only as we extend our visit in time and move farther into the eighteenth century does the character become truly distinct.

8. Circles

Every individual of the human race has a circle whereof
he is the centre, from the king to the beggar; but when
out of that place they become of no account, and so it is
in this County, for a man is great, learned and wise in
the sphere of his friends and relations, but elsewhere he
is a mere cypher.

— James Reid. *The Religion of the Bible And Religion of
K.W. County Compared*

TRAVEL THE ROAD from the
Essex boundary southeastward toward Stingray Point again.
Time—some seventy years—has passed since we traveled it in
the late 1660s. The imprint of men and women on the land is
considerably greater than it was then. The woods are still about
us as we walk, at some places untouched, virginal, but elsewhere second-growth scrub coming up in "old fields" left idle
after years of tobacco and corn to allow reinvigoration by a
long fallow. There are more openings in the woods, too, more
farms and plantations. In all there are some 280-odd families
in the county, where in 1668 there had been just over 80. And
the network of roads and paths linking them forms a more
elaborate web. There is even something of a second main road
crossing the old one halfway between Mickleburrough's bridge
and the courthouse. Coming to the crossing from the northwest and turning to the left would lead us down the neck of
land formed by Robinson's Creek and the Rappahannock on
the one side and Rosegill Creek on the other to Urbanna;
turning to the right, the road would lead us to a new bridge
across the Dragon, built in 1718, then on into King and Queen
County. The bridge effectively enhanced Urbanna's hinter-

land, and, like so much involving the town, it had stirred controversy. Harry Beverley and some other "well disposed persons" had proposed its construction, even agreeing to build it at their own cost; the Middlesex court had refused; Beverley had carried the matter to the Virginia assembly in Williamsburg, obtaining from that august body special legislation allowing the work.[1]

For the most part, the fields we pass as we walk the road look as they looked before—hills of corn and tobacco among rotting stumps, crooked rail fences, and ramshackle tobacco houses. But there are occasional oxen now, pulling carts or hogsheads of tobacco or, in the spring, plows. Here and there we spy a field completely cleared of stumps, the soil turned and dressed with plow and harrow. (Were the stumps laboriously removed when green? Or, more likely, simply knocked out when well rotted? We do not know for certain.)

Some of the fields sport wheat now, "English grain" as distinguished from "Indian corn." Old Ralph Wormeley was growing winter wheat as early as the 1680s, planting in the late fall, grazing livestock on the mid-winter shoots, then harvesting in the spring. The presence "in the Barne" of a pair of "French Burr millstones" when Rosegill was inventoried in 1701 indicates that he intended grinding wheat as well as corn in his mill.[2] At the turn of the century, too, Thomas Landon sought to make his livelihood raising wheat on rented ground. Unfortunately, William Gardner thought so little of Landon's oxen that he shot one for its meat. Landon prized the beast at twenty-five pounds sterling and sued for damages; a jury awarded him only six, three times the value of a cow. Shortly thereafter Landon died, ending the experiment.[3] In the eighteenth century, roughly one out of ten inventories from the county lists the wherewithal for the cultivation of wheat—plows, plow chains, harrows, oxen—the proportion steadily increasing with time. Most reflect larger than average estates; a few suggest that the owners rented out the oxen and equipage to neighbors. Still, Middlesex in 1740 remains essentially a part of the "tobacco coast." Wheat, like corn, although traded locally, is primarily for home consumption. Tobacco is the export crop.

The houses we pass are also much the same as they were, "Virginia common built" houses, more often than not one or

two rooms and a loft, of weathering wood and inevitably in
some degree of disrepair. Some are larger and more elaborate than others, boasting brick end chimneys and founda-
tions, two full stories, occasionally a jutting "porch room" with
its "little room above," the structure set in the midst of a clut-
ter of outbuildings. The largest and most elaborate of the
houses cannot be seen from the road. These are the houses
of the preeminent gentlemen, fronting on the rivers and
approachable only by long paths or by boat. Even at this date
most are, like Rosegill, of wood. The great brick piles we normally associate with early Virginia—the Robinsons' "Hewick"
just upriver from Urbanna, for example—are for the most
part still to be built.

For all the sameness, however, Middlesex is not the same.
Walking the road in our imagination we see evidence of the
greatest single difference: blacks laboring in the fields where
once there were whites. When we assume the omniscient role
of historian, we sense other changes, some of which we have
already traced in detail: the greater profusion of goods in the
houses of the county, but also the greater disparity in wealth
between rich and poor, the former, in effect, growing away
from the latter and, indeed, increasingly separating themselves even from the middling sort; the presence of Urbanna
as a retail center for all but those few major planters who
retained their own connections to English merchants. There
are, however, other differences.

The county, for one thing, was regularly losing white population where once it received it. Newcomers still entered, true.
But more left than arrived. In absolute numbers, the net loss
does not seem particularly important. Just after the turn of
the century, the white population had peaked at around 1,440
persons and some 308 families; by 1740 there were roughly
100 fewer whites and 279 families. Yet absolute numbers hide
the full extent of the exodus. Those leaving—15 to 25 a year
from 1720 to 1750—were more often than not young married adults who, had they not left, would have added their
own families to the count of families and their children to the
total count. With the young leaving, the mean age of those
remaining was a bit higher, and, given the natural course of

things demographic, this group tended on average to add fewer children to the population.[4] The true loss, in other words, was the absolute loss plus what would have been gained had there been no loss at all.

That Middlesex would have come to the point of losing its sons and daughters is not at all surprising. The county was a developing cluster of farms and plantations on the edge of what was thought of as an empty wilderness. We cannot read into the mentality of our people a driving urge to exploit the vastness. They were innately conservative, concerned with the mundane affairs of farms, families, and neighborhoods, rather than consumed with a desire to follow what we would conceive to be the main chance to self-aggrandizement. Neither can we, in talking about emigration from the county, leave the impression that ours were or were becoming a restlessly mobile people. The continuity of family names in the county is one indication of the opposite. When, in 1783, after the American Revolution, an enumeration of Middlesex was undertaken, 60 percent of the family names listed dated to the period before the establishment of Urbanna (1706), 82 percent to that before 1750.[5] Of the "new" family names, moreover, fully half were new only in the sense of men from outside the county entering to marry county women. And while the very nature of our study of a single place precludes following any significant number of emigrants out of the county—hence we cannot say as a matter of fact what in the main befell them—it is far more likely that the young married couples leaving Middlesex soon encapsulated themselves in new neighborhoods rather than spent their lives wandering here and there.[6]

That said, however, we must nevertheless acknowledge the impact of the empty continent upon our people, indeed, upon all the ordinary Englishmen who came as farmers to the Anglo-American coast stretching from New England through the Chesapeake and southward. For notably we are talking about a general process. Word of new areas opening to the west, carried into established neighborhoods, was an offer of release from perceived difficulties, and impatient men everywhere seized upon the succor proferred.[7] To the men of York in the 1650s, the peninsula that became Middlesex had itself been such an offer; King and Queen, Spotsylvania, and Albemarle served the same purpose to the men of Middlesex as the eighteenth century progressed.

Equally to the point is the fact that perceived difficulties were bound to increase as our (or any) cluster of farms developed, an inevitable concomitant of fathers begetting sons in an essentially agricultural and finite area. We noted the phenomenon earlier, citing the Daniells as an example—William Daniell, the founder of the family in Middlesex, who divided 600 acres among four sons, and his grandson Robert, who had 340 acres and six sons. An analysis of 152 wills of fathers with lands to bequeath and two or more sons is indicative of the general trend in the county. In wills dated through 1699, 93 percent of the younger sons were provided with Middlesex land, a percentage dropping to 71 in wills dated 1700 to 1719, and to 62 in those dated after 1719.[8] At least in Middlesex primogeniture as a custom seems to an extent a product of population growth and a maturing landscape.

The well-to-do who had land in several counties could provide for their younger sons. Recall Ralph Wormeley's bequeathing Rosegill to his first son, Ralph, and York County lands to John. Such divisions were a commonplace among the better sort, although as the century progressed more and more bequests involved partially developed or undeveloped lands in the interior counties. The son of a less well-to-do father, left landless, could perhaps gain control of land at home by marrying the daughter of a father without sons or, in this land of early death, a landed widow of the neighborhood. Failing that, he could only leave the county altogether, departing with a wife and in some cases young children in the hope of replicating elsewhere the rise to landed status of his father or grandfather. For to remain landless in the county was to face a grim future.

Slavery clearly exacerbated the population loss inevitable in our maturing county. We saw that as the county took "the negro road" the microeconomics of the farm shifted to the disadvantage of the lesser sort, that slavery was a matter of winners and losers, and that on occasion losers left the county. Zacharias Gibbs comes to mind, leaving with his own family and in company with his sisters and their families for Spotsylvania rather than rebuild a labor force decimated by epidemic.

When we consider the options open to the landless of the county we see the impact of slavery again. Perspicacious parents (or the county court if a son were orphaned early) might bind a boy to a craftsman to learn a trade. But for all the talk earlier of towns encouraging crafts, it did not happen to any great extent in Middlesex. And whatever was gained in the way of crafts by virtue of Urbanna was all but negated as the slave population grew and, at least on the larger holdings, native-born blacks began to be put to trades. Thomas Smith's will of 1723, for example, referred to his Bob as "bound to a Carpinter" and Tom "who is to be bound to a trade." The comment of a later governor (1766) points to the end product of the trend: "Every Gentleman of much property in Land and Negroes, have some of their own Negroes bred up in the Trade of black-smiths, and make axes, Hoes, plough shares, and such kind of coarse Work for the use of their Plantations. I do not know that there is a white-smith or maker of Cutlery in the Colony."[9] The landless son might rent, but, again, as the slave population grew, opportunities tended to be foreclosed. More and more, properties once rented or put out on shares by the well-to-do over time became quarters worked by blacks. In desperation the young man might incorporate himself into the very system that so restricted his options and become an overseer—the opportunity for escape from his difficulties that Benjamin Davis appears to have spurned. But even this might take the youth out of Middlesex. Benjamin Pace, the third son of John Pace, after struggling in the county for a number of years, left with his wife and four children to oversee a King and Queen County quarter being opened by Edwin Thacker.

In still another way, we see the impact of slavery on the emigration of whites. Those prospering with slaves tended to enlarge their holdings, buying or taking for debt and merging with their own the lands of less prosperous neighbors. Freeholds, in effect, like tenancies, were transformed into slave quarters for an ever-growing black population. One small neighborhood located on either side of the main road five miles below the Lower Church illustrates this phenomenon, although in exaggerated terms. In 1704 the twelve landed families of the neighborhood, their holdings ranging from John Mann's 460 acres to John Sandeford's 130, were already hemmed in by the lands of paramount families: William Churchill's principal holding (1,250 acres) and that of the Kemps (1,200) to the west, to the east one of the many Middlesex properties of the Armisteads of Gloucester and another Churchill plantation. Two decades later, only one of the original families remained, and there were but four freeholds in all. Even at the time, the exodus of white families was such as to cause concern, a petition of 1727 commenting on the high proportion of blacks in the county in general, but emphasizing the lower precinct, where "the meaner sort of the people (in whom consists the strength of all Countrys) are daily moving higher up, so that there is some danger of this Extream part of the Country being entirely abandon'd by them."[10]

As important as the loss of families, however, was a change in the social air of the county. We sense it when, as visitors, we consider our own appearance. Before when, in imagination, we traveled the roads of the county in the hopes of seeing its various facets, we had minimal concern for our dress and demeanor. Now we had better have maximum concern or chance being denied admission to all but the lowliest house. We must heed the advice given in 1738 to John Bartram, a Pennsylvania Quaker, by an English correspondent. "Make up thy drugget Cloths, to go to Virginia," Bartram's friend wrote. "I should not esteem thee the less, to come to me in what dress thou will,—yet those Virginians are a very gentle, well dressed people—and look perhaps more at a man's outside than his inside. For these and other reasons go very clean, neat, and handsomely dressed." Emulating Devereux Jarratt leaving his New Kent County neighborhood in the early 1750s to make his way in the world, we ought to buy ourselves wigs "that [we] might appear something more than common, in a strange place, and be counted somebody." The fact that we come as scholars might serve us to an extent. Philip Fithian, a New Jerseyite in Virginia as a tutor later in the century, tells us as much. Virginians, he wrote home in 1774, "are exalted as much above other Men in worth and precedency, as blind stupid fortune has made a difference in their property; excepting always the value they put upon posts of honour and mental acquirements." "If you should travel through this Colony, with a well-confirmed testimonial of your having finished with Credit a Course of studies at Nassau-Hall [Princeton]; you would be rated, without any more questions asked, either about your family, your Estate, your business, or your intention, at 10,000 *li;* and you might come, and go, and converse, and keep company according to this value; and you would be dispised and slighted if yo[u] rated yourself a farthing cheaper." But scholarship would carry us only so far. An array of idle accomplishments was coming to define the gentle-born, and we would inevitably fail the ultimate test. Fithian again: "Any young gentleman travelling through the Colony . . . is presum'd to be acquainted with Dancing, Boxing, playing the Fiddle, and Small-Sword, and cards; . . . and if you stay here any time your Barrenness in these must be detected."[11]

The new air was a surface manifestation of deeper changes in the fabric of the society. In the seventeenth century—that is, before the county took "the negro road"—the social world that was Middlesex can be described in terms of concentric circles centered on individual families. Living within a settled family, the individual looked out at the families immediately about in the neighborhood, a comfortable circle of friends and kin (and increasingly the latter). The precinct embraced a second, wider circle of families at least familiar from regular encounters at church and militia musters. Court day involved one with a still larger circle, although more often than not a circle of mere acquaintances, persons not quite familiar but not entirely strange either. There were servants, true, but *white* servants, largely English, sharing a common culture with the settled families, if not their freedom, and common aspirations. Surviving servitude, they would seek land, marriage, children, and the companionship of a neighborhood. There were, too, the cosmopolitan few—Burnhams, Beverleys, Robinsons, Wormeleys, and the like. With their properties and relations increasingly scattered across several counties, with connections to English merchant houses, and with access to the politics of Jamestown, the few were part of a circle of their own, the circumference of which exceeded the little society of the county. And yet, with the exception of Wormeley, they remained a part of the everyday life of Middlesex. One could rent land from Mr. Burnham, buy a hoe from Mr. Beverley's store promising tobacco from a future crop, or take corn to Mr. Robinson's mill, paying his miller a toll out of what was ground. Among the county-oriented families, there were gradations of wealth and status. But no person was so far removed from oneself as to be unapproachable. Gradations, moreover, were not immutably fixed. Ex-servants became freedmen, and some even gained a middling rank in the society. Some of the middling sort culminated a life of service to the county with a seat on the justices' bench or among the vestrymen, or both, there to rub elbows, so to speak, with the most esteemed of men, sharing to at least an extent in their highest status.

History being essentially a narrative and the human affairs narrated being a matter of process—of the perpetual flowering of what was and the seed of what is to be—we must admit immediately that this depiction of Middlesex catches only a single moment of time. Forced to date it, we would choose 1681 and the duty visit Jane Olney paid to the deathbed of John Burnham. Among so many things, the scene shows clearly that at least at that moment the distance between the preeminent (Burnham) and the common sort (Jane) was not so great as to bar whatever Christian charity or curiosity prompted Jane's husband to bid her "goe down to see" if Burnham "was dead or alive."

By the 1730s and 1740s, such a visit as Jane's would be unlikely, and a description of Middlesex in terms of concentric circles inappropriate. Race, rank, and commerce had imposed a different geometry, one of tangential circles.

In and between their separate quarters, the blacks lived out their lives. Contemporaries saw them at work among themselves, "very busy at framing together a small House" on a Sunday, a day on which they did not labor for the master, "digging up their small Lots of ground allow'd by their Masters for Potatoes, peas, &c," and setting out at night along "the Negro road" to "meet together and amuse themselves with Dancing to the Banjo" and satirizing in song "the usage they have received from their Masters or Mistresses."[12] The discerning eye of the historian dissects the entries in a master's diary and thereby glimpses the complicated web of personal relationships in their quarters forming circles that touch upon but never really encompass the family in the great house.[13] The blacks shared the land with the whites, but not at this point in time a culture.

In Urbanna the storekeepers and tradesmen lived largely within circles of their own. Town and countryside met to bargain goods for tobacco. Townsmen watched the weather and were aware when "the first glut" of tobacco worms attacked the crop, for the economy was unified and what affected the farms and plantations affected the town. But the townsman's interest in such things was less immediate than that of the countryman who must hurry to pinch the worms from the leaves (or send his blacks to do it) else lose a crop. Townsmen eyed with more concern the overall size of the Chesapeake tobacco crop and its effect on the market overseas, the ebb and flow of prices, and the comings and goings of ships. And they acted in concert in their own interest, the Urbanna merchants in 1727, for example, petitioning the governor to remove the customshouse from the home of a major planter and place it in the town as "the most proper and Convenient place" inasmuch as "the far greater part of the Tobacco Exported from this River, is purchased in the Country for merchants at home" by the men of Urbanna. Not a single countryman (as distinct from townsman) was among the signers.[14]

For their part, the cosmopolitan families, masters of many slaves, lived in increasing splendor but were increasingly isolated from the lesser families. They were "of Middlesex"— that was where they lived—and they took precedence within the county. But with their lands and kin and connections elsewhere they could as easily be "of Gloucester," "of Essex," or "of Caroline." The Corbins are an example. Concomitant with Urbanna's rise, Gawin Corbin turned his attention more and more to King and Queen County, where his second wife had property; then, sometime before 1720, he moved his residence there completely, returning to Middlesex only periodically to oversee the overseers of his lands along the

Rappahannock. In the mid-1730s, a Corbin was again "of Middlesex," in the person of Gawin's son Richard, who moved onto the family land. But in 1745 Richard moved out and again there was no Corbin "of Middlesex."

Their apartness was more a matter of mundane things, however, With blacks to labor for them, the cosmopolitan gentlemen sought no laborers from the county, and few sharecroppers or renters relative to the numbers sought a half-century before, only overseers. Urbanna, moreover, had largely usurped the gentlemen's economic role as retailers to their neighbors. County families—those without their own connections to English merchants—dealt now with Reid and Cheap, not with an Armistead Churchill. Or, to put the point the other way, Armistead did not deal with his neighbors as his father had and was the more apart from them because of it. And apartness in fact was matched by a growing apartness in attitude. In 1733, for example, the vestry gave permission to John Grymes, "in behalf of himself Mr. Wormely's, Colonel Churchill's and Major Berkeley's families," and to Armistead Churchill and Edmund Berkeley, "in behalf of themselves, Colonel Grymes's and Mr Wormely's families," to build small additions to the Middle and Lower churches at their own expense—small wings where these most preeminent of men and their ladies might have pews separate from, indeed, not even visible to, the body of the congregation. Equally to the point, the same families were to have private wings at *both* the Lower and Middle churches. Neighborhoods and precincts had no meaning for the cosmopolitan sort. The minister circulated among the three churches of the parish, administering to each in turn: the gentlemen would be driven in their carriages or phaetons to either of two churches and miss the minister's service only one week out of three.[15]

Yet there were still the neighborhoods, circles unto themselves of purely county families, some eking out a slim living (or trying to) from a few acres without bound labor, most with slaves of their own, even a few with many blacks, but none with the great wealth and wide outlook of the cosmopolitan families. Some of the neighborhoods, particularly in the lower and middle precincts, were hemmed in by large holdings worked by blacks. Within neighborhoods, families lost members regularly to emigration—John Minor and his sister Diana (Minor) Goodloe, for example, grandchildren of the Elizabeth Montague whose wedding we attended in 1671, left for Spotsylvania in the early 1730s. But kinship and friendship among the families remaining still form tight clusters when plotted on a modern map. We readily envision the neighborhood matrons gathering to gossip, supporting each other in childbirth, and families and friends coming together for weddings, clustering about deathbeds. And now there was a new reason to gather. Devereux Jarratt, having left his New Kent neighborhood as a youth of nineteen, returned for a visit a few years later and recalled in old age the ensuing celebration: "My brothers and their wives, and all the black people on the plantation, seemed overjoyed at my coming. . . . Nothing was thought too good for me, which their houses afforded. . . . A considerable company of people, of different sexes and ages" gathered "for the purpose of drinking cider and dancing. . . . Without [doors], the tankard went briskly round, while the sound of music and dancing was heard within."[16]

Tangential circles—circles that touch each other but circumscribe no common area: In the way of metaphors, the imagery exaggerates when applied to the web of relationships found in Middlesex in the third and fourth decades of the century. "The blacks on the plantation," in Jarratt's recollection, joined his brothers and their wives in greeting his return. The men of separate neighborhoods came together for militia musters, and neighborhood men and women met at the churches for services part social, part religious. The importance attached to the last is indicated by a bid for an independent parish on the part of "sundry Freeholders and Inhabitants" of the upper precinct in 1736. We alluded to the petition in our first chapter when stipulating the central question that we carried into our visit to Middlesex: What form did communities take in the Chesapeake? Now all falls into place.

The scene is reminiscent of 1657 when Henry Corbin brought together the heads of families of the upper part of the peninsula to begin the process that led to the formation of old Lancaster Parish. In 1736 Edwin Thacker played Corbin's role. The third generation of the name in the county,

Thacker was wealthy, a member of the court and vestry, and
even at the moment opening land across the Dragon in King
and Queen. But he was still a county man in orientation, trading through Urbanna and tied by kinship and friendship to
other Thackers (his cousin Henry, for one), to Vivions, Prices,
Seagers, Montagues—county families all and for the most part
upper precinct families. Their precinct was by far the largest
at the moment, encompassing almost half the white families
of the county; indeed, at the very meeting at which the vestry
voted to allow the cosmopolitan gentlemen their private wings,
it had acknowledged the overcrowding of the Upper Church
and voted funds for an addition that almost doubled its size.
Yet some of the upper precinct families felt they were getting
short shrift from the vestry. Their church (and its addition)
were of wood, the others brick. Where previous to 1728 the
parish had appointed three churchwardens, one for each precinct, it had since that date appointed only two to serve at
large; since 1732, none had been an upper precinct man. And
following the death in 1734 of Bartholomew Yates, the parish
minister for thirty-one years (and Thacker's uncle), the minister seems to have given his attention largely to the Middle
and Lower churches, riding up-county only one week in four,
if that. In August 1736, probably at Thacker's on the south
side of Sunderland Creek, roughly two miles from the site of
Corbin's earlier meeting on the north side, the disaffected
upper precinct men met to frame their petition to the legislature. Stipulating their "great Grievance" in being without
regular services, they asked to be set off as a separate parish.
The petition was ultimately denied, although perhaps it had
some effect. In November the then-minister announced he
was leaving the parish, and the vestry ordered the churchwardens to write to Yates's son, then in England, "to desire him
immediately to come over."[17] The point, however, is not
effectiveness but the importance attached to the church by
men whose weekday lives were spent within the more limited
circles of the neighborhoods.

The image of tangential circles shows itself again as an
exaggeration when we consider the county as a whole. Court
and vestry, as they did from the very beginning, encompassed
in effect representatives from the various parts of the county.
Thus on the court in the 1730s and 1740s were purely county

men from the several precincts (Thacker and William Montague of the upper precinct, for example, George Hardin of the lower), Urbanna merchants (James Reid, Patrick Cheap), and cosmopolitan gentlemen (Armistead Churchill, Edmund Berkeley), the latter as a type more regular in attendance than had been the case earlier, even coming to dominate the meetings of the court in the 1740s, displacing the purely county gentlemen who had dominated until then. Elevated on their platform, more concerned now with the letter of the law than with its spirit, with the correct wording of writs and pleas, the gentlemen justices seem more aloof and distant than when they had gathered in Richard Robinson's hall or even in George Wortham's made-over house.[18] In not a few years, they would build themselves still another and more splendid brick courthouse in Urbanna. But when we scan the men who actually did the work of the county and parish during these decades, serving as jurymen, constables, surveyors of highways, tobacco agents, and the like, we see a drawing into the public business of men from all parts and levels of the county society and the silent operation not simply of wealth but of family ties and personal worth in determining the level of the public's business accorded to individuals. And when, in the mind, we stand by the courthouse door on court day listening to the litigious voices from within and the hurly-burly of the crowd without, we see it still as a periodic coming together of the county, part business, part social.[19]

Yet the metaphor exaggerates only to an extent. Jarratt, away from his New Kent neighborhood and called upon to enter the home of a "gentleman and his lady" well above him in wealth and status, was awkward and ill at ease. "I knew not how to introduce myself to strangers, and what style was proper for accosting persons of their dignity. . . . I felt miserable, and said little, the whole evening. I was truly out of my element." For his part, the gentleman was equally nonplussed, assuming Jarratt on his first entrance to be "the son of a very poor man, in the neighbourhood."[20] How very different from Jane Olney's visit to the Burnham house in 1681?[21]

Our visit to Middlesex ends not with a great event but simply at a point in time: the mid-century mark. A hundred years have elapsed since Englishmen moved onto the peninsula between the Rappahannock and Piankatank. Their history has obviously been one of process rather than events, of adjustments and readjustments to changing situations, and of conservative adjustments at that when we consider the similarity of scene between Corbin's gathering of heads-of-family in 1657 and Thacker's in 1736. Indeed, events—Bacon's Rebellion, the plant-cutting riots, the comings and goings of royal governors—have actually had minimal effect. It would, therefore, be inappropriate to end with an event.

Still, we must characterize Middlesex as we leave it, acknowledging immediately that our characterization applies only to the white society of the county. What is going on in the quarters is too shadowy for generalization when seen from the vantage point of a single county.

The private wings attached to the Lower and Middle churches by the cosmopolitan families and the discomfort of Devereux Jarratt in the presence of his "betters" are obvious clues. The one is evidence of the proud aloofness emerging in an elite—a ritual assertion of wealth, gentle birth, and rightful dominance, of the character we glimpsed in the Robinson brothers and Harry Beverley as they fought for Urbanna just after the turn of the century, and in Ralph Wormeley before them. The other is evidence of the social distance that had come to separate men of one sort from those of another in this society as land and blacks—wealth or at least the appearance of it—came to define the gentle-born as a breed distinct from the common sort, building on but exaggerating social distinctions that had existed in the county from the beginning.[22]

It is not enough, however, to characterize the society in terms of gentle-born and common sort. When we trace the connections of men and women to see with whom they dealt, whom they married, and who were their friends and who their kin, when we categorize them by wealth and offices held—by status—we see no dichotomy but a continuum stretching downward from the top, the boundaries between types almost imperceptible except for the distinction between cosmopolitan and county. When we place county families within the landscape and look again, we see their connections forming a scattering of neighborhoods. And when we follow them to their churches on a Sunday, to Urbanna's stores, and to musters and to court day, we see the whole as a single community. Ritual assertions and social distinctions are part of the picture, but only a part. They, the tobacco economy, and slavery mark our Chesapeake community as a unique place in time and, as such, important to historians. But stripped of these attributes and reduced to timeless fundamentals—stratified, open-country neighborhood networks, a small retail center— Middlesex in 1750 was simply that rural society toward which and from which American society has proceeded.

Notes

Preface

*For convenience we list them:

"Little Communities: Viewpoints for the Study of the Early South—Report From Middlesex," presented to the Southern Historical Association, Nashville, Tenn., November 1970.

"The Social Web: A Prospectus for the Study of the Early American Community," the Phi Alpha Theta Lecture, the University of Rhode Island, May 1971, published in William L. O'Neill, ed., *Insights and Parallels: Problems and Issues of American Social History* (Minneapolis, Minn., 1973), 57–123.

" 'Now-Wives and Sons-in-Law': Parental Death in a Seventeenth-Century Virginia County," presented at a conference on the seventeenth-century Chesapeake, College Park and St. Mary's, Md., November 1974, published in Thad W. Tate and David L. Ammerman, eds., *The Chesapeake in the Seventeenth Century: Essays on Anglo-American Society* (Chapel Hill, N.C., 1979), 153–82.

"Of Agues and Fevers: Malaria in the Early Chesapeake," presented at a conference on early American social history, Stony Brook, N.Y., June 1975, published in *William and Mary Quarterly*, 3d ser., XXXIII (1976), 31–61.

"The Evolution of Religious Life in Early Virginia," presented at the fourth annual Lawrence Henry Gipson Symposium, Bethlehem, Pa., September 1976, published in *Lex et Scientia: The International Journal of Law and Science*, XIV (1978), 190–240.

"Community Study," presented at the Newberry Library Conference on Quantitative and Social Science Approaches in Early American History, Chicago, Ill., October 1977, published in *Historical Methods*, XIII (1980), 29–41.

"Rhythms of Life: Black and White Seasonality in the Early Chesapeake" (with Charles Wetherell), presented to the Organization of American Historians, New Orleans, La., April 1979, published in *Journal of Interdisciplinary History*, XI (1980), 29–53.

"Middle Virginians: Status in Early Chesapeake Bay Society," the Society of the Cincinnati Lecture, the University of Virginia, May 1979, and included here (revised) in chapter 5.

" 'More True and Perfect Lists': The Reconstruction of Censuses for Middlesex County, Virginia, 1668–1704," *Virginia Magazine of History and Biography*, LXXXVIII (1980), 37–74.

"*In Nomine Avi:* The Naming of Children in a Chesapeake County, 1650–1750," presented to the Social Science History Association, Bloomington, Ind., November 1982, and included here as "Child-Naming Patterns" in the *Explicatus.*

1. The Visitors

1. Darrett B. Rutman, *Winthrop's Boston: Portrait of a Puritan Town* (Chapel Hill, N.C., 1965); Rutman, *Husbandmen of Plymouth: Farms and Villages in the Old Colony, 1620–1692* (Boston, 1967).

2. H. R. McIlwaine and J. P. Kennedy, eds., *Journals of the House of Burgesses of Virginia* (Richmond, Va., 1905–15), VI, 262.

3. John Winthrop, "A Modell of Christian Charity," *Winthrop Papers*, II ([Boston],

1931), 294. Note the use of this quotation by Michael Zuckerman in *Peaceable Kingdoms: New England Towns in the Eighteenth Century* (New York, 1970), 51.

4. The Dedham church covenant of 1636, quoted in Kenneth A. Lockridge, *A New England Town: The First Hundred Years, Dedham, Massachusetts, 1636–1736* (New York, 1970), 4–5.

5. Jonathan Edwards, quoted in Richard L. Bushman, *From Puritan to Yankee: Character and the Social Order in Connecticut, 1690–1765* (Cambridge, Mass., 1967), 3.

6. See, for example, chapter 2 ("In Quest of Community") of Paul Boyer and Stephen Nissenbaum, *Salem Possessed: The Social Origins of Witchcraft* (Cambridge, Mass., 1974).

7. R[oger] G[reen], *Virginia's Cure: Or An Advisive Narrative Concerning Virginia* (London, 1662), in Peter Force, comp., *Tracts and Other Papers, Relating Principally to the . . . Colonies in North America* (Washington, D.C., 1836–47), III, tract XV, 5–6.

8. Robert Beverley, *The History and Present State of Virginia*, ed. Louis B. Wright (Chapel Hill, N.C., 1947), 319.

9. John J. Waters, "Patrimony, Succession, and Social Stability: Guilford, Connecticut, in the Eighteenth Century," *Perspectives in American History*, X (1976), 131. The theoretical considerations that follow are developed more fully in Darrett B. Rutman, "Community Study," *Historical Methods*, XIII (1980), 29–41, and idem, "The Social Web: A Prospectus for the Study of the Early American Community," in William L. O'Neill, ed., *Insights and Parallels: Problems and Issues of American Social History* (Minneapolis, Minn., 1973), 57–89.

10. Lockridge, *New England Town*, 91; Zuckerman, *Peaceable Kingdoms*, 4; John J. Waters, "The Traditional World of the New England Peasants: A View from Seventeenth-Century Barnstable," *New England Historical and Genealogical Register*, CXXX (1976), 21; Bushman, *Puritan to Yankee*, ix, x. Zuckerman is something of an exception. In *Peaceable Kingdoms*, 256–57, communalism survives into modern America and "belies the belief that we are a liberal society which . . . has always known 'the reality of atomistic social freedom.'" In "The Fabrication of Identity in Early America," *William and Mary Quarterly*, 3d ser., XXXIV (1977), 183–214, atomism and communalism (or "self and society") are in antagonistic juxtaposition from early modern Europe to modern America. Among scholars of the Middle colonies, the "world we have lost" never crossed the ocean; Bushman's open, pluralistic, and voluntaristic social order, summarized as "privatism," was there from the beginning. See e.g., Stephanie Grauman Wolf, *Urban Village: Population, Community, and Family Structure in Germantown, Pennsylvania, 1683–1800* (Princeton, N.J., 1977). Yet the "community" considered by these scholars to be absent is that defined by Lockridge et al. in New England terms. See also Rhys Isaac, *The Transformation of Virginia, 1740–1790* (Chapel Hill, N.C., 1982), 115–18. Isaac feels compelled to explain why "the Virginia parish was no simple, traditional Christian village sustained by a strong sense of continuity between the past and the present."

11. Ferdinand Toennies, *Community & Society* (1887), trans., Charles P. Loomis (East Lansing, Mich., 1957), 33–34. We have taken the liberty of completing the translations, using "community" and "society" in the quotations.

12. Oscar Lewis, *Life in a Mexican Village: Tepoztlan Restudied* (Urbana, Ill., 1951), 428.

13. Lockridge, *New England Town*, 18, 167–68, 172–73.

14. Alan Macfarlane, in "History, Anthropology and the Study of Communities," *Social History*, V (1977), 632, writes of Toennies's *Gemeinschaft*: "The belief in such 'communities' is one of the most powerful myths in industrial society, shaping not only policy and government . . . but also affecting thought and research. Expecting to find 'communities,' the prophecy fulfilled itself and communities were found." See also the Introduction to Colin Bell and Howard Newby, eds., *The Sociology of Community* (London, 1974) and their *Community Studies: An Introduction to the Sociology of the Local Community* (London, 1971), 13.

15. Charles Abrams, *The Language of Cities: A Glossary of Terms* (New York, 1971), 59–60.

16. Talcott Parsons, "The Principal Structures of Community," in Carl J. Friedrich, ed., *Community* (New York, 1959), 250.

17. Gerhard E. Lenski, *Power and Privilege: A Theory of Social Stratification* (New York, 1966), 25; John Donne, *Devotions Upon Emergent Occasions* (1624), ed. John Sparrow (Cambridge, Eng., 1923), 98.

18. See Ronald Abler et al., *Spatial Organization* (Englewood Cliffs, N.J., 1971), chapters 8, 10, and 11 for a general discussion of these basic concepts.

19. Macfarlane, "History, Anthropology and the Study of Communities," 649.

20. Rutman, "Community Study," 37–41, briefly reviews this literature and the mathematics of the analysis.

21. Rutman, "The Social Web," 77–78.

22. The most significant records missing for Middlesex are tithable lists. These can be extracted from Lancaster County records for the period prior to the formation of Middlesex, but no lists from Middlesex itself have been located. One, possibly two, books of Middlesex County Court records covering 1668 to 1673 are missing, as are court orders for 1727 to 1731 and 1738 to 1739. Pages from the vestry records seem to have been purposefully destroyed during Bacon's Rebellion. The parish register is generally scant for the earliest years, while a near-hiatus of marriage entries begins in the 1730s and of death records in the 1740s; but this deterioration can be partially compensated for with other sources. On balance, our data are strongest for the period 1678 to 1726.

23. We have described the process of record stripping in Darrett B. and Anita H. Rutman, " 'Now-Wives and Sons-in-Law': Parental Death in a Seventeenth-Century Virginia County," in Thad W. Tate and David L. Ammerman, eds., *The Chesapeake in the Seventeenth Century: Essays on Anglo-American Society* (Chapel Hill, N.C., 1979), 175–77; Rutman and Rutman, " 'More True and Perfect Lists': The Reconstruction of Censuses for Middlesex County, Virginia, 1668–1704," *Virginia Magazine of History and Biography*, LXXXVIII (1980), 37–74; and Rutman, "Community Study," 35–37.

24. The principal sources for the Davis entry are *The Parish Register of Christ Church, Middlesex County, Va. from 1653 to 1812* (Richmond, Va., 1897), 16, 70, 72, 80; H. R. McIlwaine and W. L. Hall, eds., *Executive Journals of the Council of Colonial Virginia, 1680–1754* (Richmond, Va., 1925–45), III, 288; Lancaster Orders, 1655–66, 173; Middlesex Wills, 1675–1798, pt. 1, 130; Middlesex Wills, 1698–1713, 192, 200–201; Middlesex Wills, 1713–34, 43; Middlesex Orders, 1680–94, 278, 347; Middlesex Orders, 1694–1705, 285, 291, 581; Middlesex Orders, 1705–10, 105, 154, 185, 206; Middlesex Deeds, 1679–94, 25–26; Middlesex Deeds, 1703–20, 47, 278–83. The register is very badly transcribed and must be checked against the original.

25. See Rutman and Rutman, " 'More True and Perfect Lists,' " 48–54, for a full assessment of the biases.

26. Rhys Isaac in his "Ethnographic Method in History: An Action Approach," *Historical Methods*, XIII (1980), 43–61, and *Transformation of Virginia*, 323–57, links this classic historiographic technique to a particular approach in anthropology.

27. That the vignettes frequently involve violence is a function of the records upon which we must draw and should not leave the impression of a violent society. Violent exchanges between people precipitate court actions and generate records; commonplace and tranquil exchanges do not. By our best estimate, accusations and conviction rates for offenses against persons and property in Middlesex (roughly equivalent to modern "crimes") computed for successive five-year periods from 1676 onward averaged roughly 2.9 and 1.6 per 1,000 population per year, about the same as has been reported for similar offenses for seventeenth-century New England and rural England of the late seventeenth and early eighteenth centuries. (See, for example, Kai T. Erikson, *Wayward Puritans: A Study in the Sociology of Deviance* [New York, 1966], chapter 4; Robert W. Roetger, "Order and Disorder in Early Connecticut: New Haven, 1639–1701," [Ph.D. Dissertation, University of New Hampshire, 1982]; J. M. Beattie, "The Pattern of Crime in England, 1660–1800," *Past and Present*, LXII [1974], 47–95.) Comparison with modern rates can only be tentative. A 1967 study of offenses roughly approximating our offenses against persons and property in nonmetropolitan areas of the north-central United States estimated a "true" crime rate of 38.6 per 1,000; the police were called in 49% of these cases (18.9 per 1,000), responded to 77% of the calls (14.6), recorded the act to be a crime 75% of the time (10.9), made an arrest in 20% of the cases (2.2), and obtained a conviction in 42% of the cases in which they made an arrest (0.9). If we accept an "accusation" in Middlesex as the rough equivalent of the police record of a crime, one's person and property were considerably safer in the rural Chesapeake of 250-odd years ago than in the safest part of the contemporary United States. Phillip H. Ennis, *Criminal Victimization in the United States: A Report of a National Survey* (Washington, D.C., 1967), 6–14, 20–30, 47–49.

28. Edmund Berkeley and Dorothy Smith Berkeley, eds., *The Reverend John Clayton: A Parson with a Scientific Mind, His Scientific Writings and Other Related Papers* (Charlottesville, Va., 1965), 81–82.

2. Entry

1. The phrase is borrowed from Arthur Pierce Middleton's title, *Tobacco Coast: A Maritime History of Chesapeake Bay in the Colonial Era* (Newport News, Va., 1953). The

early history of the Chesapeake is excellently recounted in Edmund S. Morgan, *American Slavery, American Freedom: The Ordeal of Colonial Virginia* (New York, 1975), 44–130; Richard L. Morton, *Colonial Virginia* (Chapel Hill, N.C., 1960), I, 1–187; and Wesley Frank Craven, *The Southern Colonies in the Seventeenth Century, 1607–1689* ([Baton Rouge, La.], 1949), 60–182.

2. Carville V. Earle, "Environment, Disease, and Mortality in Early Virginia," in Thad W. Tate and David L. Ammerman, eds., *The Chesapeake in the Seventeenth Century: Essays on Anglo-American Society* (Chapel Hill, N.C., 1979), 96–125. Cf. Karen Ordahl Kupperman, "Apathy and Death in Early Jamestown," *Journal of American History,* LXVI (1979), 24–40.

3. Darrett B. Rutman, "The Virginia Company and Its Military Regime," in Rutman, ed., *The Old Dominion: Essays for Thomas Perkins Abernethy* (Charlottesville, Va., 1964), 1–20.

4. Jerome E. Brooks, *The Mighty Leaf: Tobacco through the Centuries* (Boston, 1952), 51, 54, 71, 83, quoting *A Counterblaste to Tobacco* (London, 1604).

5. U.S. Bureau of the Census, *Historical Statistics of the United States, Colonial Times to 1970, Part 2* (Washington, D.C., 1975), 1168, 1191; Morgan, *American Slavery, American Freedom,* 404. See also Russell R. Menard, "Secular Trends in the Chesapeake Tobacco Industry, 1617–1710," *Working Papers from the Regional Economic History Research Center,* I (1978), 1–34; Menard, "The Tobacco Industry in the Chesapeake Colonies, 1617–1730: An Interpretation," *Research in Economic History,* V (1980), 109–77.

6. William Strachey, *The Historie of Travell Into Virginia Britania (1612),* eds. Louis B. Wright and Virginia Freund (London, 1953), 122–23; John Smith, *The Generall Historie of Virginia, New England and the Summer Isles,* ed. Edward Arber, *Travels and Works of Captain John Smith* (Edinburgh, Scotland, 1910), II, 535.

7. Tobacco cultivation seems to have been an adaptation of Indian corn cultivation to tobacco. On Indian cultivation see e.g., Smith, *A Map of Virginia. With a Description of the Countrey, the Commodities, People Government and Religion,* ed. Arber, *Smith,* I, 61–63; Robert Beverley, *The History and Present State of Virginia,* ed. Louis B. Wright (Chapel Hill, N.C., 1947), 143–45. On tobacco cultivation see C. T., *An Advice How to Plant Tobacco* (London, 1615), reprinted in part in Warren M. Billings, ed., *The Old Dominion in the Seventeenth Century: A Documentary History of Virginia, 1606–1689* (Chapel Hill, N.C., 1975), 182–84; George Alsop, *A Character of the Province of Maryland,* ed. Clayton Colman Hall, *Narratives of Early Maryland, 1633–1684* (New York, 1910), 363; Thomas Glover, *An Account of Virginia, Its Situation, Temperature, Productions, Inhabitants and Their Manner of Planting and Ordering Tobacco* (Oxford, 1904, [orig. publ. London, 1676]), 28–30; John Clayton's 1688 description in Edmund Berkeley and Dorothy Smith Berkeley, eds., *The Reverend John Clayton: A Parson with a Scientific Mind, His Scientific Writings and Other Related Papers* (Charlottesville, Va., 1965), 59–64, 79–83; Joseph Ewan and Nesta Ewan, eds., *John Banister and His Natural History of Virginia, 1678–1692* (Urbana, Ill., 1970), 360–61; and Gregory A. Stiverson and Patrick H. Butler III, eds., "Virginia in 1732: The Travel Journal of William Hugh Grove," *Virginia Magazine of History and Biography,* LXXXV (1977), 42–43.

8. Susan Myra Kingsbury, ed., *The Records of the Virginia Company of London,* (Washington, D.C., 1906–35), III, 504.

9. See *Explicatus,* "Tobacco Prices" and "Tobacco Productivity."

10. William Tatham, *An Historical and Practical Essay on the Culture and Commerce of Tobacco* (London, 1800), as reprinted in G. Melvin Herndon, *William Tatham and the Culture of Tobacco* (Coral Gables, Fla., 1969), 13.

11. The timing of the tobacco year would, of course, vary from year to year depending upon the weather. The year described here and in the illustration is a generalization based upon the descriptions cited in note 7 and, additionally, Gilbert Chinard, ed., *A Huguenot Exile in Virginia: Or Voyages of a Frenchman exiled for his Religion with a description of Virginia and Maryland* (New York, 1934), 118, and Jack P. Greene, ed., *The Diary of Colonel Landon Carter of Sabine Hall, 1752–1778* (Charlottesville, Va., 1965). Even a generalized year would vary according to latitude. Thus Glover and Banister, writing from the James, noted that the seedbeds were prepared and planted in the twelve days between Christmas and Epiphany (Glover, *Account of Virginia,* 28; Ewan and Ewan, eds., *Banister,* 361); Clayton, living in Gloucester, specified mid-January (Berkeley and Berkeley, eds., *Clayton,* 65–66); Carter, on the Northern Neck, planted between mid-January and mid-February and thought the crop doubtful when weather forced a delay until late February and early March (Greene, ed., *Carter,* I, 140, 200, 252, 364, 535); and Alsop, in Maryland, wrote of planting "between the months of March and April" (Alsop, *Character of . . . Maryland,* 363). The timing depicted reflects roughly the latitude of Middlesex.

12. These figures based on Middlesex prices and productivity discussed in the *Explicatus.* For Maryland see e.g., Carville V. Earle, *The Evolution of a Tidewater Settlement System: All Hallow's Parish, Maryland, 1650–1783* (Chicago, 1975), 27; *Historical Statistics,* 1198.

13. Middlesex Orders, 1694–1705, 483.

14. Philip L. Barbour, ed., *The Jamestown Voyages under the First Charter, 1606–1609* (Cambridge, Eng., 1969), II, 404.

15. The John Smith map of Virginia of 1612 places two Indian communities in what would become Middlesex, that of the "Payankatank" with a "Kings Howse" village indicated, and the "Opiscopank." Smith located the former on the north shore of the Piankatank River at about where it emerges from the Dragon Swamp, the latter on the southern shore of the Rappahannock six to ten miles from its mouth. However, "Opiscopank" appears nowhere else in Smith's work. All of his accounts of Indians along the south shore of the Rappahannock begin "far within" the river, while modern ethnological research places the first major Indian town on the river upstream from modern Leedstown. Moreover, in Smith's *True Relation* of 1608, in describing his first visit to the Rappahannock-Piankatank area (prior to June 2 of that year), he wrote of a "Desert," that is, uninhabited, although "exceeding fertil, good timber, most hils and dales, in each valley a cristall spring"; in late July or August, however, he visited the Payankatank, finding "the people were most a hunting, save a few old men, women and children, that were tending their corne." William Strachey's 1612 *Historie of Travell* suggests that Smith's explorations came at a moment of transition on the Middlesex peninsula. Strachey recounts the story of the destruction of what he called "the naturall Inhabitantes of *Payankatank*" by Powhatan in 1608 and the repopulation of their territory (with Powhatan's permission) by survivors of Kecoughtan, another Indian community destroyed by Powhatan. The story, plus Strachey's reference to the Rappahannock being called "Opiscatumeck" by "the Naturalls of old," indicates that the Opiscopank on Smith's map was gone and that the Payankatanks—that is, the displaced Kecoughtans—were the sole inhabitants of the peninsula. Strachey set the total number of Payankatanks at 40 to 50, while Smith in 1612 cited "40 serviceable men" and in his *Generall Historie* of 1624, 50 to 60 warriors. The best modern estimate is 200. In all probability, English activity along the Piankatank ultimately led to the abandonment of the town there. Later English records do not mention it. Perhaps the Payankatanks moved for a while to the banks of streams flowing into the Rappahannock. A patent of 1649 refers to "the Indian Townes of old and new Nimcock"; Nimcock is the modern Urbanna Creek. Another of 1652 refers to "Indyan quarters" on modern Lagrange Creek. All were apparently abandoned as the English entered. Perhaps, too, individual Indian families abandoned village life entirely, dispersing in the face of English attacks on their towns during the wars. This would account for the many indications in the records of isolated "Indian Cabins." Barbour, ed., *Jamestown Voyages,* I, 185, II, 336–37, 341, 374; David Ives Bushnell, Jr., "Indian Sites below the Falls of the Rappahannock, Virginia," *Smithsonian Miscellaneous Collections,* XCVI, no. 4 (Washington, D.C., 1937), 15–16; Arber, ed., *Smith,* II, 430; Strachey, *Historie of Travell,* eds., Wright and Freund, 44–45; Ben C. McCary, *Indians in Seventeenth-Century Virginia* (Williamsburg, Va., 1957), 5; Nell Marion Nugent, *Cavaliers and Pioneers: Abstracts of Virginia Land Patents and Grants* (Richmond, Va., 1934–79), I, 181; Lancaster Deeds, 1652–57, 157.

16. Virginia State Library, Richmond, State Land Office, Patents, bk. I, pt. 2, 803, 807. See chapter 3, note 18.

17. Beverley Fleet, comp., *Virginia Colonial Abstracts* (Richmond, Va., 1937–48), XXV, 7; William W. Hening, comp., *The Statutes at Large: Being a Collection of all the Laws of Virginia from the First Session of the Legislature in 1619* (Richmond, New York, and Philadelphia, 1809–23), I, 323–26, 353. It is sometimes argued that actual settlement was made in the region prior to 1644 and that settlers were removed in accordance with the Indian treaty. See e.g., George Maclaren Brydon, *Virginia's Mother Church and The Political Conditions Under Which It Grew* (Richmond and Philadelphia, 1947–52), I, 135. There is, however, no evidence for this; on the contrary, an act of June 1642, referred to in March 1643, specified that the Rappahannock River *remain* unseated. Hening, comp., *Statutes at Large,* I, 274.

18. Lancaster Deeds, 1654–1702, 363. The dispute involved land on the north side of the Rappahannock. Haddaway and Moone eventually settled on the south side in what would become Middlesex.

19. Kenneth A. Lockridge, *A New England Town: The First Hundred Years, Dedham, Massachusetts, 1636–1736* (New York, 1970), 4–7.

20. *A Voyage to Virginia. By Colonel Norwood,* in Peter Force, comp., *Tracts and Other*

Papers, Relating Principally to the . . . Colonies in North America (Washington, D.C., 1836–47), III, tract X, 49. The two were Chicheley and Sir Thomas Lunsford.

21. Lancaster Deeds, 1652–57, 90–94. The number of acquaintances and relationships in the text is a minimum figure. There are undoubtedly relationships and acquaintanceships undiscoverable from the record base.

22. Miguel de Cervantes Saavedra, *The First Part of the Life and Achievements of the Renowned Don Quixote de la Mancha*, trans. Peter Motteux (New York, 1946 [Illustrated Modern Library Edn.]), 212.

23. Lancaster Deeds, 1652–57, 68. This was one of a number of gifts to Connoway children, including one from William Eltonhead, the Maryland councillor and brother of the Middlesex sisters. See also Lancaster Deeds, 1654–1702, 151.

24. "Causes of Discontent in Virginia, 1676. Winder Papers, Virginia State Library," *Virginia Magazine of History and Biography*, III (1895–96), 40n.

25. John C. Rainbolt, *From Prescription to Persuasion: Manipulation of [Seventeenth] Century Virginia Economy* (Port Washington, N.Y., 1974), 58.

26. This is generally held with regard to New England; it applies as well to English-born Virginians, whatever attitudes might have ultimately developed in the Chesapeake. See E. M. W. Tillyard, *The Elizabethan World Picture* (New York, 1943), 9–17; Wallace Notestein, *The English People on the Eve of Colonization, 1603–1630* (New York, 1954), 25–35; Peter Laslett, *The World we have lost* (New York, 1965), 53–80; Darrett B. Rutman, *American Puritanism: Faith and Practice* (Philadelphia, 1970), 41–47, 53–80. Joan Thirsk, ed., *The Agrarian History of England and Wales, 1500–1640* (Cambridge, 1967), IV, and Lawrence Stone, *The Family, Sex and Marriage in England, 1500–1800* (New York, 1977), from their different vantage points, describe the England from which the Virginians came; Notestein (pp. 202–49) briefly sketches the principal English offices transplanted to the Chesapeake community: sheriff, justice of the peace, constable, churchwarden, and vestryman.

27. Hening, comp., *Statutes at Large*, I, 286, 311–12, 433, 525, 542, II, 103; "Ducking as Punishment," *Virginia Magazine of History and Biography*, V (1897–98), 353.

28. Chinard, ed., *Huguenot Exile*, 148; Louise E. Gray et al., *Historical Buildings in Middlesex County, Virginia, 1650–1875* (n.p., 1978), 28.

29. Lancaster Orders, 1655–66, 20; Lancaster Deeds, 1654–1702, 141.

30. Lancaster Orders, 1655–66, 6, 39.

31. The argument is more fully developed in Darrett B. Rutman, "The Evolution of Religious Life in Early Virginia," *Lex et Scientia: The International Journal of Law and Science*, XIV (1978), 198–200.

32. Lancaster Deeds, 1652–57, 152, 315–16.

33. The neighborhoods can be isolated during this early period using the Lancaster tithable lists, in this instance that of 1657 in Lancaster Orders, 1655–66, 40–44. Jackson was at the time selling off the greater part of the Brocas land, most of it to Chicheley.

34. Ibid., 6. The order appointing Cole minister for the whole specified the division of the county into two parishes (Northside and Southside) but recognized three churchwardens, including Keeble for Piankatank.

35. Hening, comp., *Statutes at Large*, I, 400, 469; Lancaster Orders, 1655–66, 35. The May order of the court is badly blurred.

36. The appeal is presumed on the basis of a reference in 1661 to Charles Hill as "in his life tyme . . . imployed by the Vestrymen of the Parishe of Pianketancke to James Cittie, for the defending of some difference between the said Parishe . . . and the Parishe of Lancaster." Ibid., 165.

37. Lancaster Deeds, 1654–1702, 374; C. G. Chamberlayne, ed., *The Vestry Book of Christ Church Parish, Middlesex County, Virginia, 1663–1767* (Richmond, Va., 1927), 5.

38. At a conservative twenty pounds tobacco per poll.

39. Chamberlayne, ed., *Vestry Book of Christ Church*, 3.

40. Lancaster Orders, 1655–66, 158; Chamberlayne, ed., *Vestry Book of Christ Church*, 2, 4, 5–6.

41. Lancaster Orders, 1655–66, 264; Lancaster Orders, 1666–80, 12.

42. Lancaster Orders, 1655–66, 285.

43. Lancaster Orders, 1666–80, 44.

44. Neither the petition (referred to in Chamberlayne, ed., *Vestry Book of Christ Church*, 13) nor the legislature's response survives, but in March 1669 the Lancaster court took note of an "order of Assembly for devideing of this County" and in May referred a criminal matter to the Middlesex court on the grounds that the act had been committed on the Southside. Lancaster Orders, 1666–80, 106a, 107.

45. Even as the parishes were uniting, the Lancaster-Piankatank rivalry was in evi-

dence; in setting this last levy, the combined vestry carefully stipulated that Piankatank collect to its "late Reputed Bounds, Includeing the Thickett Plantacion and Harwoods Pattent and noe more." Chamberlayne, ed., *Vestry Book of Christ Church,* 5.

46. Ibid. The site was referred to as "next the head of Capt. Brocas his ground." This seems to be the Timberland Neck tract, purchased from Brocas's heir and incorporated into the Wormeley holding.

47. R[oger] G[reen], *Virginia's Cure: Or An Advisive Narrative Concerning Virginia* (London, 1662), in Peter Force, comp., *Tracts and Other Papers, Relating Principally to the . . . Colonies in North America* (Washington, D.C., 1836–47), III, tract XV, 5–6.

48. A 1665 order of the Lancaster vestry. Chamberlayne, ed., *Vestry Book of Christ Church,* 4.

3. The Road

1. Middlesex Orders, 1694–1705, 335. For the location of the Upper Chapel, see George Carrington Mason, *Colonial Churches of Tidewater Virginia* (Richmond, Va., 1945), 280–82.

2. William W. Hening, comp., *The Statutes at Large: Being a Collection of all the Laws of Virginia from the First Session of the Legislature in 1619* (Richmond, New York, and Philadelphia, 1809–23), II, 156; H. R. McIlwaine and J. P. Kennedy, eds., *Journals of the House of Burgesses of Virginia* (Richmond, Va., 1905–15), II, 48; Middlesex Orders, 1673–80, 21, 22.

3. Gilbert Chinard, ed., *A Huguenot Exile in Virginia: Or Voyages of a Frenchman exiled for his Religion with a description of Virginia and Maryland* (New York, 1934), 142.

4. Edmund Berkeley and Dorothy S. Berkeley, "Another 'Account of Virginia' By the Reverend John Clayton," *Virginia Magazine of History and Biography,* LXXVI (1968), 421.

5. Ibid., 426.

6. Chinard, ed., *Huguenot Exile,* 119.

7. Cary Carson et al., "Impermanent Architecture in the Southern American Colonies," *Winterthur Portfolio,* XVI (1981), 135–96, is a superb treatment of the subject; Carson, "Doing History with Material Culture," in Ian M. G. Quimby, ed., *Material Culture and the Study of American Life* (New York, 1978), 56–57, is a flawed preliminary statement. H. Chandlee Forman, *Old Buildings, Gardens, and Furniture in Tidewater Maryland* (Cambridge, Md., 1967), 189–200, describes an extant house that originally used tree trunks as piers and includes a photograph of a much decomposed remnant.

8. For obvious reasons, the glebe house is the best documented in Middlesex. Its history can be followed in C. G. Chamberlayne, ed., *The Vestry Book of Christ Church Parish, Middlesex County, Virginia, 1663–1767* (Richmond, Va., 1927). The quotations are from pp. 21, 46, 107–8, 115, 218–19.

9. By H. Chandlee Forman in *The Architecture of the Old South: The Medieval Style, 1585–1850* (Cambridge, Mass., 1948), *Virginia Architecture in the Seventeenth Century* (Williamsburg, Va., 1957), 23, and other works. While perhaps technical misnomers, "medieval" and "gothic" convey the texture of the style.

10. See *Explicatus,* "Child-Naming Patterns."

11. We use "traditional" and "modern" as ideal types delimiting a scale, full well recognizing that societies always fall somewhere between ideals. A good short statement is in Richard D. Brown, *Modernization: The Transformation of American Life, 1600–1865* (New York, 1976), 7–16. Note also the argument against a modern entrepreneurial mindset in James A. Henretta, "Families and Farms: *Mentalité* in Pre-Industrial America," *William and Mary Quarterly,* 3d ser., XXV (1978), 3–32.

12. On the growth and changing nature of the population, see *Explicatus,* "Population Estimates."

13. See generally Abbot Emerson Smith, *Colonists in Bondage: White Servitude and Convict Labor in America, 1607–1776* (Chapel Hill, N.C., 1947), and specifically: Mildred Campbell, "Social Origins of Some Early Americans," in James Morton Smith, ed., *Seventeenth-Century America: Essays in Colonial History* (Chapel Hill, N.C., 1959), 63–89; David Galenson, " 'Middling People' or 'Common Sort'? The Social Origins of Some Early Americans Reexamined," *William and Mary Quarterly,* 3d ser., XXXV (1978), 499–524, and "Mildred Campbell's Response," 525–40; Campbell, " 'Of People Too Few or Many': The Conflict of Opinion on Population and Its Relations to Emigration," in William Appleton Aiken and Basil Duke Henning, eds., *Conflict in Stuart England: Essays in Honour of Wallace Notestein* (London, 1960), 171–201; Galenson, "British Servants and the Colonial Indenture System in the Eighteenth Century," *Journal of Southern History,* XLIV

(1978), 41–66; Galenson, "Immigration and the Colonial Labor System: An Analysis of the Length of Indenture," *Explorations in Economic History*, XIV (1977), 360–77; James Horn, "Servant Emigration to the Chesapeake in the Seventeenth Century," in Thad W. Tate and David L. Ammerman, eds., *The Chesapeake in the Seventeenth Century: Essays on Anglo-American Society* (Chapel Hill, N.C., 1979), 51–95; and David Souden, " 'Rogues, whores and vagabonds': Indentured Servant Emigrants to North America, and the Case of Mid-Seventeenth Century Bristol," *Social History*, III (1978), 23–41. Galenson's *White Servitude in Colonial America: An Economic Analysis* (New York, 1982) appeared too late to be of direct use.

14. On early blacks and the shift to Africans, see Philip D. Curtin, *The Atlantic Slave Trade: A Census* (Madison, Wis., 1969), 118–19, 142–43; Russell R. Menard, "The Maryland Slave Population, 1658 to 1730: A Demographic Profile of Blacks in Four Counties," *William and Mary Quarterly*, 3d ser., XXXII (1975), 29–54; Allan Kulikoff, "The Origins of Afro-American Society in Tidewater Maryland and Virginia, 1700 to 1790," *William and Mary Quarterly*, 3d ser., XXXV (1978), 226–40.

15. On mortality see *Explicatus*. There is no way to establish an exact percentage for those surviving servitude. Edmund S. Morgan, *American Slavery, American Freedom: The Ordeal of Colonial Virginia* (New York, 1975), 180–85, argues that mortality rates in general improved from the 1640s on. Our calculations indicate a radical deterioration in Middlesex in the last quarter of the century. These separate conclusions suggest that servant survival rates in Middlesex were high during the first twenty years of settlement, then declined. It is unlikely, however, that more than 50 percent of arriving servants survived to freedom.

16. Middlesex Orders, 1673–80, 23. Lois Green Carr and Russell R. Menard, "Immigration and Opportunity: The Freedman in Early Colonial Maryland," in Tate and Ammerman, eds., *Chesapeake in the Seventeenth Century*, 208–9, estimate that 40% of those immigrating under indentures died. Formal indentures usually involved a shorter term of servitude than was required of those entering without indentures or as minors and serving according to the "custom of the country." When service categories involving these longer periods are included, the 40% estimate rises to some 60%.

17. The more frequent approach and that of Carr and Menard in ibid.; Menard, "From Servant to Freeholder: Status Mobility and Property Accumulation in Seventeenth-Century Maryland," *William and Mary Quarterly*, 3d ser., XXX (1973), 37–64; Lorena S. Walsh, "Servitude and Opportunity in Charles County, Maryland, 1658–1705," in Aubrey C. Land et al., *Law, Society and Politics in Early Maryland* (Baltimore, Md., 1977), 111–33; Menard, P. M. G. Harris, and Carr, "Opportunity and Inequality: The Distribution of Wealth on the Lower Western Shore of Maryland, 1638–1705," *Maryland Historical Magazine*, LXIX (1974), 169–84.

18. The patenting system flowed from the headright system, i.e., for every "head" transported into Virginia, the person paying the cost of transportation gained the right to fifty acres of land. Robert Beverley, *The History and Present State of Virginia*, ed. Louis B. Wright (Chapel Hill, N.C., 1947), 277–78, described the system as of the turn of the seventeenth to eighteenth century. To paraphrase: (1) The headrights were "proved" by entering a list of persons transported to the clerk of a court and swearing to the truth of the list. They were then forwarded to and certified by the secretary of the colony. Notably, certified headrights ("certificates") circulated almost as money. (2) The applicant selected the land and obtained an official survey. (3) A copy of the survey, with certificates sufficient for the size of the tract, was forwarded to the secretary, who, if there were no objections or contravening patents, made out the patent itself, which was subsequently "passed" by the governor and council. The patent was conditional upon paying a quitrent of twelvepence per fifty acres and "seating" the land within three years, that is, clearing, planting, and tending an acre of corn or building a house and running cattle for a year. A patent could "lapse" if not seated or it could "escheat" upon the death of the patentee intestate and devoid of "heirs of the body." In both instances, a second party had to act to obtain the lapse or escheat; the loss of the land was, therefore, neither automatic nor inevitable. The patenting of land purchased or inherited as a way of insuring title was a very common phenomenon. This and the multiple entry of headrights makes the use of patents for any other purpose than tracking particular properties very hazardous, and even in tracking, patents considered without a scrutiny of wills and conveyances in county records can be misleading. Extant patents are on file at the Virginia State Library, Richmond; specific patents can be located using the manuscript Index and Abstracts of Patents and Grants, Counties, Nos. 19 (Lancaster) and 21 (Middlesex), or Nell Marion Nugent, *Cavaliers and Pioneers: Abstracts of Virginia Land Patents and Grants* (Richmond, Va., 1934–79). We have invariably gone back to the full patent as the source of the most complete information.

19. Middlesex Deeds, 1679–94, 138. Old Nash's partner, Needles, also earned enough to buy and followed the same course of selling and renting parts of his land.

20. The terms of the lease in this case are embodied in Tuggle's will in Middlesex Wills, 1675–1798, pt. 1, 27–28.

21. In Middlesex subdivision continued well beyond the abrupt decline of the servant body in the 1680s and 1690s; it was not, therefore, a case of exhausting the supply of land when there were still freed servants wanting it, but the reverse. The number of freed servants (demand) gave out before the supply. Sons of those with land replaced the freedmen on the demand side, but this created an altogether different psychological problem.

22. Based upon our own analysis of prices and values from a variety of Middlesex sources and Menard's analysis of values found in Maryland and Virginia inventories as reported in his "From Servants to Slaves: The Transformation of the Chesapeake Labor System," *Southern Studies*, XVI (1977), 372. See also Paul G. E. Clemens, *The Atlantic Economy and Colonial Maryland's Eastern Shore: From Tobacco to Grain* (Ithaca, N.Y., 1980), 62.

23. Middlesex Wills, 1713–34, 80.

24. Middlesex Wills, 1675–1798, pt. 1, 27–28.

25. Bevèrley, *History*, 78. Wilcomb E. Washburn, *The Governor and the Rebel: A History of Bacon's Rebellion in Virginia* (Chapel Hill, N.C., 1957) remains the best account.

26. "Proclamations of Nathaniel Bacon," *Virginia Magazine of History and Biography*, I (1893–94), 60–61; "A True Narrative of the Late Rebellion in Virginia, By the Royal Commissioners, 1677," in Charles M. Andrews, ed., *Narratives of the Insurrections, 1675–1690* (New York, 1915), 122.

27. "Virginia in 1677–1678 [Sainsbury Abstracts]," *Virginia Magazine of History and Biography*, XXIII (1915), 148–49.

28. Brent's route is surmised from Bacon's, as the latter moved to counter Brent's approach.

29. "The History of Bacon's and Ingram's Rebellion, 1676," in Andrews, ed., *Narratives*, 87.

30. Chamberlayne, ed., *Vestry Book of Christ Church*, 25; "Persons Who Suffered by Bacon's Rebellion. The Commissioners' Report," *Virginia Magazine of History and Biography*, V (1897–98), 64–70; Hening, comp., *Statutes at Large*, III, 569. Sir Henry Chicheley was also imprisoned, but not in the county. Despite extensive genealogical research on the Wormeley family both by us and others (e.g., *Virginia Magazine of History and Biography*, XXXV [1927], 455–56, XXXVI [1928], 98–101, 283–93, 385–88), there is no evidence of a connection between the two Wormeley families of Middlesex, one stemming from the Ralph Wormeley who settled Rosegill and the other from the Christopher referred to here. The latter makes his first appearance in the county records in 1667. By then he was already married to Frances Armistead, widow of both Justinian Aylmer and Anthony Elliott. (Armistead, Aylmer, and Elliott were all prominent names in the colony and Anthony Elliott a major Middlesex landowner.) Wormeley is not a common name, however, suggesting a connection between the two families. The fact that "Christopher" does not appear in the line from Ralph although it was the given name of Ralph's grandfather, father, and brother hints at a "left-handed" connection displeasing to the Rosegill family. The most obvious possibility is that Christopher of Middlesex was Ralph II's uncle Christopher's illegitimate son. The earlier Christopher had been governor of Tortuga in the 1630s and had come to Virginia following the Spanish capture of that island, settling in York. A justice of the York County Court and member of the colony council, he died in the early 1640s, his widow marrying William Brocas.

31. Middlesex Orders, 1673–80, 61, 77–78, 81, 90.

32. We can at least estimate the age of twenty-one of the defendants. We report the median.

33. It might be argued that Wormeley (whose suit gives us most of the Baconians) could name only those of Boodle's troop he knew and that he would have recognized long-term residents more readily than others. In the nature of seventeenth-century judicial proceedings, however, what was common knowledge of the vicinage was as admissible as particular knowledge. Wormeley need not even have had to be on his property at the time of the raid to cite as defendants those whom common knowledge associated with the trespass. Moreover, in returning their verdict the jury specifically found against "Dr. Robert Boodle . . . with the rest of his Troope." Middlesex Orders, 1673–80, 78.

34. Five separate random drawings of twenty-four Middlesex men resident in the 1670s produced only five men in all whose life histories displayed incidents similar to those in the text.

35. Middlesex Orders, 1673–80, 71.

36. T[homas] M[athew], "The Beginning, Progress and Conclusion of Bacon's Rebellion, 1675–1676," in Andrews, ed., *Narratives*, 40.

37. Eventually their eleven hundred acres would lapse for lack of seating; Hooper would lose his plantation next to Richens's in a debt proceeding.

38. Lancaster Orders, 1655–66, 135.

39. Our agreement with Washburn, *Governor and the Rebel*, 83, and disagreement with the thesis of Book III of Morgan, *American Slavery, American Freedom*, 215–92, is self-evident. The dichotomization of the latter fails to encompass both the totality of the early Chesapeake system we see operating in the county and the nature of the county's Baconians.

40. Middlesex Orders, 1673–80, 60; C.O. 1/40, 129, Public Record Office, London.

41. In the absence of general court records, we do not know the results of the appeals. However, by the time they reached the general court (if, indeed, they did), the official climate was against such prosecutions. If the appeals had gone against the defendants, one would expect the county court records to reflect the fact in executions and distraints for the actual collection of the damages awarded. There are none.

42. There is no evidence from Middlesex to support the description by other authors of a Berkeleian "terror" following the suppression of the rebellion. Notably, such descriptions are documented by recounting the executions of twenty-three Baconian leaders and quoting descriptions sent to England by royal commissioners intent on painting the governor in the worst possible light. See e.g., Thomas J. Wertenbaker, *Virginia under the Stuarts, 1607–1688* (Princeton, N.J., 1914), 200–207. Both of the "lucrative lawsuits" entered in Middlesex by followers of Berkeley intent on enriching themselves—part of what Morgan, *American Slavery, American Freedom*, 274–75, calls "the legalized plundering by which the loyal party were accumulating property at the expense of everyone they could label a rebel," which extended into 1680—are recounted in the text. Robert Beverley, alleged to be one of the chief plunderers, filed neither.

43. Middlesex Orders, 1673–80, 71.

44. Ibid., 45.

45. Lancaster Orders, 1666–80, 208. We have reordered the rules and omitted ellipses for effect.

46. Hening, comp., *Statutes at Large*, II, 478.

47. We have shortened and in part paraphrased the Middlesex commission of May 1684 found in Middlesex Deeds, 1679–94, 144–45.

48. Lancaster Deeds, 1652–57, 213; Middlesex Orders, 1694–1704, 424; 1710–21, 111–12; 1721–26, 6; "Some helps for the Grand Jury of Middlesex," Middlesex Deeds, 1679–94, 672–73. In this early period, the forms of law were only loosely followed. See Henry Hartwell, James Blair, and Edward Chilton, *The Present State of Virginia and the College*, ed. Hunter Dickinson Farish (Williamsburg, Va., 1940), 44–45. Published originally in 1727, the description was written thirty years earlier. The justices' principal guide was Michael Dalton, *The Countrey Justice, Containing the practise of the Justices of the Peace out of their Sessions. Gathered, for the better helpe of such Justices of the Peace as have not been much conversant in the studie of the Lawes* (London, 1622) and their knowledge of Virginia's statutes. The description in the text, however, is based upon actual proceedings at the Lancaster and Middlesex courts. These frequently were at variance with both Dalton and statute.

49. The councillors had a customary and legal right to attend and even vote in any county court, although they did not do so ordinarily. Hening, comp., *Statutes at Large*, II, 358. 390.

50. Quoted in Washburn, *Governor and the Rebel*, 109.

51. Sir Thomas Grantham, *An Historical Account of Some Memorable Actions, Particularly in Virginia* (London, 1716), 3–4; "The Corbin Family," *Virginia Magazine of History and Biography*, XXIX (1921), 378–79.

4.   Family, Friends, Neighbors

1. We have silently transferred a description of a 1687 Gloucester wedding to Middlesex and given it to Elizabeth in 1671. See Gilbert Chinard, ed., *A Huguenot Exile in Virginia: Or Voyages of a Frenchman exiled for his Religion with a description of Virginia and Maryland* (New York, 1934), 137–39. For Shepherd's fee, see Middlesex Orders, 1673–80, 33, a reference to William Montague's debt to Shepherd for presiding at William's marriage. (William was one of Elizabeth's brothers.) For the silver drinking cup, see Middlesex Wills, 1675–1798, pt. 1, 35, the will of Marie [Mary] Minor, a.k.a. Mary Doodes,

Elizabeth's mother-in-law. For the carousing and shooting, see William W. Hening, comp., *The Statutes at Large: Being a Collection of all the Laws of Virginia from the First Session of the Legislature in 1619* (Richmond, New York, and Philadelphia, 1809–23), I, 401–2, 480; II, 126. Deco had been purchased by Doodes Minor in Nansemond in 1656 as a servant for life, with the provision that if Minor sold him the service would last no more than ten years. (Lancaster Orders, 1655–66, 370.) In 1671 Deco was still with Minor, along with Phillis, his daughters Mary and Jane (born 1663 and 1666 respectively), and his son James (1670). Alice Morse Earle, *Home Life in Colonial Days* (New York, 1898), 76–107, and extant inventories of the estates of Elizabeth's relatives have informed our description of the wedding feast.

2. We are, of course, simply placing people on the scene, selecting on the basis of known presence in the vicinity at the time and known connections to the Montagues or Minors.

3. Chinard, ed., *Huguenot Exile*, 138. Note that the traveler was describing the wedding of a former servant.

4. What follows is based on the analysis reported in *Explicatus*, "Social Networks."

5. Middlesex Wills, 1675–1798, pt. 1, 51–52.

6. Edmund Berkeley and Dorothy Smith Berkeley, eds., *The Reverend John Clayton: A Parson with a Scientific Mind, His Scientific Writings and Other Related Papers* (Charlottesville, Va., 1965), 32; Marion Tinling, ed., *The Correspondence of the Three William Byrds of Westover, Virginia, 1684–1776* (Charlottesville, Va., 1977), I, 56; Chinard, ed., *Huguenot Exile*, 111, 128–29. See also Michael Zuckerman, "William Byrd's Family," *Perspectives in American History*, XII (1979), 255–311. Although perhaps exaggerating the absence of familial affection, Zuckerman does an excellent job of associating early Virginia attitudes (primarily through the diaries of the second William Byrd) with the premodern "interpenetration of public and private spheres" so sweepingly presented by Philippe Ariès in his *Centuries of Childhood: A Social History of Family Life* (New York, 1962). Daniel Blake Smith, *Inside the Great House: Planter Family Life in Eighteenth-Century Chesapeake Society* (Ithaca, N.Y., 1980), 175–230, imaginatively exploits four diaries, including Byrd's, to delineate friendship and kinship networks.

7. The quotations are from Middlesex Wills, 1675–1798, pt. 1, 66, 132, 141; Middlesex Deeds, 1679–94, 200.

8. Hening, comp., *Statutes at Large*, II, 166.

9. Richard Beale Davis, ed., *William Fitzhugh and His Chesapeake World, 1676–1701: The Fitzhugh Letters and Other Documents* (Chapel Hill, N.C., 1963), 358. Laurel Thatcher Ulrich's *Good Wives: Image and Reality in the Lives of Women in Northern New England, 1650–1750* (New York, 1982), chapter 3, although set far to the north of our county, is an extraordinarily sensitive depiction of such support networks. We happily acknowledge the many conversations with Dr. Ulrich over the years that awakened our own sensitivity to the matter.

10. Middlesex Orders, 1705–10, 265.

11. Middlesex Deeds, 1703–20, 30.

12. From the depositions concerning Burnham's will (Middlesex Deeds, 1679–94, 22–32), it is unclear how much of this activity took place in Rappahannock County (where Burnham fell ill) and how much took place at Burnham's home in Middlesex (where he died). Radford was a Middlesex resident, for example, but we have no record of Doctor Read; yet the two were together with Burnham at one point. The gathering of a support network is, however, the point at issue; conceivably Middlesex relatives and neighbors (the Creykes, Elizabeth Weekes) went upriver to bring Burnham home.

13. Ibid., 31. Partially modernized for readability.

14. Middlesex Wills, 1675–1798, pt. 1, 15.

15. Middlesex Orders, 1710–21, 149.

16. Middlesex Orders, 1673–80, 186, 193.

17. Ibid., 224, 227.

18. Middlesex Orders, 1680–94, 214, 216–17, 228; Middlesex Deeds, 1679–94, 202–205. The following month Stapleton obtained a judgment of one hundred pounds sterling against Augustine (satisfied in March 1686) that resolved the issue of Augustine's land. The fate of Sarah's horse is unknown.

19. The statement is based upon a conjunction of theory and empirical data. Insofar as it applies to the Chesapeake, we clearly subscribe to the position associated most often with Peter Laslett, viz., that the small nuclear household has been predominant in Western history and that other household forms are variations (usually related to demographic phenomena) on this as an ideal. See e.g., the various essays in Peter Laslett and Richard Wall, eds., *Household and Family in Past Times* (Cambridge, Eng., 1972) and Ken-

neth W. Wachter, with Eugene A. Hammel and Peter Laslett, *Statistical Studies of Historical Social Structure* (New York, 1978). When households are reconstructed using the "census" technique described in Darrett B. and Anita H. Rutman, " 'More True and Perfect Lists': The Reconstruction of Censuses for Middlesex County, Virginia, 1668–1704," *Virginia Magazine of History and Biography*, LXXXVIII (1980), 38–55, and in *Explicatus*, "Population Estimates," the percentage of nuclear households (Fa, Mo, Ch, plus any servants) or a clear cyclic variant of the nuclear (Fa, Mo; Fa, Ch; Mo, Ch) ranges from 76% in 1687 to 89% in 1724 and 1740. The low percentage in 1687 is accounted for by a significant number of households containing single males, in a few cases two unmarried males (e.g., brothers). Note that the test did not distinguish children by parentage, that is separate children of both parents from the children of one or the other or unrelated wards. Because of the high mortality rate, parental loss was, as we shall see, high, and the children were most often a mixed lot. But this does not derogate the ideal of the nuclear unit.

20. It did not happen this way, however. Augustine sold the property in 1695; shortly after, he and Sarah died. Charity moved to a neighbor's and was supported on the public dole until she died in 1702. Margaret disappeared, perhaps dying, perhaps marrying. The buyer of the Williamson land soon sold the property—to Charles Williamson.

21. See *Explicatus*, "Mortality" and "Parental Loss."

22. What follows draws heavily from Darrett B. and Anita H. Rutman, " 'Now-Wives' and Sons-in-Law': Parental Death in a Seventeenth-Century Virginia County," in Thad W. Tate and David L. Ammerman, eds., *The Chesapeake in the Seventeenth Century: Essays on Anglo-American Society* (Chapel Hill, N.C., 1979), 153–82.

23. For children born from 1690 to 1709, the percentages were 21 and 35 respectively; for those born from 1710 to 1750, 21 and 31.

24. Middlesex Wills, 1698–1713, 139–41, 245–46, 231, 236–37; Middlesex Wills, 1713–34, 267–68, 311.

25. Middlesex Wills, 1675–1798, pt. 1, 136–38; Middlesex Orders, 1680–94, 679; Middlesex Wills, 1675–1798, pt. 1, 132; Lancaster Deeds, 1654–1702, 1–2.

26. One result was that the law was extremely restrictive regarding the marriage (even the solicitation to marriage) of minor girls. See, for example, Hening, comp., *Statutes at Large*, II, 281; III, 149–51, 441–46.

27. Middlesex Wills, 1675–1798, pt. 1, 136–38; 1698–1713, 244–45.

28. Lancaster Orders, 1655–66, 307; Middlesex Orders, 1680–94, 47, 100, 240; Middlesex Wills, 1698–1713, 179.

29. Gawin Corbin to Thomas Corbin, April 22, 1676, *Virginia Magazine of History and Biography*, XXIX (1921), 244; Wormeley Estate Papers, 1701–16, with Christ Church, Lancaster Processioners' Returns, 1711–83, Virginia State Library, Richmond. (Extensive extracts of the latter are printed with the Wormeley genealogy in *Virginia Magazine of History and Biography*, XXXVI (1928), 287–91, and in "Robert Carter and the Wormeley Estate," *William and Mary Quarterly*, 1st ser., XVII (1909), 252–64.

30. See this volume, chapter 3, and "Child-Naming Patterns" in the *Explicatus*.

31. Tinling, ed., *Correspondence of the Three William Byrds*, I, 39; Middlesex Wills, 1698–1713, 93; Middlesex Deeds, 1703–20, 57–59, 181; Middlesex Wills, 1675–1798, pt. 1, 1.

32. Davis, ed., *Fitzhugh and His Chesapeake World*, 358.

33. A rationale for distinguishing these particular levels is offered in *Explicatus*, "Social Networks." Militia records are all but nonexistent. The few that remain, however, indicate that the county was organized as a single military unit but mustered generally by precinct-oriented companies. See, for example, the manuscript "List of the Lower Troop of Middlesex County as they Appeared at the place of Exercise the 1st day of August 1730," Middlesex County Records, Virginia Historical Society, Richmond. The unit was a company of forty-five horsemen and included only men from the lower and middle precincts at a time when the lower precinct was all but depopulated of whites (see chapter 8).

34. Middlesex Wills, 1713–34, 329.

35. In 1694, following the deaths of both Nicholas Paine and Dodson's wife, Mabel returned to the lower parts and married Dodson. Subsequently she bore him four daughters. Mabel's story is inferred from bits and pieces. John Hackney Dodson was baptized simply as the "sone of Francis Dodson" (no mention of his mother), but when he died in 1726 his property was divided according to the terms of his will among his sisters Rachel, Mabel, and Rebecca (Mabel's surviving daughters by Dodson) by his cousin William Hackney (son of Mabel's brother William). Elizabeth, born to Mabel three months after her marriage to Nicholas Paine, was not acknowledged in Paine's will although she

was still alive and Paine left bequests to his daughters by Mabel—Mary and Ann. Father Hackney's disapproval of Mabel's relationship to Dodson is clear in his 1700 will. To Mabel he left one shilling, the traditional disinheritance; her children "born whilst she was Nickolas Pains wife"—a phrase carefully excluding John Hackney Dodson and Mabel's legitimate children by Dodson—were named contingency heirs. Oddly enough, Elizabeth Paine was acknowledged by her grandfather and given a specific bequest—featherbed, furniture, plates, spoons. *The Parish Register of Christ Church, Middlesex County, Va. from 1653 to 1812* (Richmond, Va., 1837), 47; Middlesex Wills, 1713–34, 294; Middlesex Wills, 1675–1798, pt. 1, 83; Middlesex Wills, 1698–1713, 95–96.

36. MS Middlesex County Court Records, Virginia Historical Society, Richmond, Va., n.d., but date approximated from contents; "An Account of the Indians in Virginia [1689]," ed. Stanley Pargellis, *William and Mary Quarterly*, 3d ser., XVI (1959), 231.

37. Hening, comp., *Statutes at Large*, II, 102; III, 530–31.

38. Lancaster Orders, 1655–66, 307; Middlesex Orders, 1680–94, 642–43; Hening, comp., *Statutes at Large*, III, 279–82.

39. *Register of Christ Church*, 33; C. G. Chamberlayne, ed., *The Vestry Book of Christ Church Parish, Middlesex County, Virginia, 1663–1767* (Richmond, Va., 1927), 35.

40. Attendance at one church or another can be established in a variety of ways. For long periods baptisms at the Upper Church are identified as such in the existent parish register, while there are occasional indications of Lower and Middle Church baptisms. Similarly, indications of burial at particular churches are found in the register. A survey of tombstones (for the most part in the extant Lower and Middle Church yards) adds others, although caution is required for graves have been moved. Appointment to precinct-oriented offices (reader, clerk, churchwarden, and, in the eighteenth century, sexton) implies residence in the particular precinct, while the presentments and charitable undertakings of the various churchwardens identify the precinct of the offender or recipient. Once it became clear that attendance was largely geographically determined, simple propinquity (as determined by mapping patents, bequests, and conveyances) became an adequate test for most assignments to a precinct; baptisms and the like were resorted to only to establish the boundaries between precincts.

41. Chamberlayne, ed., *Vestry Book of Christ Church*, 48, 68.

42. Ibid., 61. For a number of years in the seventeenth century, the middle and lower precincts—the latter the smallest of the three—shared a clerk/reader. For a while too (1679 to 1689), Joseph Harvey was the only individual paid by the parish to perform the office. It is clear in the records, however, that the upper precinct maintained its own clerk/reader during these years. The various functions associated with the office in the 1689 regulations—reader, clerk, sexton—ultimately separated.

43. Ibid. The squabble followed the death of Harvey, when the middle and lower precinct vestrymen tried to continue the practice of paying only one clerk (officiating at their churches) and the upper precinct vestrymen insisted on paying three.

44. John Nash of the upper precinct was an occasional exception.

45. But see Darrett B. Rutman, "The Evolution of Religious Life in Early Virginia," *Lex et Scientia: The International Journal of Law and Science*, XIV (1978), 190–240, where we are able to draw upon materials from the whole of Virginia.

46. Omitting temporary appointments: John Shepherd, 1668–83; Deuel Pead, 1683–90; Matthew Lidford, 1691–93; Samuel Gray, 1693–98; Robert Yates, 1698–1702; Bartholomew Yates (his brother), 1703–34; John Reade, 1734–36; Bartholomew Yates (son of Bartholomew), 1737–63.

47. Chamberlayne, ed., *Vesty Book of Christ Church*, 44, 86, 177ff., 180–81; William Stevens Perry, comp., *Historical Collections Relating to the American Colonial Church* (Hartford, Conn., 1870–78), I, 348–50. There is one extant example of a Pead sermon: "A Sermon Preached at James City in Virginia the 23d of April 1686," ed. Richard Beale Davis, *William and Mary Quarterly*, 3d ser., XVII (1960), 371–94.

48. Yates's response to the bishop of London's queries, June 15, 1724, Perry, comp., *Historical Collections*, I, 296–98. See also Patricia U. Bonomi and Peter R. Eisenstadt, "Church Adherence in the Eighteenth-Century British American Colonies," *William and Mary Quarterly*, 3d ser., XXXIX (1982), 245–86.

49. Chinard, ed., *Huguenot Exile*, 118; Hunter Dickinson Farish, ed., *Journal & Letters of Philip Vickers Fithian, 1773–1774: A Plantation Tutor of the Old Dominion* (Williamsburg, Va., 1957), 167. The constant disrepair of the churches—like that of the glebe—can be sensed in the repairs and rebuildings recorded in Chamberlayne, ed., *Vestry Book of Christ Church*. The brick churches (the Lower and, much changed, the Middle still standing) were built in the early eighteenth century.

5. Strata

1. See for example William W. Hening, comp., *The Statutes at Large: Being a Collection of all the Laws of Virginia from the First Session of the Legislature in 1619* (Richmond, New York, and Philadelphia, 1809–23), I, 127—a very early example of a pervasive philosophy of punishment.

2. Middlesex Wills, 1675–1798, 146–47; Middlesex Deeds, 1679–94, 80; C. G. Chamberlayne, ed., *The Vestry Book of Christ Church Parish, Middlesex County, Virginia, 1663–1767* (Richmond, Va., 1927), 4.

3. The building is described in Middlesex Orders, 1694–1705, 570.

4. Lancaster Orders, 1666–80, 206. See also Chamberlayne, ed., *Vestry Book of Christ Church*, 62–63.

5. "The Autobiography of the Reverend Devereux Jarratt, 1732–1763," *William and Mary Quarterly*, 3d ser., IX (1952), 361. The autobiography was originally published as *The Life of the Reverend Devereux Jarratt, Rector of Bath Parish, Dinwiddie County, Virginia, Written by Himself, in a series of Letters Addressed to the Rev. John Coleman* . . . (Baltimore, 1806). We cite the *William and Mary Quarterly* version of the first part, published with introduction and notes by Douglass Adair, as the most convenient.

6. Gilbert Chinard, ed., *A Huguenot Exile in Virginia: Or Voyages of a Frenchman exiled for his Religion with a description of Virginia and Maryland* (New York, 1934), 116–17.

7. Abbot Emerson Smith, *Colonists in Bondage: White Servitude and Convict Labor in America, 1607–1776* (Chapel Hill, N.C., 1947), 261, describes as "negligible" "a disposition to general rebellion" among the servants. For the fear of servant rebellion, see, e.g., Hening, comp., *Statutes at Large*, II, 395, 509–10. In the first, "evile disposed servants" are allegedly taking advantage of Bacon's Rebellion. In the second, inhabitants of York, Gloucester, and Middlesex in 1670 express their fear of "fellons and other desperate villaines" being carried into Virginia as servants and hark back to the "barbourous designe of those villaines" who plotted servant revolt in Gloucester in 1663. See also Middlesex Orders, 1680–94, 309–10, a reference to a plot among Wormeley servants unmasked in 1687.

8. Nicholas Spencer to Lord Culpeper, 1676, quoted in Edmund S. Morgan, *American Slavery, American Freedom: The Ordeal of Colonial Virginia* (New York, 1975), 236; Chinard, ed., *Huguenot Exile*, 93, 95; Louis B. Wright, ed., *An Essay upon the Government of the English Plantations on the Continent of America (1701): An Anonymous Virginian's Proposals for Liberty Under The British Crown* . . . (San Marino, Calif., 1945), 30.

9. Middlesex's Ralph Wormeley blamed the proprietors of other colonies, particularly William Penn, for putting out false stories about Virginia and drawing off would-be servants. "This Art of getting and keeping People from us, is a piece of very ill Neighbourhood in them," he wrote in *An Essay upon the Government of the English Plantations*, 35. We follow the attribution of this pamphlet to Wormeley argued by Virginia White Fitz, "Ralph Wormeley: Anonymous Essayist," *William and Mary Quarterly*, 3d ser., XXVI (1969), 586–95, rather than Wright's attribution of it to Robert Beverley (p. xi) or Carole Shammas's attribution in "Benjamin Harrison III and the Authorship of *An Essay upon the Government of the English Plantations*. . . ," *Virginia Magazine of History and Biography*, LXXXIV (1976), 166–73. Robert Beverley's *The History and Present State of Virginia*, ed., Louis B. Wright (Chapel Hill, N.C., 1947) is also in part an effort to refurbish Virginia's reputation. See e.g., p. 297: "That which makes this Country most unfortunate is, that it must submit to receive its Character from the Mouths not only of unfit, but very unequal Judges."

10. Middlesex Orders, 1694–1705, 428, 483.

11. Hening, comp., *Statutes at Large*, II, 117–18. Almost half a century later, Robert Beverley included a digest of the laws relating to servants for much the same reasons. See his *History and Present State of Virginia*, 272–73.

12. Hening, comp., *Statutes at Large*, II, 167; Chamberlayne, ed., *Vestry Book of Christ Church*, 90; Middlesex Orders, 1705–10, 28.

13. Hening, comp., *Statutes at Large*, II, 116–18, 266, 277–79. Whites running away with blacks—whose service never ended—were required to serve additional time technically owed by the black.

14. Ibid., 115, 266. We have no real way of establishing anything like a precise offense rate. In 1682 Middlesex men were awarded three thousand pounds of tobacco from the colony levy in accordance with a law establishing a two hundred–pound reward for apprehending a runaway more than ten miles from the master's house. H. R. McIlwaine and J. P. Kennedy, eds., *Journals of the House of Burgesses of Virginia* (Richmond, Va., 1905–15), II, 175. (An earlier one thousand–pound tobacco reward had proved prohib-

itively expensive.) Assuming all of the runaways for whom rewards were claimed were white servants and belonged in Middlesex, and estimating two hundred white servants in the county that year—extreme assumptions meant to compensate for runaways not apprehended—suggests a rate of seventy-five per one thousand.

15. Lancaster Orders, 1655–66, 179; Middlesex Deeds, 1679–94, 4–5; Middlesex Orders, 1680–94, 428.

16. Lancaster Orders, 1655–66, 139, 149, 242.

17. Lancaster Orders, 1666–80, 47, 72, 75.

18. Joseph Ewan and Nesta Ewan, eds., *John Banister and His Natural History of Virginia, 1678–1692* (Urbana, Ill., 1970), 355; Edmund Berkeley and Dorothy Smith Berkeley, eds., *The Reverend John Clayton: A Parson with a Scientific Mind, His Scientific Writings and Other Related Papers* (Charlottesville, Va., 1965), 107; Beverley, *History and Present State of Virginia,* 309–10.

19. Middlesex Orders, 1680–94, 527.

20. We have met Marter before. In 1689 he had married Robinson's runaway servant Ann. By 1696 Ann was dead.

21. Middlesex Orders, 1694–1705, 105–10.

22. In the absence of general court records, there is no direct evidence that Ann Davis was executed, but everything points to that conclusion. County records indicate that she was dispatched for trial and that the "Tryall of Ann Davis (a Criminall)" was held in March 1696. (Middlesex Orders, 1694–1705, 126.) She never returned from Jamestown, and Henry, at his death in 1697, left no widow. In July 1698, Alice Davis was referred to as "fatherless and motherless" and placed in the care of Adam and Hannah Barwell. (Ibid., 230.) Hannah was the widow of Nicholas West, Ann's brother, who died shortly before or after the murder. To complete the dissolution of the household: Rose Gates was removed from Henry's care at the same court at which Ann was remanded for trial. John Marter disappears from the records after receiving 120 pounds tobacco as a fee for testifying against Ann. We know nothing of Marter's "boy."

23. In chapter 1, as an illustration of the extent of the prosopography underlying the computerized biographies.

24. Middlesex Orders, 1705–10, 206, 104.

25. Middlesex Deeds, 1703–20, 277–83. We have taken the liberty of transforming the third person, past tense recital of the depositions into first person, present tense dialogue.

26. Unfortunately, Gloucester County records are not extant.

27. Wortham was convicted of murder but, "it being found by the jury that the fact was committed *se defendendo,*" was pardoned by the governor. H. R. McIlwaine and W. L. Hall, eds., *Executive Journals of the Council of Colonial Virginia, 1680–1754* (Richmond, Va., 1925–45), III, 288.

28. See e.g., Roland Mousnier, *Social Hierarchies: 1450 to the Present,* trans. Peter Evans (New York, 1973), 9–20; Robert A. Nisbet, *The Social Bond* (New York, 1970), 187–97.

29. James A. Henretta, *The Evolution of American Society, 1700–1815: An Interdisciplinary Analysis* (Lexington, Mass., 1973), 93. See also the works of Rhys Isaac (e.g., "Evangelical Revolt: The Nature of the Baptists' Challenge to the Traditional Order in Virginia, 1765 to 1775," *William and Mary Quarterly,* 3d ser., XXXI [1974], 345–68) and T. H. Breen (e.g., "Horses and Gentlemen: The Cultural Significance of Gambling among the Gentry of Virginia," *William and Mary Quarterly,* 3d ser., XXXIV [1977], 239–57). The last chapters of Edmund S. Morgan's *American Slavery, American Freedom* project into the eighteenth century a society at variance with that assumed in these works; in Morgan's hands, however, Virginia's seventeenth-century society tends to fit the Henretta-Isaac-Breen pattern.

30. See *Explicatus,* "Status."

31. Franchise requirements varied, but from 1677 on franchises were limited to the freeholder, defined in 1684 as a "person who holds lands, tenements or hereditaments for his owne life, for the life of his wife, or for the life of any other person or persons." Hening, comp., *Statutes at Large,* III, 26. Subsequent acts refined the definition to male, twenty-one years of age or older, with a freehold of twenty-five acres with a house or one hundred acres without, and excluded convicted recusants. Ibid., III, 172–75, 236–46; IV, 475–78.

32. Specifically 36.5 percent of the 230 male heads of household on the reconstructed census of 1699 reported in Darrett B. and Anita H. Rutman, " 'More True and Perfect Lists': The Reconstruction of Censuses for Middlesex County, Virginia, 1668–1704," *Virginia Magazine of History and Biography,* LXXXVIII (1980), 37–74. Twenty-five

years later, 86 men held 156 offices, 34.4 percent of the 250 male household heads.

33. Middlesex Wills, 1698–1713, 132, tobacco converted to current using *Explicatus,* table 1.

34. See e.g., Hening, comp., *Statutes at Large,* I, 433; II, 353–55, 389–91; III, 168–71; "Extracts from Proceedings of the House of Burgesses of Virginia, 1652–1661," *Virginia Magazine of History and Biography,* VIII (1900–1901), 393–94; Middlesex Orders, 1694–1705, 562.

35. Petit jury duty was restricted to freeholders with "visible" lands and goods worth fifty pounds sterling in 1699; and grand jury duty to "freeholders" in 1705. Hening, comp., *Statutes at Large,* III, 175–76, 367–71. In Middlesex the sheriff was charged with the selection of grand juries "of the ablest freeholders and Inhabitants" (1688) and juries of "the hone[st] men of the Neighbourhood" (1680), "the Antientest and Discreetest Freeholders of the Neighbourhood" (1686). Middlesex Orders, 1673–80, 226; 1680–94, 265, 336.

36. Middlesex Orders, 1694–1705, 186.

37. *The Parish Register of Christ Church, Middlesex County, Va. from 1653 to 1812* (Richmond, Va., 1897), 41.

38. E.g., Charles Edgar Gilliam, " 'Mr.' in Virginia Records before 1776," *William and Mary Quarterly,* 2d ser., XIX (1939), 142–45. Gilliam argued that honorifics spread so far down through the society that they could not be indications of status by birth, but that they were an indication of some sort of status based upon "personal worth." We agree. See *Explicatus,* "Status."

39. Middlesex Wills, 1698–1713, 113–32.

40. Chinard, ed., *Huguenot Exile,* 142.

41. The Huguenot exile wrote of Wormeley renting one house to the governor, who ate one meal a day in his own house and the other in Wormeley's; the houses were arranged in such a way as to form what the French traveler thought of as a "courtyard" (ibid., 142, 147). That they were in some fashion joined together is a conjecture based upon the order of the rooms designated in the 1701 inventory. On the first day, the appraisers seem to have proceeded through a four-room structure typical of the time and economic level of the deceased (viz., "parlor," "chamber," "chamber over said chamber," and "chamber over the parlor," each with a fireplace), ending "at the Stair head in the passage." On the second day, they moved through "the nursery" and "old nursery" to "the room over the Ladyes Chamber," then down to "the Ladies chamber," an "entry," and into the two "closets." If we assume that the "passage" led in some fashion into a connecting structure containing the nursery above and Esquire Wormeley's closet below, then the old nursery, the room over the lady's chamber, the lady's chamber, and Madam Wormeley's closet form a second, typical house, and the progression through the structure would be logical. The house presently standing, while it may contain elements of an older structure, is clearly eighteenth-century. We are indebted to Jonathan H. Poston, who, in 1979, arranged for our examination of the present structure and subsequently shared with us his extensive knowledge of the site, and to Mr. and Mrs. Charles R. Longsworth of Rosegill and Williamsburg, who graciously gave us entry to the house.

42. The buildings are specified in the inventory. See Middlesex Orders, 1694–1705, 28, for reference to the building of the kitchen; Middlesex Deeds, 1679–94, 123–24 for the mill; Philip Alexander Bruce, *Institutional History of Virginia in the Seventeenth Century* (New York, 1910), II, 167, for the battery. At some point in time, a mill dam was erected on the home farm, forming a lake. We suspect this was done around 1701 and that millstones in the inventory were designed for the mill then being built or planned.

43. Middlesex Wills, 1698–1713, 116; Chinard, ed., *Huguenot Exile,* 104.

44. Louis B. Wright, *The First Gentlemen of Virginia: Intellectual Qualities of the Early Colonial Ruling Class* (San Marino, Calif., 1940), 197–211, explores the Wormeley library.

45. See *Explicatus,* "Literacy."

46. The titles of Wright's *First Gentlemen* and Jackson Turner Main's "The One Hundred," *William and Mary Quarterly,* 3d ser., XI (1954), 355–84.

47. Some Middlesex examples: Ralph *Wormeley* (Agatha Eltonhead's son) married first his local cousin, Lady Katherine Lunsford, then Elizabeth Armistead of Gloucester. He was related to and friends with London merchants Gawin and Thomas Corbin, Edmund Jennings of York (who married his cousin, Frances Corbin), and Robert Carter of Lancaster (who married his wife's sister, Judith Armistead); they, along with William Armistead of Gloucester, were named overseers of his estate in his will. Of his children, daughter Katherine married her cousin, Gawin Corbin of Middlesex; Elizabeth married John Lomax of Essex; Judith married Mann Page of Gloucester; John married Elizabeth Ring of York. John, at his death, owned lands in Middlesex, Gloucester, King William,

York, Caroline, and King George. Henry *Corbin* arrived from England via Westmoreland to marry Alice (Eltonhead) Burnham. His merchant brothers, Gawin and Thomas, remained in England and were his major London connections. Of his children: Lettice married Richard Lee of Westmoreland; Alice married Philip Lightfoot of Charles City: Winifred married Leroy Griffin of Rappahannock; Ann married William Tayloe of Richmond; Frances married Edmund Jennings of York. Corbin's son Thomas went to England and became a London merchant. Another, Gawin, married Ralph Wormeley's daughter by the Lady Lunsford, then successively Jane (Lane) Wilson of King and Queen and Martha Bassett of New Kent. Robert *Beverley* married Katherine (Armistead) Hone of the Gloucester Armisteads and widow of Theophilus Hone of Elizabeth City. His son Peter married Elizabeth Peyton of Gloucester; Robert Beverley, Jr., married Ursula Byrd, daughter of William Byrd of Westover; his daughter Mary married William Jones of King and Queen. The first Beverley, at his death, owned lands in Gloucester, Rappahannock, and New Kent, as well as in Middlesex, some in parnership with his brother-in-law, John Armistead of Gloucester. He was a business partner of William Fitzhugh of Stafford. And for some years he had London connections with Gawin Corbin. The first John *Grymes* arrived in Middlesex already married to Alice Townley, daughter of Lawrence and Sarah (Warner) Townley of Gloucester. At his death in 1709 he owned land in Richmond, Gloucester, King and Queen, and Middlesex. His executors were not Middlesex but Gloucester men. His son Charles married Frances Jennings of York; John junior married Lucy Ludwell of James City. John junior's 1748 will indicates land ownership in Orange, Gloucester, Caroline, King and Queen, and Middlesex. In his will he left a diamond ring to England's Horatio Walpole "as my Acknowledgment of the many Obligations I lie under through a Long Continuance of his Savour and Protection" (Middlesex Wills, 1675–1798, pt. 1, 231).

48. Quoted in Morgan, *American Slavery, American Freedom*, 274, 275; Stephen Saunders Webb, *The Governors-General: The English Army and the Definition of the Empire, 1569–1681* (Chapel Hill, N.C., 1979), 366.

49. Middlesex Orders, 1680–94, 51, 55.

50. Quoting Morgan, *American Slavery, American Freedom*, 285, and Webb, *Governors-General*, 403–404, 408, 415. See also John C. Rainbolt, *From Prescription to Persuasion: Manipulation of [Seventeenth] Century Virginia Economy* (Port Washington, N.Y., 1974), 117–20; Thomas J. Wertenbaker, *Virginia under the Stuarts, 1607–1688* (Princeton, N.J., 1914), 232–37.

51. Richard Beale Davis, ed., *William Fitzhugh and His Chesapeake World, 1676–1701: The Fitzhugh Letters and Other Documents* (Chapel Hill, N.C., 1963), 119; Hening, comp., *Statutes at Large*, III, 544.

52. We do not have full export figures for these years, but London imports in 1681 (the crop of 1680) were 14.5 million pounds, up 2.5 million from 1680 and 1.5 million from 1679. U.S. Bureau of the Census, *Historical Statistics of the United States, Colonial Times to 1970, Part 2* (Washington, D.C., 1975), 1190.

53. Chinard, ed., *Huguenot Exile*, 141–42.

54. For Morgan, *American Slavery, American Freedom*, 338–62, this sort of "populism" was purely an eighteenth-century development.

55. County records and Chamberlayne, ed., *Vestry Book of Christ Church* indicate presence at court and vestry meetings. Robert Beverley appeared at 32.5% of the court sessions during the years he was a member and 23.7% of the vestry meetings; Ralph Wormeley appeared at 5.5% of the courts and 43.2% of the vestries; John Burnham at 44.1% and 33.3% respectively. These examples of cosmopolitan gentlemen are in sharp contrast to the records of county-oriented gentry. John Wortham attended 86.7% of the courts and 91% of the vestry meetings following his appointments; Randolph Seager 88.8% of the courts and 66.6% of the vestries; William Daniell 89.4% and 78.7%.

56. Middlesex Orders, 1680–94, 314.

57. Middlesex Orders, 1705–10, 275.

6. "The Negro Road"

1. Middlesex Deeds, 1703–20, 400.

2. Lancaster Deeds, 1652–57, 202–3; 1654–1702, 56; William Berkeley, "Enquiries to the Governor of Virginia . . . with the Governor's Answers," *Virginia Historical Register*, III (1850), 10.

3. Elizabeth Donnan, ed., *Documents Illustrative of the History of the Slave Trade to America* (Washington, D.C., 1930–35), I, 250, IV, 58; Richard Beale Davis, ed., *William Fitzhugh and His Chesapeake World, 1676–1701: The Fitzhugh Letters and Other Documents*

(Chapel Hill, N.C., 1963), 93, 175; Marion Tingling, ed., *The Correspondence of the Three William Byrds of Westover, Virginia, 1684–1776* (Charlottesville, Va., 1977), I, 26.

4. Donnan, ed., *Slave Trade*, IV, 11, 12n.; Gilbert Chinard, ed., *A Huguenot Exile in Virginia: Or Voyages of a Frenchman exiled for his Religion with a description of Virginia and Maryland* (New York, 1934), 141, 148; William P. Palmer et al., eds., *Calendar of Virginia State Papers and Other Manuscripts [1652–1869]* (Richmond, Va., 1875–93), I, 30, 34, 36–37.

5. "An Account of the Indians in Virginia [1689]," ed. Stanley Pargellis, *William and Mary Quarterly*, 3d ser., XVI (1959), 242; Donnan, ed., *Slave Trade*, IV, 65, 67.

6. See *Explicatus*, "Population Estimates." In 1705, perhaps only coincidentally, Gawin Corbin, a London merchant with strong business and kinship ties to Middlesex, was himself on the African coast outbidding others for slaves. See Donnan, ed., *Slave Trade*, II, 43; IV, 174n.

7. Darrett B. and Anita H. Rutman, " 'More True and Perfect Lists': The Reconstruction of Censuses for Middlesex County, Virginia, 1668–1704," *Virginia Magazine of History and Biography*, LXXXVIII (1980), 58.

8. Chinard, ed., *Huguenot Exile*, 142, describes Wormeley's labor force at the beginning of 1687 as 26 "negro slaves" and 20 "Christian"—the latter presumably white servants. The 26 blacks would be 22.2% of the 117 we estimate to have been in the county at the time. The 85 Wormeley blacks inventoried in 1701 (see note 9) are 18.2% of the 466 we estimate for that year. The reconstructed censuses described in Rutman and Rutman, " 'More True and Perfect Lists,' " 37–74, unweighted and organized by household heads, allow us to make minimal determinations of the number of households with at least a given number of blacks. Thus in 1699, 18.8% of all household heads owned at least 1; 11.8% at least 3; 7% at least 6; 4.4% at least 11; and 1.1% at least 21. In 1704, 19.5% owned at least 1; 12.7% at least 3; 8.1% at least 6; 3.9% at least 11; and 1.6% at least 21. Inventories are frequently used for such calculations but are a poor source unless weighted to reflect the living population. Our weights would most appropriately be based upon the reconstructed censuses. Using the censuses themselves is a more direct procedure. The censuses, however, are inferior as a source when exact sizes of individual holdings are required for a calculation. The reconstructions understate the number of blacks, and while weights can correct an aggregation they cannot be applied to a single holding. We have, consequently, used inventories in the discussion of returns from slave capital in the text.

9. Middlesex Wills, 1698–1713, 113–31. See *Explicatus*, "The Aggregate Black," for our methods of estimating ages. The labor force in the quarters included 32 adult males (adult being defined as sixteen years of age and over), 27 adult females, and 21 children. The average population of a quarter was 6.6 adults and 2.3 children; excluding Crumwell's—a geriatric quarter to all appearances—7 and 2.5. The average black adult (again excepting Crumwell's) found himself or herself in a group of 7.3 adults and 3.6 children, reporting Smith's C-Means (see Daniel Scott Smith, "Averages for Units and Averages for Individuals within Units: A Note," *Journal of Family History*, IV [1979], 84–86). Using the weighted 1704 census, we estimate the mean slave holding in the county to have been 8.4 and that the average black lived in an establishment of 40.3 slaves. By "establishment" we mean the total holdings of a slaveowner; it is not to be confused with "quarter"—the actual social group within which so many of the blacks lived.

10. See infra in the text for both the incident and evidence of the absence of overseers on at least some properties.

11. Rosegill's ratio of children (zero to fifteen years old) to adult women (sixteen and over) was 0.78, Berkeley's 1.65. Unfortunately, very few of the inventories of large holdings break down the blacks into quarters, although all other evidence points to quartering as a common practice.

12. Middlesex Wills, 1713–34, 138–48. The inventory contains no evaluations but includes ages through fifteen. The average adult black on a quarter found himself in a group of eleven adults and between four and five children.

13. Middlesex Wills, 1698–1713, 98–106, 176–79.

14. The case is to be found in Middlesex Orders, 1694–1705, 490–98.

15. Condensing the divergent theses of Edmund S. Morgan, *American Slavery, American Freedom: The Ordeal of Colonial Virginia* (New York, 1975), and Russell R. Menard, "From Servants to Slaves: The Transformation of the Chesapeake Labor System," *Southern Studies*, XVI (1977), 355–90.

16. See, for example, Allan Kulikoff, "The Beginnings of the Afro-American Family in Maryland," Aubrey C. Land et al., eds., *Law, Society and Politics in Early Maryland* (Baltimore, Md., 1977), 171–96; Kulikoff, "The Origins of Afro-American Society in

Tidewater Maryland and Virginia, 1700 to 1790," *William and Mary Quarterly*, 3d ser., XXXV (1978), 226–59; the early chapters of Gerald W. Mullin, *Flight and Rebellion: Slave Resistance in Eighteenth-Century Virginia* (New York, 1972). Although the setting is South Carolina, Peter H. Wood's *Black Majority: Negroes in Colonial South Carolina from 1670 through the Stono Rebellion* (New York, 1974) is suggestive. Among the better recent studies of nineteenth-century slave culture are Eugene D. Genovese, *Roll, Jordan, Roll: The World the Slaves Made* (New York, 1972); Herbert G. Gutman, *The Black Family in Slavery and Freedom, 1750–1925* (New York, 1976); Robert William Fogel and Stanley L. Engerman, *Time on the Cross: The Economics of American Negro Slavery* (Boston, 1974); John W. Blassingame, *The Slave Community: Plantation Life in the Antebellum South* (2d edn.; New York, 1979); and Leslie Howard Owens, *This Species of Property: Slave Life and Culture in the Old South* (New York, 1976). See also Lawrence W. Levine, *Black Culture and Black Consciousness: Afro-American Folk Thought from Slavery to Freedom* (New York, 1977). Stanley M. Elkins, *Slavery: A Problem in American Institutional and Intellectual Life* (3d edn.; Chicago, 1976) is an invaluable introduction to the historiography of its subject, particularly chapters 1, 5, and 6.

17. J. Graham Cruikshank, *Black Talk: Being Notes on Negro Dialect in British Guiana* (1916), quoted in J. L. Dillard, *Black English: Its History and Usage in the United States* (New York, 1972), 137–38. Translation:

"English! Where would I learn it?"

"You didn't know any English at all when you came to the white man's country?"

"None at all!"

"Who taught you when you came?"

"Who taught me? Eh-eh! Who else but my friend?"

"How did he teach you? Did he give you a book and so on?"

"Book! You gotta be kiddin'! Does our people have books? . . ."

"In what manner did you learn?"

"It was Uncle whom I lived with who taught me himself. Uncle would say 'Boy, take this calabash—the calabash would be in his hand—and go dip water. Water—water, the thing inside the barrel.' So Uncle did, until I picked up English little by little."

"So you all picked up white man's talk, little by little?"

"Yes, that's it. A friend would teach a friend, that friend would be teaching another friend. Haven't you ever seen how a child learns to talk—when his father is talking he'll be watching his father's mouth?"

18. Louis B. Wright and Marion Tinling, eds., *The Secret Diary of William Byrd of Westover, 1709–1712* (Richmond, Va., 1941), 19, 34, 483; Tingling, ed., *Correspondence of the Three William Byrds*, I, 355. See Mullin, *Flight and Rebellion*, chapter 1, for a number of other expressions of the same import.

19. Middlesex Orders, 1680–94, 535.

20. Middlesex Orders, 1694–1705, 234–42. Italics inserted.

21. Genovese's argument in *Roll, Jordan, Roll*, 4–7.

22. Middlesex Deeds, 1679–94, 359, partially modernized to improve readability. See also Peter Laslett, *The World we have lost* (New York, 1965), 2.

23. The historian's sources are such that we tend generally to think in terms of formal names. In baptismal records, legal appearances, contracts, and the like, peoples' names were set down (for us to read) as John, Matthew, Francis, Henry, Mary, Susanna, and so forth. Yet it is important to realize the widespread use of diminutives: "Jack" Wormeley, "Matt" Kemp, "Frank" Dodson, "Harry" Daniell, "Poll" Cole, "Molly" Byrd, "Sukey" Carter. The analysis of the setting in which the diminutive was used—the conversation between Madam Creyke and Jane Olney, for example—allows reconstruction of the rules of usage. It is on this basis that we construe the diminutive as familial. Diminutives occasionally trespassed into the realm of formal names in the seventeenth century, but they did so increasingly in the eighteenth. Some examples from the baptismal records: Betty George (1722), Betty Blackey (1723), Aggy Mosely (1729), Peggy Jones (1744), Sukey Kidd (1747). The appearance of these names seems an ironic consequence of the fact that with slavery the diminutive forms were so much more publicly expressed.

24. See *Explicatus*, "Child-Naming Patterns." We give there our evidence for rejecting completely the argument that black names reflected in any significant ways African roots or patterns. Cf. Dillard, *Black English*, 123–35.

25. Tinling, ed., *Correspondence of the Three William Byrds*, II, 488.

26. Winthrop D. Jordan, *White over Black: American Attitudes toward the Negro, 1550–1812* (Chapel Hill, N.C., 1968), 41.

27. William W. Hening, comp., *The Statutes at Large: Being a Collection of all the Laws of Virginia from the First Session of the Legislature in 1619* (Richmond, New York, and Philadelphia, 1809–23), III, 86. See also Jordan, *White over Black,* 138–40.

28. Tinling, ed., *Correspondence of the Three William Byrds,* II, 488.

29. Hening, comp., *Statutes at Large,* II, 481, 493; III, 86–88, 102–3; V, 16–24; *The Parish Register of Christ Church, Middlesex County, Va., from 1653 to 1812* (Richmond, Va., 1897), 57–58; Middlesex Orders, 1694–1705, 383; H. R. McIlwaine and J. P. Kennedy, eds., *Journals of the House of Burgesses of Virginia* (Richmond, Va., 1905–15), III, 266. The petition of 1700, signed by twenty-four middle-level householders, was rejected in 1701 on the grounds that previous laws "sufficiently provide" concerning the same. The previous law (1692) provided that damage done by slaves "living at a quarter where there is noe christian overseer" be recompensed by the owner. Hening, comp., *Statutes at Large,* III, 103.

30. We have used an estimate of the number of servants or slaves at the midpoints of five-year periods (e.g., 1678 for 1676 to 1680) and multiplied by 5 to establish servant- and slave-years-lived during the period, computing ratios by dividing the number of accusations before the court by years-lived and multiplying by 1,000. Servant rates for the years 1676 to 1680 = 12.1; 1681 to 1685 = 33.7; 1686 to 1690 = 25.1. Slave rates, 1711 to 1715 = 6.2; 1716 to 1720 = 1.9; 1721 to 1725 = 2.5. The rates in the text are averages of the period rates. For overall offense rates, see chapter 1, note 27. Robinson also had trouble with his white servants and was frequently complained against for "immoderate correction," "insufficiency of clothing," and the like. See e.g., Middlesex Orders, 1710–21, 404, 468, 473, 502; 1721–26, 130, 136, 179.

31. Waverly K. Winfree, comp., *The Laws of Virginia: Being a Supplement to Hening's The Statutes at Large, 1700–1750* (Richmond, Va., 1971), 257–59.

32. Middlesex Orders, 1705–10, 129, 328; 1710–21, 40, 93, 336; H. R. McIlwaine and W. L. Hall, eds., *Executive Journals of the Council of Colonial Virginia, 1680–1754* (Richmond, Va., 1925–45), III, 242–43.

33. Middlesex Orders, 1694–1705, 519. We do not know the result.

34. Jack P. Greene, ed., *The Diary of Colonel Landon Carter of Sabine Hall, 1752–1778* (Charlottesville, Va., 1965), II, 635.

35. On disease exchange in general, see William H. McNeill, *Plagues and Peoples* (New York, 1976); on malaria, Darrett B. and Anita H. Rutman, "Of Agues and Fevers: Malaria in the Early Chesapeake," *William and Mary Quarterly,* 3d ser., XXXIII (1976), 31–60.

36. See chapter 3, note 22.

37. Hening, comp., *Statutes at Large,* II, 479–80; Henry Hartwell et al., *The Present State of Virginia, and the College* (1699), ed. Hunter Dickinson Farish (Williamsburg, Va., 1940), 5–6.

38. The assumptions and procedures involved in the calculation of capital gains and profits here and in the examples following are the same as those used in the simulation reported in *Explicatus,* "The Aggregate Black," with the exception of the fertility and mortality rates incorporated in the latter. All values are standardized to a 1723 base. The estimated gain from Sharlott is minimal, for in the absence of birth records from the late 1740s on, we are undoubtedly missing grandchildren.

39. Middlesex Wills, 1713–34, 357, 361–62; 1740–48, 193–95.

40. In generalizing we have again used the age-specific production and cost factors given in *Explicatus,* "The Aggregate Black," and have filled in missing ages in inventories by the methods sketched there. Where the data available in an inventory defied all efforts to estimate an age, we assumed a prime black. Missing values were estimated by applying the age-value curve depicted in the *Explicatus,* figure 35. All values representing monetary sums (capital, gross income, costs) were adjusted to a constant 1723 base. The analysis was based upon 162 complete inventories listing 1,124 slaves. The inventories were broken into three groups according to the number of slaves listed by an iterative least-squares procedure testing all possible cutpoints to find the best-fitting categorization of return on capital (*eta* squared = .222). The declining variance in the categories is indicative of the relatively tight fit about the mean among large holders (individual returns on slave capital more apt to approximate the mean) and a relatively loose fit among small holders (individual returns more likely to stray toward extremes). The results:

NUMBER OF SLAVES	NUMBER OF INVENTORIES	RETURN ON SLAVE CAPITAL (%)		
		MEAN	MEDIAN	VARIANCE
1–3	68	14.9	15.0	24.4
4–9	64	12.1	12.8	14.8
10+	30	8.9	9.5	5.6

41. Thomas Percy, "Sir Cauline," pt. II, lines 1–2, in *Reliques of Ancient English Poetry* (1765), ed. Henry B. Wheatley (London, 1886), I, 70; Middlesex Wills, 1713–34, 333–34.

42. Based upon unweighted census reconstructions for the year (see note 8) 45.6% of household heads owned at least 1, 30.1% at least 3, 17.9% at least 6, 9.1% at least 11, and 4.7% at least 21. In 1740—the date of our last census—50.2% owned at least 1 slave, 33.7% at least 3, 21.5% at least 6, 12.2% at least 11, and 5.0% at least 21. Using the weighted censuses, we estimate the average holding of 1724 to have been 8.5 and the average black to have lived in an establishment of 30; in 1740 the average holding was 8.3 and the average black lived in an establishment of 21.5.

43. The examples that follow are drawn from the biographies described in chapter 1. See note 40 above for the assumptions and procedures underlying the calculations of gains and losses.

44. Middlesex Wills, 1698–1713, 161.

45. See *Explicatus* and particularly table 45.

46. See *Explicatus* and particularly table 34.

47. Lancaster Deeds, 1652–57, 202–4; Middlesex Wills, 1698–1713, 98–106, 176–79; 1713–34, 37–39.

48. Middlesex Orders, 1694–1705, 28; Middlesex Wills, 1698–1713, 55–76, 89–90, 140; Louise E. Gray et al., *Historic Buildings in Middlesex County, Virginia, 1650–1875* (n.p., 1978), 154.

49. Lancaster Deeds, 1654–1702, 16–17; Middlesex Wills, 1698–1713, 8, 147–48; 1713–34, 364.

50. Lois Green Carr and Lorena S. Walsh, "Inventories and the Analysis of Wealth and Consumption Patterns in St. Mary's County, Maryland, 1658–1777," *Historical Methods*, XIII (1980), 81–104, also see a spread of amenities through the society and (pp. 93, 96) suggest a number of possible explanations.

51. Michael Dalton, *The Countrey Justice, Containing the practise of the Justices of the Peace out of their Sessions. Gathered, for the better helpe of such Justices of Peace as have not been much conversant in the studie of the Lawes* (London, 1622), 82; Hening, comp., *Statutes at Large*, II, 246; Middlesex Orders, 1680–94, 375. See also Virginia Bernhard, "Poverty and the Social Order in Seventeenth-Century Virginia," *Virginia Magazine of History and Biography*, LXXXV (1977), 141–55; Howard Mackey, "The Operation of the English Old Poor Law in Colonial Virginia," *Virginia Magazine of History and Biography*, LXXIII (1965), 29–40; Mackey, "Social Welfare in Colonial Virginia: The Importance of the English Old Poor Law," *Historical Magazine of the Protestant Episcopal Church*, XXXVI (1967), 357–82.

52. Lancaster Orders, 1655–66, 323; C. G. Chamberlayne, ed., *The Vestry Book of Christ Church Parish, Middlesex County, Virginia, 1663–1767* (Richmond, Va., 1927), 4.

53. Chamberlayne, ed., *Vestry Book of Christ Church*, 9, 10, 17, 26, 28, 29.

54. Ibid., 26, 29, 31.

55. The law only spoke to the matter of parents and children (e.g., Hening, comp., *Statutes at Large*, II, 298; Winfree, comp., *Supplement to Hening*, 255), although Dalton, *Countrey Justice*, 84–85, was specific on the equal responsibility of grandparents and grandchildren. We infer custom from practice.

56. Welfare cases are identified by application to the biographies described in chapter 1. See *Explicatus* for population estimates. Welfare costs have been extracted from county and parish budgets found throughout the manuscript county records and from Chamberlayne, ed., *Vestry Book of Christ Church*. Budgeted welfare costs per se are an understatement because the churchwardens (who had a special role in dispensing charity) rarely recorded full accounts. We have attempted to fill the hiatus by estimating on the basis of fines received (they were dispensed to the poor by the churchwardens) and reimbursements to the churchwardens when they expended their own funds. The figures in the text are averages of five-year aggregations.

57. See *Explicatus* and particularly table 41.

58. McIlwaine and Kennedy, eds., *Journals of the House of Burgesses*, V, 12; Chamberlayne, ed., *Vestry Book of Christ Church*, 153.

59. Middlesex Deeds, 1687–1750, 10–11, 35, 45–46; Middlesex Orders, 1694–1705, 350, 546, 570.

60. The remodeling and building of the churches can be followed in Chamberlayne, ed., *Vestry Book of Christ Church*, 67–147; George Carrington Mason, *Colonial Churches of Tidewater Virginia* (Richmond, Va., 1945), 282–88.

61. Middlesex Orders, 1680–94, 200–201; Marcus Whiffen, *The Eighteenth-Century Houses of Williamsburg: A Study of Architecture and Building in the Colonial Capital of Virginia* (Williamsburg, Va., 1960), 73–74.

62. The building directions are in Middlesex Orders, 1694–1705, 546, 570 (courthouse); Chamberlayne, ed., *Vestry Book of Christ Church*, 118–23 (Upper Church), 126–31 (Middle), 139–40, 144–47 (Lower).

63. The Lower Church. The Upper Church was replaced again in the 1770s; the Middle Church fell into ruins in the early nineteenth century, was rebuilt at mid-century, and has been extensively remodeled since; the courthouse was abandoned in 1748 when a new one was built in Urbanna. The fate of the buildings can be followed in Mason, *Colonial Churches of Tidewater Virginia*, 288–91; Gray et al., *Historic Buildings in Middlesex*, 12–15, 93–96, 127–29, 158–65.

7. Urbanna

1. We take the phrase from a 1692 case involving the estate of Oswald Cary. Middlesex Orders, 1680–94, 541.

2. Middlesex Wills, 1698–1713, 141–45.

3. Ibid., 104–6.

4. Wormeley Estate Papers, 1701–16, with Christ Church, Lancaster Processioners' Returns, 1711–83, Virginia State Library, Richmond, 148. A Middlesex hogshead (sweetscented) held roughly 500 to 600 pounds at this time. Note, for example, Middlesex Orders, 1680–94, 457, a report of the weighing of two of Matthew Kemp's hogsheads in 1690 (626 and 612 pounds, less 74 and 77 pounds "tare" or weight of the cask itself); C. G. Chamberlayne, ed., *The Vestry Book of Christ Church Parish, Middlesex County, Virginia, 1663–1767* (Richmond, Va., 1927), 74–76, an accounting of seven hogsheads averaging 659 pounds gross and 579 pounds net (deducting tare) and four weighing 510 pounds net; Middlesex Orders, 1694–1705, 42, a hogshead weighed at 542 pounds net. They were increasing in size, however. Chamberlayne, ed., *Vestry Book of Christ Church*, 112 (1707), specifies "Eight hundred Neat"; Middlesex Orders, 1705–10, 286, a 1710 Middlesex case involving thirty-one hogsheads averaging 815 pounds net; Waverly K. Winfree, comp., *The Laws of Virginia: Being a Supplement to Hening's The Statutes at Large, 1700–1750* (Richmond, Va., 1971), 75–90 and 185–91 (1713, 1720), 700 pounds sweetscented and 600 pounds oronoco; William W. Hening, comp., *The Statutes at Large: Being a Collection of all the Laws of Virginia from the First Session of the Legislature in 1619* (Richmond, New York, and Philadelphia, 1809–23), IV, 247–71 (1730) specifies at least 800 pounds. Still later a hogshead would exceed 1,000 pounds. See Paul G. E. Clemens, *The Atlantic Economy and Colonial Maryland's Eastern Shore: From Tobacco to Grain* (Ithaca, N.Y., 1980), 170–71; Arthur Pierce Middleton, *Tobacco Coast: A Maritime History of Chesapeake Bay in the Colonial Era* (Newport News, Va., 1953), 101–4; James F. Shepherd and Gary M. Walton, *Shipping, Maritime Trade, and the Economic Development of Colonial North America* (Cambridge, Eng., 1972), 65–68. On a ship's cargo, see William Fitzhugh's proposal to load a ship for Thomas Clayton, 1686, in Richard Beale Davis, ed., *William Fitzhugh and His Chesapeake World, 1676–1701: The Fitzhugh Letters and Other Documents* (Chapel Hill, N.C., 1963), 180–83.

5. Henry Hartwell et al., *The Present State of Virginia and the College* (1699), ed. Hunter Dickinson Farish (Williamsburg, Va., 1940), 12–13; John Oldmixon, *The British Empire in America* (1708), quoted in Lewis Cecil Gray, *History of Agriculture in the Southern United States to 1860* (Washington, D.C., 1933), I, 410.

6. Middlesex Orders, 1680–94, 521, 634; 1694–1705, 132.

7. "Brothers of the Spade: Correspondence of Peter Collinson, of London, and of John Custis, of Williamsburg, Virginia, 1734–1746," ed. E. G. Swem, *Proceedings of the American Antiquarian Society*, LVIII (1948), 68, 79–80.

8. Middlesex Orders, 1694–1705, 276.

9. In war the ships arrived and departed in convoy. See Middleton, *Tobacco Coast*, chapter 10.

10. Edmund Berkeley and Dorothy Smith Berkeley, eds., *The Reverend John Clayton: A Parson with a Scientific Mind, His Scientific Writings and Other Related Papers* (Charlottesville, Va., 1965), 53; Hartwell et al., *Present State of Virginia*, 10–11.

11. Nicholas Spencer to Mr. Secretary Coventry, July 9, 1680, quoted in John W. Reps, *Tidewater Towns: City Planning in Colonial Virginia and Maryland* (Williamsburg, Va., 1972), 67; R[oger] G[reen], *Virginia's Cure: Or An Advisive Narrative Concerning Virginia* (London, 1662), in Peter Force, comp., *Tracts and Other Papers, Relating Principally to the . . . Colonies in North America* (Washington, D.C., 1836–47), III, tract XV, 5; John C. Rainbolt, *From Prescription to Persuasion: Manipulation of [Seventeenth] Century Virginia Economy* (Port Washington, N.Y., 1974), 49–50, 149–50.

12. Hening, comp., *Statutes at Large*, I, 412–14, 476; Lancaster Deeds, 1652–57, 201; [William Sherwood], "Virginias Deploured Condition: Or an Impartiall Narrative of the Murders Comitted by the Indians there, and of the Sufferings of his Majesties Loyall Subjects under the Rebellious Outrages of Mr. Nathaniell Bacon Junior . . . ," *Collections of the Massachusetts Historical Society*, 4th ser., IX (1871), 164.

13. For the acts in general, see Edward M. Riley, "The Town Acts of Colonial Virginia," *Journal of Southern History*, XVI (1950), 306–23; Rainbolt, *Prescription to Persuasion*, 113–17, 132–35, 157–68. For the growth of towns in Virginia and the South in general—a matter unfortunately confused by the use of the words "urban" and "urbanization"—see Joseph A. Ernst and H. Roy Merrens, " 'Camden's turrets pierce the skies!': The Urban Process in the Southern Colonies during the Eighteenth Century," *William and Mary Quarterly*, 3d ser., XXX (1973), 549–74; Hermann Wellenreuther, "Urbanization in the Colonial South: A Critique," *William and Mary Quarterly*, XXXI (1974), 653–71; Jacob M. Price, "Economic Function and the Growth of American Port Towns in the Eighteenth Century," *Perspectives in American History*, VIII (1974), 123–86; Carville Earle and Ronald Hoffman, "Staple Crops and Urban Development in the Eighteenth-Century South," *Perspectives in American History*, X (1976), 7–78.

14. Middlesex Wills, 1698–1713, 84–87; Louis B. Wright, *The First Gentlemen of Virginia: Intellectual Qualities of the Early Colonial Ruling Class* (San Marino, Calif., 1940), 187–211.

15. Louis B. Wright and Marion Tinling, eds., *William Byrd of Virginia: The London Diary (1717–1721) and Other Writings* (New York, 1958), 455; William Cowper, *The Task* (1785), in Robert Southey, ed., *The Works of William Cowper* (London, 1835–37), IX, 92–93; Hunter Dickinson Farish, ed., *Journal & Letters of Philip Vickers Fithian, 1773–1774: A Plantation Tutor of the Old Dominion* (Williamsburg, Va., 1957), 32. The gallery is still extant.

16. Hartwell et al., *Present State of Virginia*, 71. John Hemphill of the Research Division, Colonial Williamsburg Foundation, is preparing a study of the administration of Virginia and in conversations has very graciously shared with us his great knowledge of Wormeley's activities as secretary.

17. Berkeley and Berkeley, eds., *Clayton*, 32; Gilbert Chinard, ed., *A Huguenot Exile in Virginia: Or Voyages of a Frenchman exiled for his Religion with a description of Virginia and Maryland* (New York, 1934), 147, 149–50.

18. Middlesex Orders, 1673–80, 224; 1680–94, 41a, 42, 50, 509–10; Hening, comp., *Statutes at Large*, III, 59; H. R. McIlwaine and J. P. Kennedy, eds., *Journals of the House of Burgesses of Virginia* (Richmond, Va., 1905–15), II, 181.

19. Middlesex Orders, 1680–94, 193, 200–201.

20. Ibid., 474, 508–10.

21. Ibid., 512, 515–18.

22. Ibid., 572–73. See also Wesley Newton Laing, "Urbanna's Tobacco Warehouse," Association for the Preservation of Virginia Antiquities, *Report on a Building at Urbanna, Virginia* ([Richmond, Va., 1961]), passim.

23. Middlesex Deeds, 1687–1750, 10–11; Middlesex Orders, 1680–94, 559, 610–11, 627, 654.

24. A younger brother, William, married Judith, daughter of Christopher Wormeley, and died in Middlesex in 1702. Harry had other even younger brothers, but they played no part in the events recounted.

25. "Will of Christopher Robinson, 1693," *Virginia Magazine of History and Biography*, VII (1899–1900), 21; Middlesex Orders, 1680–94, 718–19 (converted from an amount listed in both sterling and tobacco).

26. Robert Carter to Thomas Corbin, [1706], *Virginia Magazine of History and Biography*, XXXVI (1928), 290.

27. Kemp and Churchill, among the old feoffees, were still alive and active.

28. Middlesex Deeds, 1703–20, 70–72.

29. When, at a later date, the same sort of movement arose on the upper James, William Byrd II expressed what undoubtedly were Churchill's sentiments as the fight over Urbanna developed, and perhaps Wormeley's before him: "I erected a very con-

venient [ware]house . . . over against the falls, which is so well customed that it brings me in at least 50 *li* per annum. But a powerful family in those parts finding the storage of their goods . . . to be very chargeable, intend to push hard . . . to have a town laid out there, that they may build warehouses of their own, and perhaps if an act should pass in their favour, the publick may give me twenty shillins an acre for 50 acres. Now behold the great injustice of this proceeding. In the first place I would not sell 50 acres, in this place for 5 *li* an acre, if I were not compelld to it. . . . In the next place what compensation shall I have for 50 *li* a year I make by the warehouses, when others will have such warehouses as well as I." Byrd to Micajah Perry, May 27, 17[29], Marion Tinling, ed., *The Correspondence of the Three William Byrds of Westover, Virginia, 1684–1776* (Charlottesville, Va., 1977), I, 398. (We have taken the liberty of silently filling in bracketed words to improve readability.) Byrd would lay out Richmond at the site a few years later. It seems that the same sort of processes were at work at different locations in the Chesapeake but proceeding within different time frames.

30. Middlesex Orders, 1694–1705, 525, 528, 536, 544, 546.

31. Ibid., 570, 578; Middlesex Deeds, 1703–20, 70–72. When George Wortham agreed to donate land he previously had offered to sell, Smith's location was abandoned.

32. H. R. McIlwaine and W. L. Hall, eds., *Executive Journals of the Council of Colonial Virginia, 1680–1754* (Richmond, Va., 1925–45), II, 391, 403, 433.

33. Middlesex Orders, 1694–1705, 602–3; Middlesex Deeds, 1703–20, 85–86; William P. Palmer et al., eds., *Calendar of Virginia State Papers and Other Manuscripts [1652–1869]* (Richmond, Va., 1875–93), I, 88.

34. Robinson had refused to join the court when first appointed in 1701; Churchill formally withdrew in 1702 after fairly regular attendance from 1687 on. Middlesex Orders, 1694–1705, 394, 401. It is quite likely that Robinson had a long-standing and deep grievance against Churchill, perhaps reciprocated, possibly dating from Churchill's activities with regard to the estate of the elder Robinson. The formality of their refusals in 1701 and 1702 might be a result. In any event, the two were together in attendance at a court or vestry meeting only three times from 1701 to 1710, years when both were active.

35. Middlesex Deeds, 1703–20, 70–72.

36. Churchill was elected in a by-election in April 1704 occasioned by the death of Edwin Thacker, elected in 1702. For the protest, see McIlwaine and Kennedy, eds., *Journals of the House of Burgesses*, IV, 134, 139.

37. Middlesex Orders, 1694–1705, 627–28; 1705–10, 77–78; Middlesex Deeds, 1703–20, 85–86. Grymes was subsequently awarded six shillings damages in open court.

38. McIlwaine and Kennedy, eds., *Journals of the House of Burgesses*, IV, 94, 100, 102.

39. Palmer et al., eds., *Calendar of Virginia State Papers*, I, 105–6.

40. Middlesex Orders, 1705–10, 112, 122, 124, 154, 179, 202.

41. Laing, "Urbanna's Tobacco Warehouse," 8.

42. See *Explicatus*, "Population Estimates."

43. Middlesex Deeds, 1703–20, 72.

44. Ibid., 122; Middlesex Orders, 1705–10, 80, 131.

45. Gregory A. Stiverson and Patrick H. Butler III, eds., "Virginia in 1732: The Travel Journal of William Hugh Grove," *Virginia Magazine of History and Biography*, LXXXV (1977), 21; Edmund Berkeley and Dorothy Smith Berkeley, *Dr. John Mitchell: The Man Who Made the Map of North America* (Chapel Hill, N.C., 1974), 17–20.

46. Winfree, comp., *Supplement to Hening*, 75–90; D. Alan Williams, "Political Alignments in Colonial Virginia Politics, 1698–1750," (Ph. D. Dissertation, Northwestern University, 1959), 142–44.

47. Palmer et al., eds. *Calendar of Virginia State Papers*, I, 181; Winfree, comp., *Supplement to Hening*, 119–24; Middleton, *Tobacco Coast*, 120–22.

48. Hening, comp., *Statutes at Large*, IV, 247–71.

49. Middlesex Orders, 1710–21, 155, 167; Middlesex Deeds, 1703–20, 361: "The Present State of Virginia . . . 1714," *Virginia Magazine of History and Biography*, II (1894–95), 8.

50. McIlwaine and Kennedy, eds., *Journals of the House of Burgesses*, V, 83, 133.

51. Middlesex Orders, 1705–10, 117; Middlesex Wills, 1713–34, 347–50.

52. Ibid., 252–56, 303–5, 335–42. By 1744 Patrick Cheap's markup was higher, on some goods 35 percent, on others 55 percent. Middlesex Wills, 1740–48, 214–32. See also Jacob M. Price, *Capital and Credit in British Overseas Trade: The View from the Chesapeake, 1700–1776* (Cambridge, Mass., 1980), 149–50.

53. Referred to in the inventory of his estate in Middlesex Wills, 1713–34, 347.

54. For evidence of a country store (Price's in the upper precinct), see Middlesex Wills, 1713–34, 298–300; 1740–48, 429; Middlesex Deeds, 1687–1750, 133. For peddlers see Middlesex Wills, 1698–1713, 153–54; 1675–1798, pt. I, 212; 1740–48, 423–24; Hening, comp., *Statutes at Large*, V, 54–57. The second Middlesex warehouse established under the 1730 act (at Kemp's on the Piankatank) seems to have served major planters in the lower part of the county and across the river in northern Gloucester. McIlwaine and Kennedy, eds., *Journals of the House of Burgesses*, VI, 202–3, 207, 424; Hening, comp., *Statutes at Large*, IV, 380–93.

55. Louis B. Wright and Marion Tinling, *The Secret Diary of William Byrd of Westover, 1709–1712* (Richmond, Va., 1941), 98, 101; Middlesex Wills, 1698–1713, 247–49. The sermons were being delivered on Wednesdays, until 1713 when they were changed to Fridays, presumably at the Middle Church. Chamberlayne, ed., *Vestry Book of Christ Church*, 136.

56. James Reid, "The Religion of the Bible and Religion of K[ing] W[illiam] County Compared" (1769), in Richard Beale Davis, ed., *The Colonial Virginia Satirist: Mid-Eighteenth-Century Commentaries on Politics, Religion, and Society*, Transactions of the American Philosophical Society, New Series, LVII, pt. 1 (Philadelphia, Pa. 1967), 48, 57.

8. Circles

1. Middlesex Orders, 1710–21, 331, 337, 350, 402, 405; H. R. McIlwaine and J. P. Kennedy, eds., *Journals of the House of Burgesses of Virginia* (Richmond, Va., 1905–15), V, 191, 196, 198, 200, 205, 207, 210; Waverly K. Winfree, comp., *The Laws of Virginia: Being a Supplement to Hening's The Statutes at Large, 1700–1750* (Richmond, Va., 1971), 167–68.

2. Gilbert Chinard, ed., *A Huguenot Exile in Virginia: Or Voyages of a Frenchman exiled for his Religion with a description of Virginia and Maryland* (New York, 1934), 119; Middlesex Wills, 1698–1713, 126; [Thomas K. Ford], *The Miller in Eighteenth-Century Virginia: An Account of Mills and the Craft of Milling* (Williamsburg, Va., 1978), 12.

3. Middlesex Orders, 1694–1705, 303–4. Landon, too, was planting winter wheat. See also Harold B. Gill, Jr., "Wheat Culture in Colonial Virginia," *Agricultural History*, LII (1978), 380–93; David Klingaman, "The Significance of Grain in the Development of the Tobacco Colonies," *Journal of Economic History*, XXIX (1969), 268–78.

4. See *Explicatus*, "Population Estimates." The downward trend would continue. In 1783 there would be 1,167 whites in 233 families and 2,282 blacks, 66.2% of the total. U.S. Bureau of the Census, *Heads of Families at the First Census of the United States Taken in the Year 1790. Records of the State Enumerations: 1782 to 1785: Virginia* (Washington, D.C., 1908), 10. Note that there was also a trickle of black emigration from roughly 1720 on—blacks being sent from Middlesex plantations to upcountry quarters.

5. U.S. Bureau of the Census, *Heads of Families . . . 1790 . . . Virginia*, 10.

6. See A. Gordon Darroch, "Migrants in the Nineteenth Century: Fugitives or Families in Motion?" *Journal of Family History*, VI (1981), 257–77, an excellent criticism of current hypotheses about "transiency." What data we have on the emigrants lend support to Darroch's argument.

7. See Darrett B. Rutman, "People in Process: The New Hampshire Towns of the Eighteenth Century," *Journal of Urban History*, I (1975), 268–92.

8. Based on samples of 21, 30, and 101 respectively.

9. Middlesex Wills, 1713–34, 263a–64; Governor Francis Fauquier quoted in Lewis Cecil Gray, *History of Agriculture in the Southern United States to 1860* (Washington, D.C., 1933), I, 454.

10. William P. Palmer et al., eds., *Calendar of Virginia State Papers and Other Manuscripts [1652–1869]* (Richmond, Va., 1875–93), I, 212–13.

11. Edmund Berkeley and Dorothy Smith Berkeley, *John Clayton: Pioneer of American Botany* (Chapel Hill, N.C., 1963), 89; "The Autobiography of the Reverend Devereux Jarratt, 1732–1763," *William and Mary Quarterly*, 3d ser., IX (1952), 367; Hunter Dickinson Farish, ed., *Journal & Letters of Philip Vickers Fithian, 1773–1774: A Plantation Tutor of the Old Dominion* (Williamsburg, Va., 1957), 161.

12. Farish, ed., *Fithian*, 96, 202–3; J. F. D. Smyth, *A Tour of the United States of America . . .* (London, 1784), 46; *The Journal of Nicholas Cresswell, 1774–1777* (New York, 1924), 18–19.

13. Rhys Isaac, *The Transformation of Virginia, 1740–1790* (Chapel Hill, N.C., 1982), 328–46.

14. William Tatham, *An Historical and Practical Essay on the Culture and Commerce of Tobacco* (London, 1800), as reprinted in G. Melvin Herndon, *William Tatham and the*

Culture of Tobacco (Coral Gables, Fla., 1969), 123; Palmer et al., eds., *Calendar of Virginia State Papers,* I, 212–13.

15. C. G. Chamberlayne, ed., *The Vestry Book of Christ Church Parish, Middlesex County, Virginia, 1663–1767* (Richmond, Va., 1927), 234–35. Grymes, Churchill, and Berkeley were present as members of the vestry at the time. On coaches, see Middlesex Wills, 1713–34, 114, 303, and Middlesex Wills, 1675–1798, pt. 1, 240—the latter the 1747 will of John Grymes. In 1720 Rosegill's chariot was ridden in by William Byrd. Louis B. Wright and Marion Tinling, eds., *William Byrd: The London Diary (1717–1721) and Other Writings* (New York, 1958), 455. Some years later there was mention of a chariot, phaeton, and chair at Rosegill. "A List of Tithables Belonging to Ralph Wormeley, May 20, 1773," Middlesex County Records, Virginia Historical Society, Richmond.

16. "Autobiography of Devereux Jarratt," *William and Mary Quarterly,* 3d ser., IX (1952), 375.

17. McIlwaine and Kennedy, eds., *Journals of the House of Burgesses,* VI, 262; Chamberlayne, ed., *Vestry Book of Christ Church,* 244.

18. We note a decided change setting in about the turn of the century, that is, an increasing concern for the niceties of the law. See, for example, Middlesex Orders, 1680–94, 549 (the court doubtful about a procedure and sending two members to "Waite upon" the governor and council "to know the Right way and method"), and Middlesex Orders, 1694–1705, 272 (the court accepting a defendant's plea that the plaintiff's writ was in error because it "did not sett forth how the said summe became due Whither by bill bond or account"). The last is hardly an example of the "care . . . taken to make the lawes and pleadings upon them easy and obvious to any mans understanding" of which Thomas Ludwell wrote in 1666 ("A Description of the Government of Virginia," *Virginia Magazine of History and Biography,* V [1897–98], 57).

19. On court day in the eighteenth century, see A. G. Roeber, *Faithful Magistrates and Republican Lawyers: Creators of Virginia Legal Culture, 1680–1810* (Chapel Hill, N.C., 1981), chapter 3.

20. "Autobiography of Devereux Jarratt," 370.

21. For a depiction of agrarian life in terms of circles in a quite different place and time, see William Morgan Williams, *A West Country Village, Ashworthy: Family, Kinship and Land* (London, 1963), 98–99.

22. For a description of Chesapeake society (and culture) at mid-century in just these terms, see Isaac, *Transformation of Virginia,* pt. I.

Index